W9-COZ-528

THE FUTURE OF THE AMERICAN PRESIDENCY

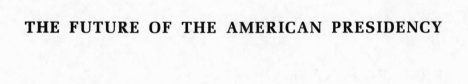

ROBERT PEABODY

EVE LUBALIN

MALCOLM B. PARSONS

DOROTHY BUCKTON JAMES

RICHARD P. NATHAN

MARIAN D. IRISH

NORMAN A. GRAEBNER

JOHN B. ANDERSON

MORRIS K. UDALL

DAVID BRODER

THOMAS E. CRONIN

AVERY LEISERSON

JAMES DAVID BARBER

THE FUTURE
OF THE
AMERICAN
PRESIDENCY

Edited by
Charles W. Dunn
Clemson University

GENERAL LEARNING PRESS
250 James Street
Morristown, New Jersey 07960

To my wife, Carol, who always walks through the valleys and climbs to the mountain tops with me.

Manufactured in the United States of America.

Published simultaneously in Canada.

Library of Congress Catalog Card Number 74-26177

ISBN 0–382–18163–8 cloth

ISBN 0–382–18164–6 paper

Preface

The American public has a warped view of the presidency. To some extent, this unrealistic view may be attributed to American government and American history textbooks. If for no other reason, the public image of the president is influenced by students who become opinion leaders and whose views of the presidency have been molded by textbook assessments. Since few students ever graduate from college or high school without courses in either American history or American government, or both, the problem is obvious.

Standard textbooks in American government and American history have frequently revealed three major weaknesses in their treatment of the American presidency.

First, there is often a textbook reverence for the presidency that contributes to an unrealistic analysis of the office. Sometimes, the president is implicitly portrayed as a magician or superhuman who is the catalyst for good and virtue in America. Descriptions of the president as "the engine of democracy" and "the American people's one authentic trumpet" readily and dramatically convey the unreality of such textbook analyses.

Second, textbooks are notoriously devoid of commentary by politicians and journalists. Yet, journalists and politicians have more direct influence over the presidency than academicians and they certainly have an equally valid position from which to offer analytical observations about the office. For example, it was journalists and politicians — not scholars — who exposed the problem of presidential isolation.

Third, there is often a disparity between what students want to know about the presidency and what the textbooks say. While students are interested in the value judgments involved in policy-making, textbook writers often obscure those value judgments in favor of institutional descriptions of the office, its structure, and its powers. The reality of power and process is only dimly illuminated by this approach.

This book is intended to shed the light that is only faintly perceived in textbooks. It is not intended to replace standard textbooks. Rather, its purpose is to analyze the critical variables that influence the future of the American presidency by presenting a cross-section of views from leading journalists, politicians, and academicians. Significantly, several of the academicians have both theoretical training and practical experience. Included in the cross-section are

- a 1973 Pulitzer Prize winner for political commentary;

- two well-known leaders of the U. S. Congress;

- a former president of the American Political Science Association;

- a principal architect of revenue sharing;

- professors from Johns Hopkins University, University of Virginia, Duke University, American University, Virginia Polytechnic and State University, Vanderbilt University, and the University of California (Santa Barbara).

The editor extends his gratitude to these men and women for their participation and to Clemson University for providing the incentive and financial means for bringing together these leading authorities on the presidency. Deserving special mention are three Clemson University officials: President Robert C. Edwards, Vice-President for Academic Affairs Victor Hurst, and Dean of the College of Liberal Arts H. Morris Cox. I would also like to express deep appreciation to the College of Liberal Arts faculty for its loyal support of the lecture series out of which this book on the presidency evolved. A personal word of appreciation should also be extended to three loyal, dedicated and efficient secretaries, Martha Morris, Sue Ling and Joan Dukes.

While working with General Learning Press, I have developed a profound respect for their intellectual acumen and editorial skills. John Hauch, Editor of General Learning Press, and Carol Rothkopf, who edited this volume, are just two of the enthusiastic and efficient staff at General Learning who deserve special commendation.

CWD

Contents

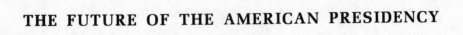

THE FUTURE OF THE AMERICAN PRESIDENCY

Introduction: The President – Servant to Sun King?

CHARLES W. DUNN
Clemson University

> The tyranny of the legislature is really the danger most to be feared, and will continue to be so for many years to come. The tyranny of the executive power will come in its turn, but at a more distant period.
>
> — Thomas Jefferson, Letter to James Madison (March 15, 1789)

WATERGATE AND ALL THAT IT SYM-bolizes places Jefferson's prophecy in historical perspective. Slightly over two years passed between June 17, 1972, the date of the Watergate break-in, and August 9, 1974, the date when Richard Milhous Nixon became the first president in American history to resign from office. During most of that time, President Nixon seemed immune from serious impeachment efforts. This seeming immunity existed despite the indictment and/or conviction of his personal attorney, two of his attorneys general, his White House legal counsel, his secretary of Commerce, his secretary of the Treasury, his two highest White House aides, plus several of his other White House staff members. The enormous growth in presidential power has placed the presidency, both the office and the officeholder, on a pedestal far above what the Founding Fathers had either imagined or intended.

How and why did this happen? To answer these questions requires an examination of the constitutional creation of the presidency, the landmarks and watersheds in the growth of presidential power, and the irony, paradox, and myth now associated with the presidency. The composite analysis of these subjects suggests that the future forebodes difficulty for both the presidency and the public.

CONSTITUTIONAL CREATION[1]

It is difficult, if not impossible, for most Americans to imagine their president as anything less than the preeminent leader of their nation and the world. This is another way of saying that we have lost sight of the office's constitutional moorings. Conceived shortly after bitter and violent reaction to the tyranny of the English Crown and King George III's colonial governors, the American presidency was originally thought of simply as one-third of the federal triangle, a fraction of a national government characterized by checks and balances to prevent abuses of power by any part of it. Yet, scarcely 200 years later, a respected political scientist said the president is like "a kind of magnificent lion who can roam widely and do great deeds . . . " [Rossiter 1960, pp. 68–69].

The Founding Fathers could hardly conceive of the president as the national leader, because there existed no well-developed concept of nationhood, or as a party leader, because there were no political parties. The first presidents were not world leaders because the United States was largely isolated from world affairs. In sum, the president was simply to be an executive who would act in certain areas generally limited to strictly executive functions. The distribution of governmental power in the American Constitution, though more balanced among the branches than in the Articles of Confederation, still maintained the balance of power on the side of the legislative branch, the Congress.

While the Founding Fathers in Philadelphia in 1787 were reacting to the tyranny of the English Crown and the royal governors, they were also substantially influenced by the organization of the national government under the Articles of Confederation and state governments in the 11-year period (1776–1787) following the American Revolution. With little or no executive power under the Articles of Confederation and in most state constitutions, the foremost governmental power in both instances was the legislative branch. This had resulted in ineffective government.

The English Crown and the royal governors may have been tyrannical, but the legislatively dominated governments of the nation and the states, which had been created largely to prevent executive tyranny, were hardly virtuous. Both executive tyranny and legislative supremacy have their pitfalls. James Madison, for example, was critical of state constitutions that expressed an overwhelming desire to preclude an "overgrown and all-grasping prerogative of an hereditary magistrate" but which were blind to the "danger from legislative usurpation, which, by assembling all power in the same hands, must lead to the same tyranny as is threatened by executive usurpations" [Federalist No. 48].

The problem confronting the Founding Fathers was to create a governmental structure providing for an executive that could act but which would not stir up visions of monarchial vices in the public mind. Not to have an executive that could act would be to have an ineffectual government, but to create an executive that would arouse popular consternation about executive tyranny would be to doom the plan for a new national government. The Founding Fathers had to balance governmental power between these two parameters.

In addition to the negative lessons of the English Crown and royal governors, the Articles of Confederation and state constitutions, there was another and positive influence acting upon the Founding Fathers: the political theories of Montesquieu and Locke. The Founding Fathers' principal derivative from their theories was the idea of a "balanced constitution," which had the following justification in Montesquieu's *The Spirit of the Laws* in which he analyzed "The Constitution of England."

> When the legislative and executive powers are united in the same person, or in the same body of magistrates, there can be no liberty; because apprehensions may arise lest the same monarch or senate should enact tyrannical laws, and execute them in a tyrannical manner.

In his *Two Treatises on Government,* Locke added the notion (in chapter 14 of his *Second Treatise*) that a somewhat broad, discretionary, and residual power should rest in the executive branch.

> . . . the good of the society requires that several things should be left to the discretion of him that has the executive power . . . . For the legislators not being able to foresee and provide by laws for all that may be useful to the community, the executor of the laws, having the power in his hands, has by the common law of Nature a right to make use of it for the good of society.

Essentially, Montesquieu and Locke developed a concept of government in which the legislative, executive, and judicial branches of government were to be separate and to have the ability to defend their respective functions from intrusion by the other branches. This would serve as a defense for the executive against legislative supremacy and for the legislative against executive tyranny. The Lockean notion of residual power for the executive reinforced the capacity of the executive to resist legislative intrusion, but perhaps more important, as will be shown in the historical context, to develop powers that were not expressly stated in the Constitution.

Emerging from these principal influences was an executive article that is probably more vague and hazy than the rest of the Constitution. The executive article sought to create a separate and independent executive branch capable of acting decisively without either permitting or tempting the executive to act in any way reminiscent of the excesses of the English Crown. The theory of the American executive branch was effectively summarized by Alexander Hamilton:

A feeble Executive implies a feeble execution of the government. A feeble execution is but another phrase for a bad execution; and a government ill executed, whatever it may be in theory, must be, in practice, a bad government.

Taking it for granted, therefore, that all men of sense will agree in the necessity of an *energetic Executive* [emphasis supplied], it will only remain to inquire, what are the ingredients which constitute this energy? . . .

The ingredients which constitute energy in the Executive are unity; duration; and adequate provision for its support; competent powers [*Federalist* No. 70].

Among the state constitutions, only New York and Pennsylvania had executives with Hamilton's concept of "energized" power. It is not surprising, therefore, that the initial support in the Constitutional Convention for an "energized" executive was weak and almost entirely limited to delegates from New York and Pennsylvania, with the very able exception of Charles Pinckney of South Carolina. The executive article evolved in the Constitutional Convention after a prolonged series of both negative and positive decisions.

Negative Decisions

The negative decisions were the discarding of the multiheaded-executive concept and the abandonment of the legislative election of the executive. By discarding and abandoning these proposals, which were part of both the New Jersey and Virginia Plans, the executive article obtained the "unity" Hamilton desired, as well as a degree of independence from legislative domination. These decisions insured a single executive and a nonlegislative election process for the executive. Consequently, executive power was centralized in one office, thus allowing the occupant of that office to act without the restraints of divided executive power, and also to become the visible symbol of the executive branch. The nonlegislative election of the executive

resulted in the creation of an electoral college system that enabled the president to establish a direct link to the people while
seeking to obtain a majority of electoral college votes. This direct
link to the people, together with the embodiment of executive
power in one office, ultimately insured that the president became the leader both of the nation and his party.

Positive Decisions

The positive decisions outlined the framework of executive
powers. Before outlining the four principal powers, however, it
is important to note another very important element, the definition of the president's length of term in office. A president, even
with broad powers, would largely be ineffective if subject to a
very limited term of office, such as 1 year with no right of succession, a condition then existing in many of the states. By granting
the president a 4-year term with the right of succession, he was
allowed time to utilize executive powers in developing policies
and programs. As the following outline makes clear, the powers
granted the president were, in many respects, indefinite and imprecise. This enabled presidents to extend the boundaries of
their office and powers as they sought to achieve their goals.

The Four Principal Presidential Powers

Power to Appoint
The decision to grant broad appointing powers to presidents
helped lead to the development of personnel and budgetary controls over an expanding administration and bureaucracy, to an
influence over the judiciary by appointments to the courts, and
to the development and guidance of foreign policy through am-
bassadorial appointments. This power, which is limited only by
senatorial confirmation and by the inability to remove from
office appointed officials who hold quasi-judicial positions (for
example, members of independent regulatory agencies, as con-

trasted with such purely executive positions as the attorney general), has enabled the president to seek to develop and administer a unified policy throughout the executive branch, and to be the principal spokesman to the Congress on matters of appropriations and policy requests.

Power to Faithfully Execute the Laws

Departments and agencies in the executive branch represent the president's principal means for implementing and enforcing the laws. Hence, cabinet departments and agencies (except for independent regulatory agencies) report directly to the president. Because enforcement and implementation of the laws involve a degree of discretion on the president's part as to how they will be enforced and implemented, the president not only has expressed powers, but also implied powers. The latter are derived from his discretionary authority and also from the constitutional declaration that "executive power shall be vested in a president of the United States." Implied powers have been construed by the United States Supreme Court to mean that the "laws" to be enforced and implemented by the president include not only statutes enacted by Congress, but also "any obligation fairly and properly inferrible from [the Constitution], or any duty . . . to be derived from the general scope of . . . duties under the laws of the United States." In the same case, In re Neagle (1890), the U. S. Supreme Court continued that executive power is not "limited to the enforcement of acts of Congress . . . according to their express terms," but also includes "the rights, duties and obligations growing out of the Constitution itself, our international relations, and all the protection *implied* [emphasis supplied] by the nature of the government under the Constitution." With only rare exceptions, the courts have upheld the president's implied powers.

Power as Commander in Chief

There was evidently little discussion about this grant of power during the Constitutional Convention, and according to *Federalist* Number 69, the power "would amount to nothing

more than the supreme command and direction of the military
and naval forces, as first General and Admiral of the Confedera-
cy." The Founding Fathers might be as much, if not more, surprised about the evolution of this power than that of any other
power or part of the Constitution. As Edward S. Corwin has
pointed out, the "President's power as Commander-in-Chief has
been transformed from a simple power of military command to a
vast reservoir of indeterminate powers in time of emergency"
[1957, p. 261]. This power, which has been broadly exercised
many times in American history and by many presidents, has
been challenged but seldom thwarted. For example, it may be
argued that the recently enacted War Powers Act, rather than
strengthening the congressional role in declaring war, simply
strengthens the president's role by giving him the freedom to
commit troops for 30 days without congressional approval,
which, it is argued, only legitimizes what modern presidents
have been doing anyway. Of course, the War Powers Act at least
forces the president into fully considering the consequences of a
military commitment should the Congress be inclined to disap-
prove of his action. Realistically, however, presidents have been
inclined to consider these consequences.

Power to Negotiate Treaties

This power, together with previously discussed powers, has
enabled the president to develop and guide American foreign
policy. Although the Senate has the power to ratify treaties, the
president has been able to circumvent this power through gener-
ous use of executive agreements that do not require Senate ratification. Executive agreements must be judiciously used, however, with an eye toward the reaction of Congress lest that reaction be an inclination to undo an agreement which, in turn,
might create a highly embarrassing situation for the president
and damage the credibility of the United States in international
relations. The necessity of keeping the Congress apprised was
vividly demonstrated by the 1974 congressional debate concerning the Middle East settlement that guaranteed nuclear energy to
Egypt. Congressional supporters of Israel were extremely wary of
this presidential commitment.

Trinitarian Fusion of Powers

Perhaps nowhere is the widely acclaimed American constitutional virtue of "flexibility" more evident than in the executive article. The executive article has been flexible enough to accommodate to new demands; or, to state it another way, the executive article has been hazy and vague enough to allow for myriad interpretations. In addition to the unclear and imprecise limits of executive power, the executive article (in conjunction with the legislative and judicial articles) establishes not so much a doctrine of separation of powers as a fusion of powers. A doctrine of strict separation of powers would have clearly specified the limits of executive power. The more accurate doctrine, fusion of powers, allowed the executive branch to develop legislative and judicial responsibilities in addition to strictly executive duties. Today, the presidency is the most important single force in the legislative process and has many judicial or quasi-judicial functions. The setting and enforcement of air pollution and civil rights compliance standards illustrate both the legislative and judicial functions within the "trinity" of the executive branch. If the Founding Fathers adopted powers in the executive article that were capable of being stretched with the passage of time and changing conditions, how and why has this stretching process occurred?

LANDMARKS AND WATERSHEDS[2]

Throughout the greater part of American history, the legislative branch maintained preeminence in power over the executive branch. This was one of the principal points made by Woodrow Wilson in his book *Congressional Government* (1885), in which he concluded that Congress was the dominant force in American government. Wilson's conclusion remained true through the early part of the twentieth century as an anecdote from the Taft administration (1909–1913) illustrates. When President Taft sent an emissary to meet with Speaker of the U. S.

House of Representatives "Uncle Joe" Cannon to request his assistance on behalf of the president, Cannon told the emissary to tell the president to come to the Speaker's office and discuss the matter with him. What an unimaginable scene in contemporary American history!

The Founding Fathers, while not allowing legislative power to be eclipsed, did reveal the possibilities and potential for the development and exercise of presidential power. The presidency of George Washington clearly established a foundation for the reverence of the presidency. In addition Alexander Hamilton as secretary of the Treasury assisted Washington in beginning to forge executive power. At least three other developments during this period also contributed to the ultimate growth of presidential power: **1.** the evolution of the party system with the very influential role of the president as party leader; **2.** the growth of a national constituency for the president as illustrated by Andrew Jackson's election to the presidency with the assistance of this new constituency; **3.** the use of emergency powers by Abraham Lincoln during the Civil War. These developments helped to demonstrate that the president could play a very important role in influencing public opinion, a key ingredient in establishing influence with the Congress, and in taking decisive action through the president's implied powers.

The principal landmarks and watersheds in the development of the preeminent power position for the American presidency occurred in the twentieth century, beginning particularly with Woodrow Wilson, but they are based on the actions and philosophical statements about presidential power made by Theodore Roosevelt. Largely, these landmarks and watersheds may be viewed as the changing conditions in America, the changing conceptions of presidential power, and the unchanging Congress.

Changing America

The agrarian society of eighteenth- and nineteenth-century America was well suited for legislative dominance in the national government. Communication and transportation were slow, and the economy was relatively simple. With economic and industrial development, however, each of these conditions changed rather rapidly, necessitating more prompt governmental responses to new, different, and more complex problems. Additionally, the crisis atmosphere of modern America, which since 1940 has produced three wars and several other military actions, such as in Lebanon (1958) and the Dominican Republic (1964), led to the deference shown the president in meeting and responding to crisis situations. Domestically, there have also been crises, particularly those associated with the Depression and the several civil rights controversies. Only the president has demonstrated the centralized leadership capacity and the control over information and communication that is necessary to respond quickly to these crises.

Changing Conceptions of Presidential Power

Historically, tension has existed between two conceptions of presidential power: the expansive and unrestricted versus the legalistic and restricted. Those presidents holding the expansive and unrestricted conception, mainly products of the twentieth century, have believed that the president's powers are not limited to defined constitutional powers and that there is an undefined residium of power, that is, implied powers, which may be tapped in the national interest. Until Theodore Roosevelt and Woodrow Wilson, the legalistic and restricted view of presidential power customarily prevailed. Roosevelt rejected the view that specific constitutional or congressional authorization must undergird executive action. He argued that executive power is limited only by specific constitutional restrictions or specific restrictions imposed by Congress under its constitutional powers [Roosevelt 1924, p. 357]. Three quotations from Woodrow Wilson illustrate a further development of the expanded and unrestricted conception of presidential power:

His office is anything he has the sagacity and force to make it . . . .

Constitution . . . is a vehicle of life, and its spirit is always the spirit of the age.

President . . . [can] be as big a man as he can. His capacity will set the limit [1911, pp. 69–71, 77–79].

In many respects, the capstone on the concept of expanded and unrestricted presidential power was laid by Franklin D. Roosevelt, who said the presidency " . . . is preeminently a place of moral leadership" and that "Without leadership alert and sensitive to change, we are bogged up or lose our way . . . " [McCormick 1932, p. 2].

Except for Dwight D. Eisenhower, the modern presidents have adhered to the conception of presidential power forged by the two Roosevelts and Woodrow Wilson. The presidency has evolved from the Founding Fathers' conception of the role of legal executive to encompass the broader and more expanded roles of national leader and party leader, which have allowed the president to act more boldly in the public or national interest, given the president's expressed and implied powers. Today, we have a president considered to be head of state, opinion molder, legislative leader, chief administrator, and party leader.

Assessments and rankings of presidential greatness generally reveal that the presidents who followed the expansive and unrestricted view of presidential power are more likely to be considered "great presidents" than those adhering to the legalistic and restricted conception. For example, Presidents Franklin D. Roosevelt and Harry Truman are customarily ranked higher on the scale of presidential greatness than are William Howard Taft and Herbert Hoover.

In large measure, the expansion of presidential power, until the presidency of Richard Nixon, was the product of policy objectives and theoretical statements about the exercise of presidential power by liberal and progressive interests. This was, of course, especially true during the New Deal period of President Franklin D. Roosevelt. Richard Nixon, by contrast, while generally pursuing more conservative policy objectives, still retained the expansive and unrestricted conception of presidential power.

Unchanging Congress

Certain very obvious and glaring differences illustrate why during periods of rapid change and increasing complexity, the president, rather than the Congress, has been the principal catalyst for developing new programs and responding to crisis situations. The legislative process, by its very nature, is properly deliberative and inherently slow. The number of congressmen, their lack of specialized training in an age of specialization, and the labyrinthian committee system contribute to their inability to act with dispatch. In addition to these limitations, the Congress until quite recently has not sought to modernize an essentially nineteenth-century organizational structure or to equip itself with the latest information-gathering tools, such as computers. Congress has both allowed and willed the growth in presidential power and the resulting decline in its own power. Congress has allowed it by not modernizing; Congress has willed it by granting successive presidents wide discretionary authority in meeting and addressing problems. The Congress often has responded to a problem by passing a bill which, in effect, lets the executive branch set up policies and programs to solve the problem.

IRONY, PARADOX, MYTH

Since the quick crescendo of presidential power associated with Franklin D. Roosevelt, each succeeding president has lived with certain public expectations about the character and the capacity of the office and the person occupying that office. These expectations, which are not always consistent with reality, have resulted in irony, paradox, and myth about the presidency which, if they continue to grow, may bring irreparable damage to the world's most powerful position. The purpose here is to indicate the several areas of irony, paradox, and myth and to suggest their inherent dangers to the nation.

Magical President

A rather dreamy-eyed and mystical view of the president has developed that looks upon the president as someone just short of superhuman. Several statements that have been made by reputable scholars and authorities illustrate this problem.

- The president is the "great engine of democracy."

- The president is the "American people's one authentic trumpet."

- "Presidential government is a superb planning institution."

- "White House is the pulpit of the nation and the President is its chaplain."[3]

All of these statements reinforce what Woodrow Wilson said many years ago.

> The nation as a whole has chosen him, and is conscious that it has no other political spokesman. His is the only national voice in affairs. Let him once win the admiration and confidence of the country, and no other single force can withstand him, no combination of forces will easily overpower him. His position takes the imagination of the country. He is the representative of no constituency, but of the whole people. When he speaks in his true character, he speaks for no special interest. If he rightly interprets the national thought and boldly insists upon it, he is irresistible; and the country never feels the zest for action so much as when its President is of such insight and calibre [quoted in Burns 1965, p. 96].

This view of the magical president creates great promise, but what of performance? The reality of Vietnam, Watergate, and other problems suggests a large gap between promise and performance. The president, we have sadly come to realize, is not necessarily superhuman.

King and His Court

As the staff and the press corps around the president have grown, so seemingly has the president's isolation from the public. This thesis, one of the principal burdens of George Reedy's *Twilight of the Presidency* [1970], illustrates one of the great ironies and paradoxes of our times. While we have greater capacity to communicate more effectively, we actually seem to communicate less effectively. Building on Reedy's thesis, Russell Baker and Charles Peters, who liken the president and his staff to the royal European courts of the seventeenth and eighteenth century, say that

> The President, needing 'access to reality' in order to govern effectively, too often has access, instead, only to a self-serving court of flunkeys, knights, earls, and dukes in business suits, whose best chances of advancing their separate fortunes usually lie in diverting reality before it can reach the President. *The result is a dangerous presidential isolation, which may be compounded in its peril because court life works to persuade the President that he is more closely in touch with reality than anyone else in the realm* [Baker & Peters 1971, p. 34, emphasis supplied].

Additionally, President Nixon unfortunately either was placed or placed himself above politics, which resulted in the loss of another restraint on him. For example, the extremes of Watergate were not caused by political party operatives, but by White House staff, other executive branch personnel, and hired hands, with little or no political experience in the traditional American sense of political party activity. The White House staff and other executive branch personnel tended to isolate President Nixon from the exigencies and vicissitudes of politics, even discouraging the president in the conduct of normally expected communication with congressmen and political party leaders. As a result the president often lacked the advice and counsel of congressional and political leaders that might have helped to provide restraint on extraordinary use of political power and have given the president a clearer view of reality. Keeping political power within legitimate political boundaries and providing a clearer view of reality are two of the purposes of the American political tradition.

The reluctant and begrudging response of President Nixon to court-ordered subpoenas of tapes and his failure to respond completely to congressional subpoenas of similar evidence vividly illustrate the problem inherent in the "king and his court" syndrome. For example, Chesterfield Smith, president of the American Bar Association, said he was "shocked" that President

Nixon had never clearly stated before the tape subpoena case
was heard by the U. S. Supreme Court that, "Yes, I am subject to
the rule of law. I'm not king, I'm only a man elected by the
people, and, when the Supreme Court decides that I have to do
something, certainly I'm going to do it" [*Washington Post,* July
6, 1974, p. A 15].

How Many Presidents?

Much recent commentary reveals that there are two presidencies rather than one. The meaning of this is dramatically
illustrated by the Johnson and Nixon presidencies. If Lyndon
Johnson were remembered only for his domestic policy
achievements, his presidency would rank much higher on the
scale of presidential greatness. The reverse is, of course, true for
Richard Nixon. The skills necessary for achievement in one area
are not necessarily the same in the other. Lyndon Johnson was a
skilled legislative strategist, but not a foreign policy expert.
Richard Nixon, by contrast, demonstrated much more skill and
interest in foreign affairs than domestic affairs. Unrealistically,
the American public tends to expect the same level of performance from a president in both areas, but the restraints on the
president in domestic policy-making are about as great as the
freedoms in foreign policy-making. In domestic policy-making,
there are numerous restraints, including the legislative process,
well-entrenched lobbyists, the members of the bureaucracy, and
many others, which are either nonexistent or less restraining in
the development of foreign policy.

Headless Bureaucracy and the Cozy Triangle

How does a president govern and manage a bureaucracy that
has close ties to the Congress and lobbyists? Historically,
bureaucratic agencies have been able to insulate themselves
from presidential influence through these ties, making the president's role as chief administrator a figment of the public imagi-

nation. The Federal Bureau of Investigation has been the best example of this phenomenon. Under the leadership of the late J. Edgar Hoover, the Bureau tended to set policy and seek congressional appropriations with little or no restraint from the president. This problem was particularly evident in the Nixon administration, which confronted not only a bureaucracy with ties to Congress and lobbyists, but also a Congress controlled by the opposite party.

Becoming and Being

The upper house of the Congress has become the principal training ground for presidential candidates and presidents. Two aspects of this senatorial training and selection process for future presidents reveal weaknesses. First, legislative skill is not the same as executive skill or, to put the issue another way, the successful senator may not be a good president. Second, a skillful campaigner is not necessarily an effective executive. Barring a major change, however, presidential candidates will most likely continue to come from the U. S. Senate where they can build a national reputation without incurring the risks of governors, who often have to make unpopular administrative and policy decisions. Senators, but not governors, are customarily expected to study and speak on foreign policy issues which, given the large presidential role in foreign policy, enhances the stature and legitimacy of a senator's campaign for president. Governors, ironically, with their greater administrative experiences have been unable to capitalize on this asset in the same way that senators capitalize on their foreign policy experience.

Unification versus Division

The president is supposed to be the nation's leader, the one who unifies the country. Ironically, as head of his party and as the principal architect of national policy proposals, he divides the country. A president who is also leader of his party automatically bears a measure of opposition from the other party, and those persons whose policy proposals are not selected and promoted by the president quite naturally may be a source of division for him. In the current setting of substantial social unrest, a president may find that his role as unifier of the nation involves a great uphill battle because of the critical priorities he must set.

Conservative versus Liberal Expectations

During much of this century, most liberals have argued for a relatively strong presidency and most conservatives for a relatively weak presidency. The means for achieving the New Deal, Fair Deal, New Frontier, and Great Society were premised upon the greater ability of the presidency to achieve the social and economic objectives of these programs. During these times, of course, conservatives largely found themselves in opposition to the programs while presidents pushed them. An irony of the Nixon presidency was that the conservatives often defended a strong president and liberals bemoaned him. It may be that whether one is for a strong or weak president depends on "whose ox is being gored." Both conservatives and liberals have seemingly lost sight of the Founding Fathers' intentions concerning the president and are more concerned with the use of presidential power to meet certain ideological and programmatic aims. The question no longer is whether presidential power should be considered in an expansive and unrestricted view, but whether that power is being used to achieve the proper policies. Today presidential power is justified by the ends it is seeking to achieve.

Trust versus Distrust

Critical social and economic problems historically have generated an increase in presidential power. Such conditions exist today in the form of rampant inflation and serious social unrest. At present, however, there are other conditions inhibiting the continued growth of presidential power. These conditions, exemplified by Vietnam and Watergate, have caused a substantial decline in public trust and confidence in governmental institutions, including the presidency. The presidency is caught, therefore, in a cross fire between conditions that have traditionally generated power growth and other conditions that are creating a loss of public trust.

The Ultimate Paradox

Substantial questions are now being raised about the effectiveness of presidential government, including critiques by such leading authorities as Edward Banfield [1970], Daniel Moynihan [1969], Theodore Lowi [1969], Peter Drucker [1969], and Andrew Hacker [1970]. From their various viewpoints each of these authorities questions different facets of presidential government. For example, Drucker contends that executive leadership has lost control of its bureaucracy, which means that the direction of policy has become divorced from the execution of policy. Even more pessimistically, Andrew Hacker contends that the United States has the most powerless government of any developed nation in the modern world. Even the titles of the books by the respective authors are indicative of the ultimate paradox of impotence amidst potency: *The Unheavenly City, Maximum Feasible Misunderstanding, The End of Liberalism, The Age of Discontinuity,* and *The End of the American Era.* This analysis suggests that the American presidency is a puzzle shrouded in a mystery and wrapped in an enigma.

CONCLUSIONS

Several conclusions may be suggested from this analysis of constitutional creation of the presidency, the landmarks and watersheds in the growth of presidential power, and the ironies, paradoxes, and myths inherent in the contemporary presidency. First, the presidency, no longer restrained by the Founding Fathers' view of the president as a legal executive, has eclipsed the Congress in governmental power and has assumed the preeminent role in American government. Second, the presidency may be at the apogee of its power both because of public distrust and authoritative reassessments of the value of continuing to strengthen the presidency; however, there are social and economic conditions that, given past experience with domestic unrest, could lead to continued growth in presidential power. Third, the ironies, paradoxes, and myths inherent in the contemporary presidency are not a good omen for either the president or the public because they distort reality for both the president and the public. Fourth, the American presidency appears to be at the same time both potent and impotent. Drawing upon the authoritative commentary of scholars, journalists, and politicians, the purpose of this book is to analyze the issues and questions distilled in this introduction as they relate to the future of the American presidency.

Charles W. Dunn, associate professor and head of the Clemson University political science department, previously served on the University of Illinois (Urbana) faculty and has published articles in several scholarly journals. He has also had substantial practical experience in national, state, and local government with Governor Daniel J. Evans (Washington), U.S. Senator Charles E. Goodell (New York), U.S. Representative Leslie C. Arends (Illinois), and as counsel to the Legislative Committee of the 1970 Illinois Constitutional Convention.

NOTES

1. See generally, Edward S. Corwin, *The President: Office and Powers, 1787–1957* (New York: New York University Press, 1957); Max Farrand, *The Framing of the Constitution of the United States* (New Haven: Yale University Press, 1913).

2. See Corwin, *The President: Office and Powers.*

3. For a full assessment of these and other quotations about the American presidency, see Thomas E. Cronin, "The Textbook Presidency and Political Science." *Congressional Record* (October 5, 1970): S17102–S17115.

BIBLIOGRAPHY

Baker, Russell and Peters, Charles. "The Prince and His Courtiers: at the White House, the Kremlin, and the Reichchancellery." *The Washington Monthly*, March 1971, pp. 34 ff.

Banfield, Edward C. *The Unheavenly City*. Boston: Little, Brown and Company, 1970.

Burns, James MacGregor. *Presidential Government*. Boston: Houghton Mifflin Company, 1965.

Corwin, Edward S. *The President: Office and Powers, 1787–1957*. New York: New York University Press, 1957.

Cronin, Thomas E. "The Textbook American Presidency and Political Science." *Congressional Record* (5 October 1970): S17102–S17115.

Drucker, Peter F. *The Age of Discontinuity*. New York: Harper & Row, 1969.

Farrand, Max. *The Framing of the Constitution of the United States*. New Haven: Yale University Press, 1913.

Hacker, Andrew. *The End of the American Era*. New York: Atheneum Publishers, 1970.

Lowi, Theodore J. *The End of Liberalism*. New York: W. W. Norton and Company, 1969.

McCormick, Anne O'Hare. "Roosevelt's View of the Big Job." *The New York Times Magazine*, 11 September 1932, pp. 2ff.

Moynihan, Daniel P. *Maximum Feasible Misunderstanding*. New York: The Macmillan Company, 1969.

Reedy, George E. *The Twilight of the Presidency.* New York: The New American Library, 1970.

Roosevelt, Theodore. *An Autobiography.* New York: Charles Scribner's Sons, 1924.

Rossiter, Clinton. *The American Presidency.* New York: The New American Library, 1960.

The Washington Post, 6 July 1974, p. A 15.

Wilson, Woodrow. *Constitutional Government in the United States.* New York: Columbia University Press, 1911.

I ☆ THE MAKING AND RATING OF PRESIDENTS

The making of presidential candidates has evoked much commentary, but there has been little concrete analysis of how the historic patterns in the process of nomination and election evolved. Robert L. Peabody and Eve Lubalin foresee continuation of the dominant "senatorial incubator" pattern of presidential nomination and election, which reveals that most presidential candidates during modern history have had substantial United States senatorial experience prior to their nomination and/or election. They note, however, at least three factors that may modify the "senatorial incubator" pattern: **1.** continued vice presidential failure to win presidential elections; **2.** increased gubernatorial tenure; and **3.** a credible campaign performance by a gubernatorial aspirant in the near future.

Having succeeded in winning an election and serving in office, the president becomes a candidate for the presidential rating game, a pastime of people in all walks of life. It has two major sides: a rating of the presidents who have held office and an analysis of those persons who might hold office. Malcolm B. Parsons examines elite perceptions of presidential performance, on the grounds that elites help to determine the perceptions of the masses. Using national survey research data of three elite groups, political scientists, historians, and economists, Parsons concludes that both the elites and the masses embrace a clear preference for an active and strong presidential style.

Robert Peabody, Johns Hopkins University political science professor, has written and edited several books, including *Organizational Authority, New Perspectives on the House of Representatives, Congress: Two Decades of Analysis, To Enact a Law,* and *Education of a Congressman.* He has had fellowships with the Brookings Institution, Social Science Research Council, and the Ford Foundation.

Eve Lubalin, Johns Hopkins University, is a graduate student and Congressional Fellow of the American Political Science Association.

Malcolm B. Parsons, Florida State University professor of government, has written articles for the *American Political Science Review, Journal of Politics, American Journal of Political Science, Journal of Criminal Law* and *Public Administration Review,* in addition to publishing *Perspectives in the Study of Politics.*

1

The Making
of Presidential Candidates

ROBERT L. PEABODY
and
EVE LUBALIN
Johns Hopkins University

As THE NINETIETH CONGRESS DREW
to a close in 1967, William S. White, the long-time chief congressional correspondent for *The New York Times* and a
Washington columnist, noted a nostalgia, and even bitterness,
among senior members of the Senate that was provoked by the
irreverent behavior of their younger colleagues. Lamenting on a
decline in the chamber's dignity, White reported that senior and
"more responsible" Senate members attributed this decline to
" . . . the vastly harsh and abrasive climbing techniques of
younger members who plainly regard the Senate as not an end in
itself but only a transitory holding place on the way up to a
Presidency or Vice Presidency." Commenting further, White
concluded,

> Among the first termers, and sometimes among the second term-
> ers, too, ambition's strident call is almost perceptibly thrumming

at Senatorial ears. Practically everybody under 50 years old is running for something he hasn't got; and running with a lack of grace and savoir faire that would have been quite shocking in the Senate of only a few years ago [1967, p. A-21].

These impressions represent more than the ruefulness of an acknowledged admirer of the Senate of Russell, Taft, and Johnson, the Senate of the 1940s and 1950s. They constitute a pungent, even agonizing, outcry about the changing role of the contemporary Senate in presidential nominating politics. For White, the Senate was and should remain a citadel — an insular body, but one with a sense of grandeur and proper perspective on its true role in the national political scene. In the mid-1950s he described the Senate as an instinctively conservative body, resistant to change, dominated by senior members with little or no ambition outside its walls, and governed by a set of informal norms stressing civility, institutional pride, legislative specialization, reciprocity, and deference to one's elders [White 1956]. Even the most cursory knowledge about presidential recruitment patterns since 1960 makes one aware of the extent to which the chamber's insularity has been breached and the career aspirations of its members deflected outward beyond its red carpets, Victorian snuff boxes, and handcrafted desks.

The pattern from 1960 on is deceptively simple — the presidential nominating conventions of both major parties have consistently granted their highest prize — the presidential nomination — to either incumbent senators or vice presidents who served in the Senate immediately before ascending to the vice presidency. Kennedy and Nixon in 1960, Goldwater and Johnson in 1964, Humphrey and Nixon in 1968, and McGovern and Nixon in 1972 — this systematic choice of individuals from one major governmental institution reveals a consistency in presidential recruitment patterns by both parties unmatched at any time in the history of the republic. Moreover, it represents a rather drastic, if not radical, departure from the political backgrounds of almost all other presidential nominees of the last century.

Before the Civil War, when the nominating process was heavily influenced by Congress, nominees often had congressional experience. Of the twenty-two pre-Civil War major party presidential nominees (1789–1860), nineteen, or 86 percent, had prior congressional experience, and five of these were incumbent senators. However, in the post-Civil War period, as nominating procedures became increasingly independent of Congress, the tendency for the major political parties to reach out to members of Congress progressively diminished. Between 1868 and 1956, only eleven, or 37 percent, of the thirty presidential nominees had served in Congress before receiving the nomination, and only three were incumbents. Two were senators and one was a member of the House of Representatives.[1]

Despite this post-Civil War diversification in nominating processes, the overall contribution of Congress as an important training ground for future presidents remains impressive. Twenty-five of the thirty-six men who have occupied the White House have a prior record of service in one or both Houses of Congress. Of the eleven exceptions, five have been governors (Cleveland, both Roosevelts, Wilson, and Coolidge); three came from a military background (Taylor, Grant, and Eisenhower); two were essentially administrators (Arthur and Hoover); and one, William Howard Taft, emerged from primarily judicial experience.

The last Democratic nomination of an incumbent senator prior to John F. Kennedy's selection was the choice of Stephen A. Douglas in 1860, a procedure that took fifty-nine ballots and two conventions to achieve [Bain & Parris 1973]. Historically, senators have seldom been favored by the Republicans either. Only two Republican senators have received their party's nomination in the post-Civil War period, Benjamin Harrison in 1888 and Warren G. Harding in 1920. Both emerged as compromise choices — Harrison's nomination took eight ballots and Harding's ten. In contrast, all senatorial nominations since 1960 have been gained on the first ballot, generally flowing out of front-running presidential primary experiences. Beyond the nominations of incumbent Senators Douglas, Harrison, and Harding, only two other post-Civil War presidential nominees have even had senatorial experience. James G. Blaine, nominated in 1884 by the Republicans, served for five years in the Senate after a long and distinguished career in the House of Representatives and just before a short stint in President Garfield's cabinet. Vice President Harry S. Truman, nominated by the Democrats in 1948, who succeeded to the presidency following Roosevelt's death, had served in the Senate from 1935 until 1945.

Perhaps even more revealing than the clear Senate monopolization of recent presidential nominations is the fact that serious contenders for the nomination, for the Democrats at least, have almost exclusively been limited to those serving in the Senate. In 1960 Senator Kennedy met serious competition for the nomination from three other colleagues, Lyndon Johnson, Stuart Symington, and Hubert Humphrey, with ex-Governor and former nominee Adlai Stevenson the only strong potential non-senatorial candidate. In 1968, the next open Democratic nominating situation, their presidential aspirants again came exclusively from the Senate, with Senators Humphrey, McCarthy, Robert Kennedy, and McGovern seriously considered for the nomination. The third party and protest candidacy of George Wallace, the former governor of Alabama, was, of course, the important exception.

In 1972, no less than ten Democratic senators, comprising almost one-fifth of that party's Senate members, were either announced or frequently discussed aspirants for the nomination. In contrast to this veritable horde of Senate hopefuls, only six other contenders of varying credibility offered themselves publicly. Former Governor Wallace was the standout once again. Once he was eliminated by an attempted assassination, no others survived the ordeal of the primary contests to emerge as a serious contender for the nomination. Only Senators McGovern, Humphrey, Muskie, and Jackson stayed in the race late into the pre-convention period. Despite Chappaquiddick and his declared intentions not to run, Senator Edward Kennedy also remained an outside possibility as a compromise draft choice [See T. White 1961, 1965, 1969, 1973].

Recent Republican presidential aspirants clearly have been a more varied group, despite the party's ultimate reliance on senators or ex-senatorial vice presidents as nominees. In the three presidential election years since 1960 when the Republican nomination was at least nominally open, governors have been as conspicuous in their efforts to secure the nomination as have senators (Rockefeller in 1960; Rockefeller, Romney, and Scranton in 1964; Rockefeller, Reagan, and Romney in 1968). In addition, Mayor Lindsay (1968), Lieutenant General James Gavin (1968), and Ambassador Henry Cabot Lodge (1964) contributed diversity to the backgrounds of recent Republican hopefuls.

What can one expect in 1976 and beyond? We will return to such speculations in the conclusion. Suffice it to point out here that, at least so far, 1976 promises to replicate this recent pattern of Democratic reliance on the Senate as a source of presidential nominees in contrast to Republican dependence on both governors and senators.

For the moment, let us withhold any attempt at explanation of these partisan differences in recent presidential recruitment patterns. First, it will prove helpful to bring together more systematically some longitudinal data on the past political careers of presidential nominees in order to set contemporary patterns in a comparative context. This will help to illustrate the magnitude of change in recruitment patterns in the recent period, as well as highlight their relative simplicity.

POST-CIVIL WAR PATTERNS OF PRESIDENTIAL NOMINATIONS

In mapping out routes to the presidential nomination in the past, we will summarize officeholding experience proximate to the nomination by making note of the last two political offices held by those ultimately running as presidential candidates of the two major parties. The method used to present these data is a so-called "frequency tree," a technique that summarizes sequential officeholding patterns so as to facilitate rapid visual inspection of prenomination career patterns [see Schlesinger 1966, ch. 6]. The frequency trees presented below will summarize aggregate career patterns for the period from 1868 to 1956 and compare them to similar data for the years 1960 to 1972.

Our data collection on career patterns begins with 1868

rather than 1832, when conventions were first used, because the national nominating conventions as we know them today did not become fully institutionalized and independent of Congress until the immediate pre-Civil War period. Thereafter, until 1868, Democratic conventions were continually disrupted by regional tensions while the Democrats' major partisan opposition, the Whigs, dissolved as a national entity and were gradually replaced by the Republican party. Since 1868 the Democratic and Republican parties have maintained themselves as the two major national partisan organizations and have used the convention system familiar to us today as the routine mechanism for making presidential nominations [See David, Goldman, & Bain 1960, pp. 8–31; Pomper 1963, pp. 12–40]. We have presented data on the political backgrounds of post-1956 nominees separately in order to underscore changes in contemporary presidential recruitment patterns. This comparison should make readily apparent the contrast in past and recent paths to the presidential nomination.

Mainly, we will combine both Republican and Democratic practices. Separate party presentations will be made to acknowledge slight party differences, but mostly to demonstrate that recent trends are consistent for both parties and in marked contrast to the past practices of both. Finally, periodized data will be presented in an abbreviated tabular form for the 1868–1956 period to demonstrate that our aggregate presentation does not mask changes in recruitment patterns over time.

The frequency trees that follow sketch out the routes to office that have been used by major party presidential nominees since the Civil War. In all cases, frequencies as well as percentages have been presented, although the percentages are the figures that have been relied on most heavily in noting trends. Each nominee has been included only once in aggregating these data, and the office entered into the totals was the last office held prior to a nominee's first nomination if he received more than one.

It will be noted that the number of cases on which the trees are based is quite small, with the total number of nominations made by both parties, exclusive of renominations of sitting incumbents between 1868 and 1956, being thirty, and the total number between 1960 and 1972 limited to six. However, these nominations represent the total universe of nominees during these periods. Furthermore, it seems doubtful that even if a larger number of nominations had been made over a longer period, given a basic two-party structure, that the trends noted here would diverge considerably [David, Goldman, & Bain, p. 125]. But, in addition to this judgment, probably the major reason why shifts in patterns based on such small numbers (N) are important for our purposes and should receive more attention than they normally might is because of the accumulated weight of precedent in American presidential nominee selection patterns.

In commenting on this phenomenon in their own study of presidential nominating patterns, David, Goldman, and Bain note the " . . . great difficulty of doing something in politics that has never been done before, compared with the ease of doing it again after it has been done once. [Similarly] . . . it is difficult to reverse a practice after it has occurred consecutively even twice, if it has the effect of producing a vested interest of some value" [David, Goldman, & Bain p. 125]. However, it should be noted that despite the logic of this argument, predictions based on seemingly well-established precedents must remain cautious ones just because counterprecedents may occur and subsequently come to be established.

Data on presidential recruitment patterns for the years 1868–1956 are presented in figure 1. The percentages on the first tier of branches indicate the frequency with which nominees have come directly from the offices appearing in the first column to the left of the decision point (the nomination). The percentages on the second tier of branches indicate the relative frequencies of office experiences immediately prior to the last office held before achieving the nomination. These data were included to see whether or not the Senate has historically been a frequent steppingstone to the nomination.

Of the seven major paths that have been followed in securing the presidential nomination between 1868 and 1956, three of them account for 70 percent of all nominees. These three, in their order of importance, are gubernatorial office (40 percent), federal

Figure 1. **Career patterns of major party presidential nominees, 1868-1956**

Pct. of nominees	No.	Next to last office	Pct. of nominees	No.	Office
6.7	(2)	Federal appointive office			
6.7	(2)	None			
6.7	(2)	Local elective office	40	(12)	Governor
13.3	(4)	Governor			
3.3	(1)	State legislature			
3.3	(1)	House			
3.3	(1)	None			
3.3	(1)	Senate			
10.0	(3)	Federal appointive office	20	(6)	Federal appointive office
3.3	(1)	Governor			
13.4	(4)	None	13.4	(4)	None
3.4	(1)	State legislature	6.7	(2)	House
3.4	(1)	None			
6.7	(2)	State elective office	6.7	(2)	Senate
3.3	(1)	State appointive office	3.3	(1)	Statewide elective office
3.3	(1)	Senate	10	(3)	
6.7	(2)	Governor			Vice president ↓ President (renomination)

Presidential nomination (30)

Figure 2. **Career patterns of Republican presidential nominees, 1868-1956**

Pct. of nominees	No.	Next to last office	Pct. of nominees	No.	Office
5.9	(1)	Governor			
5.9	(1)	None			Federal
5.9	(1)	Senate	29.4	(5)	appointive
11.8	(2)	Federal appointive office			office
5.9	(1)	Governor			
5.9	(1)	House			
5.9	(1)	None	23.5	(4)	Governor
5.9	(1)	Local elective office			
11.8	(2)	State elective office	11.8	(2)	Senate
5.9	(1)	State legislature	5.9	(1)	House
5.9	(1)	State appointive office	5.9	(1)	Statewide elective office
11.8	(2)	None	11.8	(2)	None
11.8	(2)	Governor	11.8	(2)	Vice president ↓ President (renomination)

Presidential nomination (17)

Figure 3. **Career patterns of Democratic presidential nominees, 1868-1956**

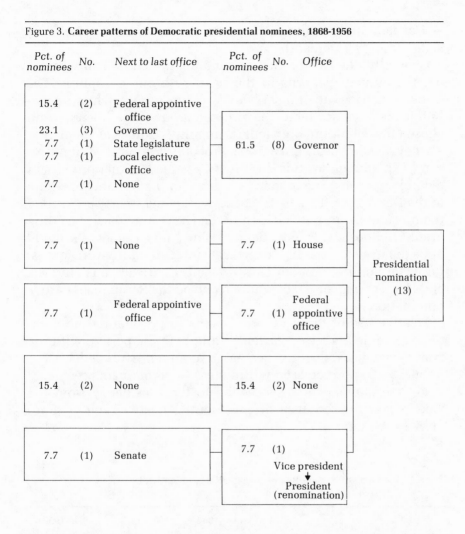

Pct. of nominees	No.	Next to last office	Pct. of nominees	No.	Office
15.4	(2)	Federal appointive office			
23.1	(3)	Governor			
7.7	(1)	State legislature	61.5	(8)	Governor
7.7	(1)	Local elective office			
7.7	(1)	None			
7.7	(1)	None	7.7	(1)	House
7.7	(1)	Federal appointive office	7.7	(1)	Federal appointive office
15.4	(2)	None	15.4	(2)	None
7.7	(1)	Senate	7.7	(1)	Vice president → President (renomination)

Presidential nomination (13)

appointive office (20 percent)[2] and succession to the presidency from the vice presidency following presidential death in office (10 percent). In addition, both parties have relied on prominent nonpoliticians, mostly military heroes and businessmen, as nominees when they were out of power. These four paths combined account for 83.4 percent of all nominations. The remainder of the nominations were scattered between two Congressmen — Garfield and Bryan (6.7 percent), two Senators

— Harrison and Harding (6.7 percent), and one former elected state judge (3.3 percent).

Generally, the two parties have not exhibited radically different recruitment patterns in the past, with one exception. The Democrats have relied most heavily on governors, while the Republicans have scattered their nominations more liberally and chosen those holding high federal appointive office as frequently as they have chosen governors. Probably the most straightforward explanation for this discrepancy is the fact that prominent federal appointees were more available to the Republicans than to the Democrats. This is true because the latter party controlled the presidency for only sixteen of the sixty-four years preceding Franklin Roosevelt's presidency. Thus, few Democrats could hope to have continuous careers as federal appointive officers as, for example, did William Howard Taft, Charles Evans Hughes, and Herbert Hoover, all of whom received the Republican party's nomination.

Relative use of these different paths to presidential nominations remained fairly consistent throughout the period, with the major changes reflecting decreased preference for federal appointees and an increased willingness to renominate presidents who had automatically succeeded to the presidency from the vice presidency because of presidential death. Table 1 summarizes the data.

TABLE 1. **Last Office Held Before Presidential Nomination by Period — Two Major Parties.**

	1868–1892	1896–1924	1928–1956
	N	N	N
Vice president succeeded to presidency		18.1% (2)	11.1% (1)
Senate	10.0% (1)	9.1% (1)	
House of Representatives	10.0% (1)	9.1% (1)	
Governor	40.0% (4)	27.3% (3)	55.6% (5)
Federal appointive	20.0% (2)	27.3% (3)	11.1% (1)
Statewide elective		9.1% (1)	
None	20.0% (2)		22.2% (2)
	100% (10)	100% (11)	100% (9)

In table 1, the longer time period has been broken into three smaller segments that correspond to changes in the electoral bases of the parties and that, additionally, consist of approximately the same number of nominations and elections. This breakdown should permit us to see if our aggregated frequency trees hide change over time and, if so, if such changes are associated with changes in the party system.

It is clear from table 1 that no dramatic changes in the career patterns of nominees emerge over time. Gubernatorial office has not only been the most frequent route to the presidency in the past, but also the most consistent. It is the only office of the seven "steppingstones" that ranks or ties for first place in each of the three time periods. In contrast to this consistent turning toward governors, a federal appointee has not won the nomination since 1928 (Hoover), and the last member of Congress before 1960 to receive a presidential nomination was Warren Harding in 1920.

The nomination of nationally prominent nonofficeholders shows no time trend, but probably indicates that such nominees are favored by parties when out of office. Under such circumstances, the Democrats nominated former Republican Horace Greeley, noted journalist and lecturer, in 1872 and General Winfield Hancock, a military hero, in 1880. In 1940, the out-of-power Republicans nominated Wendell Willkie, who mounted an unusually successful last-minute preconvention campaign based on the newly emerging mass media and his prior commercial contacts, and in 1952, General Eisenhower.

Probably the most meaningful trend has been the increase in nominating success exhibited by vice presidents who succeeded automatically to the presidency upon the death of the directly elected incumbent. This trend is not dramatized by the table because so few nominations were gained this way and because data have not yet been presented on the denial of nominations to vice presidents who became presidents and subsequently were nominated for an additional term in their own right. However, twentieth century adherence to this tradition, starting with Theodore Roosevelt and continuing with Calvin Coolidge, Harry Truman, and Lyndon Johnson, represents a sharp contrast to nineteenth-century practices. Of the four nineteenth-century incumbent presidents who succeeded automatically to the presidency, all sought renomination and none achieved it. In this century we have seen a complete reversal of this pattern.

More recently, the vice presidency has become important for the presidentially ambitious in yet another way. Since 1956, each time a presidential incumbent has not sought renomination, the incumbent vice president — Nixon in 1960 and Humphrey in 1968 — has received the nomination of the party in power. Polls showed that while President Ford was still vice president, he was the preferred candidate of Republican and independent voters for the 1976 Republican nomination.

It is clear from these data on pre-1960 presidential recruitment patterns that the aggregate congressional contribution to the major parties' pool of presidential candidates has been quite negligible. Altogether the House and Senate have contributed only four nominees (13 percent), and none of these congressmen were first ballot nominations. Of all thirty nominations during this period, two-thirds have required less than five ballots to achieve, but all four congressional nominations required more.

Two of the congressional nominations, Congressman James Garfield's (R., Ohio) and Senator Warren G. Harding's (R., Ohio), were the results of deadlocked conventions, and both candidates can be characterized as proverbial "dark horses." Neither nominee received any delegate votes in the initial convention balloting, and Garfield's nomination required thirty-six ballots, while Harding's required ten. Of the two, only Garfield can appropriately be called a career Congressman. He served in the House for eighteen years before his nomination and had been elected to the Senate by the Ohio state legislature several months before his nomination. Harding served one full term in the Senate before his nomination and held minor state elective offices prior to that.

The other two congressional nominees during this period, Congressman William Jennings Bryan (D., Neb.) and Senator Benjamin Harrison (R., Ind.), were clearly more serious contenders for their party's nomination than either Garfield or Harding were initially. Both nominees received substantial support in the early convention balloting and both clearly represented factions within their parties. However, neither of them had made Congress the major focus of their careers. Bryan served in the House for only two terms prior to his first nomination and had been out of office for over a year before receiving it in 1896. After losing this election he remained politically active as a journalist and lecturer rather than as an officeholder. He was renominated in 1900 and 1908. Harrison served one term in the Senate immediately before his nomination, but had not held formal office for thirteen years before his appointment to the Senate in 1881. That prior office was a minor state elective one. In the interim he was very active in the Indiana Republican party and attended national conventions regularly as a delegate. His political roots clearly lay in the Republican state political organization and not in the Senate.

Thus, it would seem that these past presidential recruitment patterns contrast vividly with those of the years 1960 through 1972. The exclusive reliance of both major parties on vice presidents and senatorial incumbents from 1960 to 1972 that has already been outlined is represented pictorially in figure 4. This frequency tree contrasts markedly with that presented in figure 1 both in its simplicity and in the kind of career patterns that proved successful in nomination contesting in this period.

The contrast with the past is especially interesting because senators seem to have been consistent, though less frequent and successful, contenders in the earlier period. Aggregate data collected on governmental positions held by presidential contenders since 1832, when nominating conventions were first used, indicate that senators were active candidates for the nomination in the years between 1832 and 1956. Senators constituted 35 percent of all losing contenders for major party nominations in both halves of the 120-year period [David, Goldman, & Bain 1960, p. 125].

Having established this historical contrast in recruitment patterns over time, we turn now to attempts at explanation. The major burden of our argument will be that changes in the nature of the presidential nominating process over the last thirty years

Figure 4. Career patterns of major party presidential nominees, 1960-1972

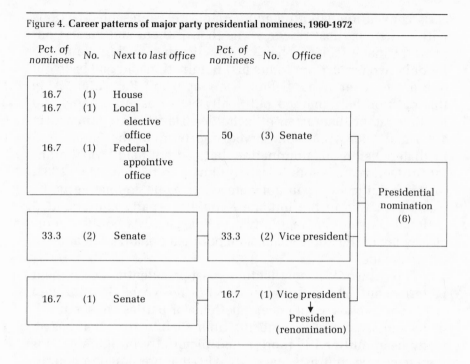

Pct. of nominees	No.	Next to last office	Pct. of nominees	No.	Office
16.7	(1)	House			
16.7	(1)	Local elective office	50	(3)	Senate
16.7	(1)	Federal appointive office			
33.3	(2)	Senate	33.3	(2)	Vice president
16.7	(1)	Senate	16.7	(1)	Vice president ↓ President (renomination)

(Presidential nomination (6))

have dovetailed with changes in the post-World War II Senate in such a way as to favor ambitious senatorial presidential aspirants over their traditional gubernatorial rivals, especially for senators of the congressional partisan majority.

THE EVOLVING NATURE OF PRESIDENTIAL NOMINATING PROCESSES

Motives in the Nominating Process

Historically, the major criterion used in selecting presidential nominees in national party conventions has been their perceived ability to win. Held together neither by ideology nor organization, political incentives have constituted the major reason for disparate party leaders to cohere at all at a national level. Examples of such incentives are the expected help of a presidential coattail in state and local elections, the exchange of patronage and other material benefits for political support, and the likely satisfaction of individual ambitions through cabinet and other federal appointments that a new president might have to dispense [David, Goldman, & Bain 1960; Polsby & Wildavsky 1971; Pomper 1963].

The direct association of American presidential nominating politics with election outcomes distinguishes American executive recruitment patterns from those of other Western nations. This distinctive political characteristic has led one recent observer of British and American practices to characterize the American system as an "entrepreneurial" one [Helco 1973; see also Epstein 1967]. What this designation is meant to convey is the premium placed in the American system on the ability of a presidential aspirant to creatively manipulate current partisan balances, political resources, and public images and preferences in such a way as to mobilize the political interests of others in his behalf. This twentieth-century view closely parallels that of a well-known nineteenth-century British observer of American presidential politics. "Who is the man fittest to be adopted as candidate?" James Bryce asked rhetorically in the 1880s. "Plainly," he answered, "it is the man most likely to win" [quoted in Pomper 1963, pp. 122–123].

One consequence of this motive force in nominating politics has been that the field from which American presidential nominees have been chosen has been comparatively flexible, wide-ranging, and inclusive [Helco 1973; Schlesinger 1967]. Prominent steppingstones, to the extent that they exist, have varied over time as changing political contexts established different opportunities and liabilities for the ambitious politician. What seems to have remained constant is the high probability that presidential nominations will go to aspirants, or entrepreneurs, who can combine political resources and opportunities in such a way as to gain support from a wide range of party leaders and, ultimately, from rank-and-file voters.

This interpretation of American nominating politics presupposes that major party conventions are composed of professional politicians and grassroots activists primarily motivated by political rather than ideological concerns. Undoubtedly, this assumption does not apply equally in every case. For example, it is not helpful in explaining the Goldwater candidacy in 1964 or the McGovern candidacy in 1972. The Goldwater and McGovern nominations, especially the latter, were made possible by the presence of a large number of issue-oriented grassroots amateurs within the delegate ranks. In both cases, amateur politicians stressed the importance of ideology rather than the more traditional concerns as a basis for candidate support, and in these two cases, the "amateur politicians" were able to capture the presidential conventions. This orientation contrasts rather sharply, for example, with the concerns of John F. Kennedy's supporters in 1960, most of whom stressed the senator's ability to win in their states [for 1960 see Tillett 1962; T. H. White 1961; for the Goldwater and McGovern candidacies see Polsby & Wildavsky 1971, pp. 35–59; T. H. White 1973]. These grassroots challenges to traditional party leadership may constitute nothing more than historical anomalies. On the other hand, they may signal the emergence of a new motive force in nominating politics. Recent changes in local party organization and reforms in the presidential nominating process may facilitate the future takeover of conventions by similarly motivated amateurs [Democratic National Committee 1970; Soule & Clarke 1970; Sorauf 1972].

Despite the possibility of such future grassroots challenges, a fundamental assumption of this paper is that a candidate's ability to persuade convention delegates that he can win the presidential election will remain crucial to his successful pursuit of the nomination. Our attempts at explaining contemporary changes in American presidential recruitment patterns flow from this perspective.

Changes in the Nominating Process

Over the past thirty years the American presidential nominating process has been transformed by three major developments that have had a pervasive impact on both delegate and aspirant behaviors: **1.** an increase in popular influence, **2.** a revolution in the American communications system, **3.** the nationalization and increasing competitiveness of American presidential politics. We shall try to indicate briefly how these developments have altered the parameters of presidential nomination contesting [Carleton 1957; David, Goldman, & Bain 1960; Davis 1967; Mendelsohn & Crespi 1970; Pomper 1963; Sorauf 1972].

Prior to the advent of mass means of communication, such as national news magazines, radio, television, and public opinion polls, the network of political contacts that made up state and local party organizations constituted the major source of political information for political leaders. Given this primitive communication system and the relative isolation of party leaders from one another, national party conventions represented unique opportunities for political leaders to meet, exchange information, cement bargains, and drum out a national ticket with a chance of winning.

Convention interaction was also important because presidential candidates traditionally limited their involvement in election campaigns, did not travel extensively, and had limited means of reaching the public directly. Thus, the support of state and local party organizations was often more important for election outcomes than personal candidate appeal. As a result, the criterion of "winnability" dictated that convention delegates find a candidate acceptable to most, if not all, major party factions who could be supported enthusiastically by established local party organizations.

As a consequence of these needs, national party conventions were truly deliberative bodies that exercised considerable discretion in the nominating process. Usually, convention deliberations were dominated by the search for a safe, "available" candidate who could win — a politician of white, Anglo-Saxon Protestant background whose personal life was uncompromised and who had not, during his political career, irrevocably offended any major party faction or interest. Beyond these criteria, one other major consideration, related to the sectional nature of American politics prior to the New Deal, seems to have been important in the selection process. This was a candidate's geo-graphical origin. Because presidential politics in the post-Civil War period was, in contrast to recent contests, relatively partisan and sectional, the selection of a nominee from a competitive, and possibly swing, state with a large number of electoral votes had unusually high strategic value. The typical result of convention deliberations in this period was the choice of a rather noncon-troversial candidate, acceptable to all party factions, whose major asset was his ability to carry a large swing state. As we have seen earlier, these candidates were often governors [see David 1972; David, Goldman, & Bain 1960; Hyman 1959; Pomper 1963; Schlesinger 1970].

These patterns in the nominating process, patterns that ob-tained as recently as forty years ago, seem almost quaint in light of contemporary preconvention campaigns. The vast changes that have occurred in the interim seem to be a result of the increasing importance of finding a candidate with national ap-peal and of the interactive effects of polls, primaries, and televi-sion on both presidential aspirants and convention delegates.

The presidential elections of 1928 and 1932 considerably eroded the sectional and intensely partisan patterns in American politics that had prevailed throughout most of the post-Civil War period. Outside the South, the impact of the Depression and the combined political campaigns of Alfred E. Smith and Franklin Delano Roosevelt led to a redistribution of partisan preferences in the electorate in such a way as to focus political contests around national rather than sectional concerns. This political realignment of the electorate, combined with the growth of na-tional mass media as the major source of political information, resulted in the spread of competitive party politics to a relatively large number of pivotal states, compared to the past, and in-creased the frequency of uniform national trends in presidential voting behavior [Burnham 1970; David 1972; Key 1955, pp. 3–18; Schattschneider 1960, pp. 78–96].

Given these political developments, the weight placed upon the geographical origins of presidential candidates in conven-tion decision making has been drastically reduced, if not entirely eliminated. The likelihood that a presidential candidate will carry one or two swing states as a result of his geographical identification has paled in significance compared to the question of whether or not a candidate will have national appeal. This, in turn, has led to the heightened importance of opinion polls, primaries, and national television coverage — all crucial components of recent preconvention campaigns.[3]

The combined impact of these forces has significantly altered the nature of preconvention campaigning and decentralized the nomination process. Pursuit of presidential nominations has become markedly more open, and lengthening preconvention campaigns have progressively focused on the cultivation of a popular national constituency as an indirect means of securing delegate support. The discretion exercised by the conventions has been reduced, and nominations have been increasingly determined before the conventions meet. Nomination is won as a result of decentralized bargaining between aspirants and delegates during which the former seek advance commitments from the latter on the basis of their poll showings [David, Goldman, & Bain 1960, pp. 273–324; Davis 1967; Mendelsohn & Crespi 1970].

This brief description of changes in the nominating process should make clear the major contrasts between recent presidential nominating contests and those conducted in the past. These modifications have confronted aspiring presidential candidates with new opportunities and liabilities in their quest for the presidency. In the words of one student of the nominating process, the traditional standard of "availability" has given way to that of "prominence" [Pomper 1963, p. 129].

THE SENATE AS AN INCUBATOR OF PRESIDENTIAL CANDIDATES

Several familiar, if not fully persuasive, arguments have been advanced to explain senatorial failures to win nomination contests over the last century [Baker 1960; Broder 1963; Harris 1959; Ranney 1971, pp. 116–117; Sorauf 1972, pp. 296–297]. First, it has been alleged that, in contrast to governors, senators were infrequently "safe" candidates, acceptable to disparate party factions, since their legislative responsibilities required that they take public stands on the whole gamut of issues that came before a Congress. Governors seldom established much of a public record, unless they had previously served in Congress, since in their role as state chief executives, they were rarely required to take positions on national issues.

Second, at a time when presidential responsibilities were largely administrative, the legislative experience of senators was not seen as directly relevant to the skills required of the president. In comparison, the experiences of governors, especially those of large states, who dealt with state legislatures and administered the affairs of an important executive office, seemed more appropriate training for the presidency than that of senators.

Third, governors usually had more influence in state party organizations than did senators and, therefore, often controlled their states' delegations to national conventions. Thus, if they themselves wanted to run for the presidency, governors were in a good position to launch their own candidacy.

Finally, senators were not popularly elected until 1914 and, therefore, usually lacked campaign experience and popular testing in their own states. Because of the special importance of nominees carrying their own states in a period of closely contested national elections, senators were seen as riskier candidates than governors fresh from one or more election victories.

Explanations for the relative failure of governors, as compared to senators, in recent conventions have often focused on many of the same dimensions but with a different twist. Governors now appear to be isolated from national policy-making, and their immersion in parochial state concerns is considered more of a liability than an asset. Moreover, the purely administrative aspects of the president's job have contracted in comparison to presidential responsibility for formulating complex national economic and social policies, conducting American foreign affairs, and leading national public opinion.

Further, governors are seen as handicapped by their state executive responsibilities because of the ostensibly unhappy political plight of most contemporary governors. Faced with increasing public demands for services and inadequate sources of revenue, governors have either had to delay improvements in public services or raise taxes to cover state expenditures. In addition, it is maintained, their effectiveness in dealing with these problems has been further reduced by antiquated state constitutions, independent state adminstrative agencies, and malapportioned, hostile state legislatures. Since they are the most visible state politicians and handiest scapegoats, incumbent governors are seen as increasingly vulnerable politically and as failing in progressively larger numbers to win their attempts at reelection. Thus governors are perceived by some as having lost most of the solid base they once possessed for launching nomination campaigns.

The final interrelated set of liabilities said to plague contemporary governors is their relative anonymity and the public's image of them as parochial figures. With the growth of national mass media centered in Washington and the shifting of political resources and responsibilities from state capitols to Washington, governors have been at a disadvantage in attracting the attention of the national media. Increasingly, because of the nationalization of American politics and disproportionate media coverage of the president and members of Congress, the latter political officials have become most familiar to the public and provide much of what national and partisan leadership of public opinion now exists.

Given the changes in the nominating process that we have outlined above, this last argument, in tandem with one other rarely mentioned gubernatorial liability — that of relatively short tenure — seems to us to be one of the most compelling explanations for recent gubernatorial failures in nomination contesting.

Recent research on the political vulnerability of governors, as reflected in actual election outcomes, contradicts the assumption that governors are in a markedly more tenuous political position now than they were earlier in this century. Although gubernatorial elections were unusually competitive during the 1950s, governors were not more vulnerable as a group in the

1960s than they had been in earlier decades. In fact, their electoral fortunes, compared to those of Congressmen, actually improved [see Schlesinger 1960, pp. 85–91; Turrett 1971, pp. 108–132].

Rather than being a recent phenomenon, relative gubernatorial vulnerability appears to be a constant attribute of state executive office compared, for example, to national legislative office. Comparison of the aggregate political fortunes of governors and senators in the 1900s reveals that during this century gubernatorial races have been more competitive than House or Senate contests. Additionally, there has been a higher rate of turnover of gubernatorial nominations and elections during this period than of senatorial ones [Hinckley 1970, pp. 836–842; Kostroski 1973, pp. 1213–1234; Schlesinger 1960, pp. 197–210; Schlesinger 1966, pp. 40–69, 142–171].

These political characteristics of senatorial and gubernatorial career patterns are reflected in data that have been collected on office tenure of presidential and vice presidential nominees. Between 1848 and 1968, 79 percent of all governors winning either of these nominations served four years or less in that office before winning their nomination. In contrast, 57 percent of senatorial recipients served eight years or more before winning their nominations, and 39 percent served 12 years or more [Schlesinger 1970].

Thus, a marked recent increase in the political vulnerability of governors does not seem to be a fully persuasive explanation for recent gubernatorial failures. However, increased gubernatorial competition in the 1950s may have constituted a temporary liability that was further aggravated by the failure of any gubernatorial nominee to win a presidential election subsequent to Franklin Roosevelt's victories. What seems a more plausible explanation in light of changes in contemporary nominating processes — or at least a necessary complement to possible perceived gubernatorial political vulnerability — is that the traditionally short office tenure of governors and long office tenure of senators, combined with the different national roles currently played by these officials, have placed Senators in an advantageous position vis-à-vis their gubernatorial rivals.

It is only about a decade since one student of political re-cruitment, Joseph Schlesinger [1966], argued that because gubernatorial tenures were short, governors were likely to have progressive ambitions and orient themselves toward higher, that is, federal, office. In contrast, Schlesinger noted that because senatorial tenures were typically extended, senators were more likely to have static ambitions and not aim for higher office. Rather, he argued, senators would view the Congress as a per-manent resting place and abide by institutional norms in order to advance quietly within its walls.

Two considerations now seem to mitigate against the force of this argument. First, the short tenure typically associated with gubernatorial office has become a distinct liability for ambitious governors because of long preconvention campaigns, the re-duced frequency of open nominations, and nomination strategies based on the gradual development of a national constituency. As David Broder has noted: "A Senator can lay siege to the Presidency; a Governor must seize it on the run" [1963, p. 93]. Contemporary patterns in presidential nominating politics and the decreasing frequency of open nominations have made this last strategy increasingly difficult.

Second, the relative paucity of senatorial nominations in the past stemmed not so much from a lack of senatorial ambition as from the liabilities intrinsic to a Senate career in relation to the criterion employed in selecting presidential nominees. As we have noted, senators frequently did contest for presidential nominations in the past, but failed to obtain them. We have already presented a number of reasons why senators seem to have fared poorly in the post-Civil War period in contests for the presidential nomination. Now we shall try to explain why recent changes in the Senate have proved to be advantageous to the presidentially ambitious senator.

The Citadel versus the Contemporary Senate

The Senate of the 1940s and early 1950s was an unlikely incubator of nationally prominent political leaders. In trying to convey a sense of Senate life during this period, we need not dwell overly long on the familiar folklore of William S. White, or the more empirically grounded contributions of Donald R. Matthews and Ralph K. Huitt.

"The Inner Club," as White described it, was an elusive construct at best, and one whose utility has been debated [Huitt 1969, pp. 159–178; Polsby 1971b, pp. 52–63]. Still, it represented the essence of the body for White, and he has since lamented its passing. Constituted of "Senate types" drawn from all sections, but dominated at its core by senior Southern members, White argued that this oligarchical assemblage ruled over the Senate through a combination of personal skills and a monopoly of the institutional bases of power within the chamber.

White's portrait of the Senate was supplemented by Donald Matthews in 1960 when he published his famous description of Senate folkways, gleaned from semistructured interviews with various participants in the Senate legislative process. Matthews' enumeration of six norms that guided Senate behavior — apprenticeship, concentration on legislative work, specialization, courtesy, reciprocity, and institutional patriotism — did not diverge appreciably from the code of conduct described by White. Rather, it seemed to make it more explicit as well as to undergird it with an empirical base. The writings of Ralph K. Huitt [1969] partially mitigated these interpretations by pointing up the range of alternative behaviors or roles available to individual senators, party leaders, and committee members.

The Senate as "Citadel" or "Establishment" contrasts vividly with characterizations of Senate behavior, influence, and function offered recently by congressional scholars, as well as by a number of White's fellow journalists. Several feature newspaper articles that appeared during the middle and late 1960s questioned the continued validity of the old model of the Senate, noting an increase in activity and initiative on the part of junior members, a decrease in the power of Southerners and committee chairmen, an erosion of traditional voting blocs premised on regional and/or economic homogeneity, and an increase in the number of senators dependent on their public image rather than a party organization for election [Albright 1968, p. A 2; Cordtz

1965, p. 8; Glass 1971, pp. 499–512; W. White 1967, p. A 21; Wicker 1965].

These journalistic assessments have been reinforced by Nelson W. Polsby [1969, pp. 61–74; 1971a, pp. 3–13 & pp. 105–110; 1971b, pp. 51–71] and Randall B. Ripley [1969] in their recent writings on the contemporary Senate. Both of these scholars have argued that the Senate can no longer be accurately portrayed as a body dominated by a limited number of powerful committee chairmen or bloc leaders engaging in habitual reciprocity on important policy questions and armed with sanctions to punish deviant members. Rather, they have submitted that changes in Senate personnel and committee structure, especially the proliferation of subcommittees, combined with the size, visibility, and rules of the chamber, have resulted in a decrease in conservative, Southern influence and a concomitant dispersion of power among individual members.

Polsby, especially, has emphasized that the opportunities available to senators in the policy-making process have made the Senate a launching pad for the presidency and a more innovative institution. In contrast to its earlier conservative, deliberative functions, Polsby notes that the Senate's main activities now consist of seizing policy initiatives, defining new issues, and cultivating national constituencies in support of them through publicized hearings, investigations, speeches, and legislative sponsorship. Given these opportunities, he finds individual senators less dependent on their senior elders for political advancement, less insular in orientation, and less willing to accept the traditional "Senate type" as an appropriate model for their own behavior.

Several other changes in internal Senate operations and institutions exogenous to the chamber may also be singled out as contributors to change in the Senate in the postwar period. Of prime importance, and probably unanticipated at the time, were the long-run consequences of stronger Democratic and Republican party leadership in the 1950s and 1960s. Elected minority leader in 1953 and majority leader in 1955, Lyndon B. Johnson reduced the power of the old Senate Inner Club in a number of ways. First, by building a formidable information network and

welding together a band of diverse senators predisposed to help
out their leader, Johnson placed himself at the center of coalition
building efforts in the chamber and thus deprived Senate elders
of one of their important functions [Evans & Novak 1966, pp.
26–224; Huitt 1969, pp. 136–158; MacNeil 1970; Peabody 1975].

Second, in his search for available resources to cement his
power, Johnson, with the approval of Senator Russell and other
Southern dignitaries, modified the seniority rule by instituting
the practice of awarding choice committee assignments to junior
senators before permitting senior members to occupy more than
one influential committee seat. This practice was also adopted by
the Republicans in 1959, and since has been codified in the
Legislative Reorganization Act of 1970. This breach in the strict
application of seniority, as well as changes in personnel, is
commonly cited as having been advantageous for Senate liberals. For although it gave more discretion to the parties' Committees on Committees, it also meant that the dispersion of leadership roles made theoretically possible by the proliferation of
subcommittees could take on further significance.

Finally, the changes Johnson instituted in the daily operation of the chamber, complemented by Senate Minority Leader
Everett Dirksen's consolidation of power, further reduced many
of the advantages that senior members had enjoyed as a function
of their mastery of chamber rules and monopolization of debate.
By employing aborted quorum calls and the unanimous consent
procedure extensively to control Senate proceedings, and by
scheduling either stop-and-go legislative activity or continuous
night sessions, Johnson reduced the role of debate and debaters
in the Senate's operations and more or less controlled its business. While Johnson's successor, Mike Mansfield, has not used
equally dramatic ploys to maintain control of the chamber, scattered observations on his leadership style suggest that the formal
Democratic leadership has maintained control over scheduling
and has supported junior members' efforts to take an active role
both within the congressional party and in the larger chamber
[Albright 1968; Bibby & Davidson 1972, pp. 145–146; Glass
1971].

A number of factors, exogenous to the internal operations of the chamber, may also be construed as contributing to change in the postwar Senate, although none have been systematically studied in that context. The first of these is the increasing degree of political competition at the state level. Donald R. Matthews [1960, p. 117] predicted that increasingly competitive two-party politics would lead to greater deviance from Senate folkways or even to their modification, as senators with marginal victories acted to decrease their political vulnerability by making a record early in their careers. Similarly, Tom Wicker of The New York Times has argued that a reduction in the political homogeneity of Senate constituencies and the national salience of new political issues has made reciprocal relationships between cohesive economic or regional blocs more difficult [1965].

In addition to changing constituency pressures, the ramifications of the growth of national mass media and polling agencies have probably had far-reaching consequences for the Senate. As political resources and activity have shifted from state capitols to Washington, national television coverage of political events also has shifted public attention to national policy makers and away from state and local politicians. Aside from the presidency and vice presidency, the Senate has been the only national institution that has shared in this publicity through its use of televised hearings and investigations [Polsby 1971b, p. 68].

This technological change has made it possible for relatively junior senators to use their subcommittee chairmenships to develop national standings probably unmatched in earlier eras. Some evidence exists that politically ambitious Senators have done just this in their quest for the nomination. Data collected on nine publicly announced Democratic senatorial presidential aspirants and nine "controls" matched for seniority, ideology, and constituency characteristics in 1971, the year before the onset of the 1972 presidential primaries, reveal that presidential aspirants held twice as many hearings, on the average, as their counterparts. These group differences could be expected by chance only three out of 100 times [Lubalin 1973].

Drawing together these observations on the contemporary
Senate, several major interrelated trends can be set forth as to
why senatorial incumbency seems to facilitate successful nomination contesting. First, and perhaps most important, is the apparent increasing dispersion of influence and initiative to a
larger number of senators, made possible by the small size of the
chamber combined with postwar dilution of the seniority principle and proliferation of subcommittees. The proliferation of
subcommittees from 1950–1970 is documented in table 2. In
addition to the gross quantitative increase in the number of subcommittees, the reorganization of the Senate committee structure reduced the relative number of unimportant subcommittees,

TABLE 2. **Senate Subcommittee Structure Between 1950 and 1970.**

	1950	1960	1970
Number of Standing			
Committee Subcommittees	60	93	116
Number of Special			
Committee Subcommittees	0	0	7
Number of Select			
Committee Subcommittees	0	6	6
Number of Joint			
Committee Subcommittees	0	10	15
Total Number of Subcommittees	60	109	144

Source: *Congressional Index,* 81st, 86th, and 91st Congresses (Commerce Clearing
House).

such as those under the jurisdiction of the Committees on the
District of Columbia, Post Office and Civil Service, and Rules
and Administration, and increased the number falling under the
jurisdiction of more politically salient and prestigious committees, such as the Committees on Armed Services, Foreign Relations, Judiciary, Labor and Public Welfare, and the nonstanding
investigatory committees. In 1950 subcommittees of the three
former committees constituted 38 percent of all subcommittees,
while in 1970 they constituted only 10 percent of all subcommittees.

By the time of the Ninety-third Congress (1973–1974) fully fifty-five of the fifty-seven Democratic senators were taking advantage of the staff assistance and other benefits flowing from the incumbency of at least one subcommittee chairmanship. Similarly, only one Republican Senator did not hold at least one ranking minority position on either of his several committees. This relatively quick absorption of junior senators into the power structure is especially advantageous for Democratic newcomers who enjoy the prerogatives of subcommittee chairmanships as a result of their membership in the majority party [Ornstein & Rohde, forthcoming].

This diffusion of organizational responsibility has probably been an important contributor to another aforementioned trend in the postwar Senate — the erosion of traditional institutional norms as, for example, apprenticeship. Compared to their forerunners, junior senators of the late 1960s and early 1970s have not hesitated to speak out. Instead, incoming members have taken an immediate and active role in legislative matters and sought to establish a visible and public record from the start. This relative independence of incoming freshmen has been further enhanced by the recent formation of active bipartisan class clubs oriented toward collective lobbying of more senior colleagues on various housekeeping matters and rules changes. Composing nearly 40 percent of the Senate membership, these clubs, if they continue to be active, represent a potentially strong force for the continuation of reforms that facilitate the exercise of initiative by individual members [Ripley 1969, pp. 218–228].

These attempts by junior members to exercise more initiative in Senate affairs have been facilitated by a third change in the Senate — the reorientation of the current party leaders, Democratic Majority Leader Mike Mansfield and Republican Minority Leader Hugh Scott. While Johnson and Dirksen, when in analogous roles, contributed to the erosion of the Inner Club in the 1950s and 1960s by centralizing party leadership, Mansfield and Scott have facilitated individualism in the Senate by reverting more to a shared pattern of leadership. Mansfield, for example, has described his role as being that of a servant to other senators [Peabody 1973, p. 18].

These modifications in Senate structure, norms, and leadership style over the last few decades have removed a number of
constraints that previously limited individual senatorial initiative and have created new opportunities for relatively junior
senators to actively participate in Senate life. By enhancing such
opportunities to lead public opinion on new issues through the
use of nationally broadcast hearings, nightly news coverage, and
guest appearances, presidentially ambitious senators, especially
those of the majority party, have exploited the potential for national leadership now inherent in Senate incumbency.

The opportunities offered senators by virtue of membership
in the contemporary Senate give them unique advantages in the
nominating process, shared or surpassed, perhaps, only by the
vice president. Politicians holding these high federal offices, if
they wish, can have access to a degree of national media coverage that gubernatorial tenure rarely merits. The popular awareness developed in this manner by senators and vice presidents
often snowballs by spurring speaking engagements that further
increase their political contacts and public recognition.

In addition to the publicity attendant on office, senators
have an advantage, as compared to governors, in rarely being
unwilling captives of specific and troublesome issues. Rather, as
a result of their membership in a collective body and their relatively large number of committee and subcommittee assignments, senators have considerable discretion in allocating their
energies and can develop public images and national constituencies in a calculated fashion. These tasks are facilitated by
their extended tenure [Broder 1963]. Similarly, vice presidents
who enjoy the respect of their presidents can expect to assume,
at least formally, national and international responsibilities that
permit them to develop the image of responsible, experienced
statesmen. Skillful exploitation of television is especially effective. Research on the political impact of television indicates that
beyond serving informational needs, this medium has been most
influential in its indirect effect on public images about politics
and politicians [Campbell 1966, pp. 318–323; Lang & Lang 1968;
Mendelsohn & Crespi 1970].

Before hazarding a few predictions about the likely future of presidential nominating patterns, the importance of precedence in the nominating process should be underscored once more. Each time a senator or vice president receives the presidential nomination, the legitimacy of these officials becoming future nominees increases. The gradual elevation of senatorial and vice presidential office to the status of presidential steppingstones, in turn, reinforces such recruitment patterns. The combination of regular interelection media coverage and the public's perception of senators and vice presidents as appropriate presidential candidates gives those incumbents who are politically ambitious an advantage over governors in the preconvention period. While governors may still make a try for the nomination by entering primaries, their assets give senators and vice presidents a headstart in nomination contesting and probably increase the likelihood that they will gain the nomination and/or win the subsequent election. Recent precedents in presidential recruitment, while shortlived, strongly condition speculation about likely future nominating patterns.

A LOOK TOWARD 1976 AND BEYOND

Speculation about future political trends is always a precarious undertaking, especially when predictions are made on the basis of such a limited number of cases. However, the material reviewed in this chapter strongly suggests the continued dominance of the nominating process by incumbent vice presidents and senators. Senatorial dominance should be especially evident for the majority congressional party. For more than four decades, Republican senators have generally suffered in their attempts to play national leadership roles, compared to their Democratic colleagues, because of their prolonged minority status and, since 1968, the presence of a Republican president.

Still, a number of factors might have the potential for altering recent presidential recruitment patterns: **1.** continued vice presidential failure to win presidential elections; **2.** increased gubernatorial tenure; and **3.** a credible campaign performance of a gubernatorial aspirant in the near future.

The last vice president to win a presidential nomination and subsequent election was Martin Van Buren in 1836. Since then, Richard Nixon and Hubert Humphrey have been the only vice presidents to gain the nomination, and both failed to win the presidential election while campaigning from that office. Although vice presidents enjoy the advantage of public recognition, and often respect, they are also saddled with the record of the previous administration. At times this may constitute a liability and make it difficult for them to establish an independent and attractive public image.

Two other sources of potential change in recent nominating patterns are lengthening gubernatorial tenure and the effect that a successful gubernatorial presidential campaign might have on public and delegate perceptions. Although gubernatorial tenure has, on the average, been shorter than senatorial tenure due to higher turnover, shorter terms, and more statutory limitations, it has increased progressively throughout the twentieth century. In the 1920s only 16.1 percent of all governors serving during that decade held office for five years or more. By the 1950s this figure had increased to 30.5 percent. This increase in tenure can be explained partially by an increase in the number of states with four-year gubernatorial terms. But it is also due, to some extent, to more gubernatorial reelection success in states with shorter terms. During the 1960s a number of states lengthened their gubernatorial terms to four years and changed their election schedules so that governors would not run in presidential election years. Both of these modifications are likely to increase average gubernatorial tenure [Schlesinger 1971, pp. 210–237]. Longer office tenure may help mitigate one of the liabilities governors have recently suffered, namely low visibility.

The other factor that might aid governors in future attempts at the presidential nomination would be a credible performance by a governor in either a preconvention or actual presidential election campaign. Such an event might counteract the impression that gubernatorial experience is not appropriate training for the presidency and alter public images as well as media coverage of governors.

Despite these possibilities, on balance it seems most likely that senators and vice presidents will continue to dominate the nominating process for the reasons noted above. Since senators are in a relatively good position to lead national-issue-oriented publics, this will probably be true even if presidential nominating politics becomes more issue-oriented.

What may change in the future is the extent of discretion exercised by the conventions themselves. Between 1968 and 1972, seven states adopted presidential primary laws, bringing the total number of states with some type of primary election to twenty-two, plus the District of Columbia. If the number of states holding primaries continues to increase, future conventions may find themselves with a majority of delegates committed to a candidate on the first ballot. In 1972, for the first time, a majority of convention delegates in both parties were chosen in primaries.

Beyond freezing larger numbers of initial delegate votes, more primaries may have the effect of making a clear reading of public opinion difficult. In turn, this might result in more candidates remaining in the contest up to the time of the convention in order to be available as compromise choices if necessary. Deadlocks, at Democratic conventions at least, may also be facilitated by reforms in the Democratic delegate selection process and convention rules, which may result in a larger number of divided state delegations in future conventions. It almost happened in the Democratic party in 1972. In sum, as a result of these developments, national nominating conventions, if not replaced by a national presidential primary, may come to exercise a degree of discretion that approaches that exercised by conventions of the past, although for different reasons. If so, we may see a period of conventions marked by more than one ballot and extensive bargaining between frontrunning aspirants reminiscent of their nineteenth-century predecessors [Parris 1972, pp. 81–86].

NOTES

1. Data on nominees' careers drawn from *Biographical Directory of the American Congress, 1774–1971* (Washington, D.C.: Government Printing Office, 1971), Senate Document 92–8; Robert Sobel, *Biographical Directory of the United States Executive Branch, 1774–1971* (Westport, Conn.: Greenwood Press, 1971); Dumas Malone, ed., *Dictionary of American Biography* (New York: Charles Scribner's Sons, 1935).

2. The federal positions included in this category were cabinet members and Supreme Court Justices.

3. One indicator of the decreasing discretion of recent nominating conventions is the number of ballots necessary to nominate a candidate. Between 1868 and 1956 only seven, or 27 percent of the twenty-six contested nominations were made on the first ballot. The abolition of the two-thirds rule at Democratic conventions in 1936 probably contributed, to some extent, to the demise of extended balloting at Democratic conventions, but long preconvention campaigns resulting in clearcut frontrunners have probably been much more important in explaining recent first-ballot nominations.

BIBLIOGRAPHY

Albright, Robert C. "Senate Youngsters Asserting Selves as Never Before." *The Washington Post*, 15 January 1968, p. A 2.

Bain, Richard C. and Parris, Judith H. *Convention Decisions and Voting Records*, 2nd ed. Washington, D. C.: The Brookings Institution, 1973.

Baker, Russell. "Best Road to the White House — Which?" *The New York Times Magazine*, 27 November 1960.

Bibby, John F. and Davidson, Roger H. *On Capitol Hill*, 2nd ed. New York: Dryden, 1972.

Biographical Directory of the American Congress, 1774–1971. Washington, D. C.: Government Printing Office, 1971, Senate Document 92–8.

Broder, David S. "What's the Best Road to the White House?" *The New York Times Magazine*, 22 September 1963.

Burnham, Walter Dean. *Critical Elections and the Mainsprings of American Politics*. New York: W. W. Norton and Company, 1970.

Campbell, Angus. "Has Television Reshaped Politics?" In *Public Opinion and Electoral Behavior*. Edited by Edward C. Dreyer and Walter A. Rosenbaum. Belmont, Calif.: Wadsworth Publishing Company, 1966.

Carleton, William G. "The Revolution in the Presidential Nominating Convention." *Political Science Quarterly* 72 (June 1957): 224–237.

Cordtz, Dan. "The Senate Revolution." *The Wall Street Journal*, 6 August 1965, p. 8.

David, Paul T. *Party Strength in the United States*. Charlottesville: University of Virginia Press, 1972.

David, Paul T.; Goldman, Ralph M.; and Bain, Richard C. *The Politics of National Party Conventions.* Washington, D. C.: The Brookings Institution, 1960.

Davidson, Roger H.; Kovenock, David M.; and O'Leary, Michael. *Congress in Crisis.* Belmont, Calif.: Wadsworth Publishing Company, 1966.

Davis, James W. *Presidential Primaries: Road to the White House.* New York: Thomas Y. Crowell Company, 1967.

Democratic National Committee, *Mandate for Reform.* DNC, 1970.

Epstein, Leon D. In *Political Parties In Western Democracies.* New York: Praeger Publishers, 1967.

Evans, Rowland and Novak, Robert. *Lyndon Baines Johnson: The Exercise of Power.* New York: The New American Library, 1966.

Glass, Andrew. "Mansfield Reforms Spark 'Quiet Revolution' in Senate." *National Journal* 10 (6 March 1971): 499–512.

Harris, Louis. "Why the Odds are Against a Governor's Becoming President." *Public Opinion Quarterly* (Fall 1959), pp. 361–370.

Helco, Hugh. "Presidential and Prime Ministerial Selection." In *Perspectives on Presidential Selection.* Edited by Donald R. Matthews. Washington, D.C.: The Brookings Institution, 1973.

Hinckley, Barbara. "Incumbency and the Presidential Vote in Senate Elections: Defining Parameters of Subpresidential Voting." *American Political Science Review* 64 (September 1970):836–842.

Huitt, Ralph K. "The Outsider in the Senate: An Alternative Role." In *Congress: Two Decades of Analysis.* Edited by Ralph K. Huitt and Robert L. Peabody. New York: Harper & Row, 1969.

Hyman, Sidney. "Nine Tests for the Presidential Hopeful." *The New York Times Magazine,* 4 January 1959.

Key, V. O., Jr. "A Theory of Critical Elections." *Journal of Politics* 17 (1955):3–18.

Kostroski, Warren L. "Party and Incumbency in Postwar Senate Elections." *American Political Science Review* 67 (December 1973): 1213–1234.

Lang, Kurt and Lang, Gladys Engel. *Politics and Television.* New York: Quadrangle Books, 1968.

Lubalin, Eve. "Political Ambition and Senatorial Behavior." Department of Political Science, Johns Hopkins University, Spring 1973.

MacNeil, Neil. *Dirksen: Portrait of a Public Man.* New York: World Publishing Company, 1970.

Malone, Dumas, ed., *Dictionary of American Biography.* New York: Charles Scribner's Sons, 1935.

Matthews, Donald R. *United States Senators and Their World.* New York: Vintage Books, 1960.

Mendelsohn, Harold and Crespi, Irving. *Polls, Television and the New Politics.* New York: Chandler Publishing Company, 1970.

Ornstein, Norman J. and Rohde, David W. "Seniority and Future Power in Congress." In *Change in Congress.* Edited by Norman J. Ornstein. Forthcoming.

Parris, Judith H. *The Convention Problem Issues in Reform of Presidential Nominating Procedures.* Washington, D. C.: The Brookings Institution, 1972.

Peabody, Robert L. "Congressional Leadership: What Difference Does It Make?" Paper delivered at American Political Science Association meeting, 7 September 1973.

Peabody, Robert L. *Leadership in Congress.* Boston: Little, Brown and Company, 1975.

Polsby, Nelson W. "Policy Analysis and Congress." *Public Policy,* 18 (Fall 1969):61–74.

Polsby, Nelson W. *Congressional Behavior.* New York: Random House, 1971a.

Polsby, Nelson W. *Congress and the Presidency,* 2nd ed. Englewood Cliffs, N. J.: Prentice-Hall, 1971b.

Polsby, Nelson W. and Wildavsky, Aaron B. *Presidential Elections: Strategies of Electoral Politics,* 3rd ed. New York: Charles Scribner's Sons, 1971.

Pomper, Gerald. *Nominating the President: The Politics of Convention Choice*. Evanston, Ill.: Northwestern University Press, 1963.

Ranney, Austin. "Parties in State Politics." In *Politics in the American States*, 2nd. ed. Edited by Herbert Jacob and Kenneth N. Vines. Boston: Little, Brown and Company, 1971.

Ripley, Randall. *Power in the Senate*. New York: St. Martin's Press, 1969.

Schattschneider, E. E. *The Semi-Sovereign People*. New York: Holt, Rinehart and Winston, 1960.

Schlesinger, Joseph A. "Stability in the Vote for Governor, 1900–1958." *Public Opinion Quarterly* 24 (Spring 1960a):85–91.

Schlesinger, Joseph A. "The Structure of Competition for Office in the American States." *Behavioral Science* 5 (July 1960b):197–210.

Schlesinger, Joseph A. *Ambition and Politics*. Skokie, Ill.: Rand McNally and Company, 1966.

Schlesinger, Joseph A. "Political Careers and Party Leadership." In *Political Leadership in Industrialized Societies*. Edited by Louis J. Edinger. New York: John Wiley & Sons, 1967.

Schlesinger, Joseph A. "The Governor's Place in American Politics." *Public Administration Review* 30 (January-February 1970):2–10.

Schlesinger, Joseph A. "The Politics of the Executive." In *Politics in the American States*. 2nd ed. Edited by Herbert Jacob and Kenneth N. Vines. Boston: Little, Brown and Company, 1971.

Sobel, Robert. *Biographical Directory of the United States Executive Branch*. Westport, Conn.: Greenwood Press, 1971.

Sorauf, Frank J. *Party Politics in America*, 2nd ed. Boston: Little, Brown and Company, 1972.

Soule, John W. and Clarke, James W. "Amateurs and Professionals: A Study of Delegates to the 1968 Democratic National Convention." *American Political Science Review* 64 (September 1970):888–898.

Tillett, Paul, ed., *Inside Politics: The National Conventions, 1960*. Dobbs Ferry, N. Y.: Oceana Publications, 1962.

Turrett, J. Stephen. "The Vulnerability of American Governors, 1900—1969." *Midwest Journal of Political Science* 15 (February 1971):108–132.

White, Theodore. *The Making of the President — 1960.* New York: Atheneum Publishers, 1961.

White, Theodore. *The Making of the President — 1964.* New York: Atheneum Publishers, 1965.

White, Theodore. *The Making of the President — 1968.* New York: Atheneum Publishers, 1969.

White, Theodore. *The Making of the President — 1972.* New York: Atheneum Publishers, 1973.

White, William S. "Ambitious Younger Members Alter Senate for the Worse." *The Washington Post,* 18 December 1967, p. A 21.

White, William S. *The Citadel.* Boston: Houghton Mifflin Company, 1956.

Wicker, Tom. "Winds of Change in the Senate." *The New York Times Magazine,* 12 September 1965.

2

The Presidential Rating Game

MALCOLM B. PARSONS
Florida State University

HOW DO ECONOMISTS, HISTORIANS, and political scientists perceive and evaluate presidential performance in the United States, and what, if any, difference does it make? In choosing to deal with these questions, one chooses to examine components of what Vilfredo Pareto called the "nongoverning elite," as opposed to what he called the "governing elite."

In the nongoverning elite, these three groups are part of a larger body known as "the intellectuals." Thus, the larger problem that is approached is the problem of the relationships between knowledge and power. The intellectuals in a society are those who engage in creating, transmitting, and criticizing ideas. They include artists, poets, writers, philosophers, scientists, journalists, teachers, commentators, and so on. It has been observed that in most countries and at most times the intellectuals are "one of the least homogeneous or cohesive of elites," and that they display "a considerable variety of opinion on cultural and political questions" [Bottomore 1964, pp. 69–70]. A society's intellectuals, however difficult to pinpoint as a group, and whatever their doctrinal persuasions or class connections, share a common and direct concern for the culture. As for the economists, historians, and political scientists among them, we shall be interested primarily in demonstrating just how varied their perceptions of presidential performance may be, and if variation can be accounted for in relation to such things as the shared values of professional association, liberal or conservative doctrines, or political party identification.

In utilizing Pareto's distinction between governing and nongoverning elites, it must be acknowledged that at times certain intellectuals leave their customary nongoverning sphere and enter the other, possibly without completely abandoning their former roles as intellectuals. Woodrow Wilson is perhaps our best example, having left political science and Princeton for politics, the governor's chair and, ultimately, the American presidency itself. John F. Kennedy, as a Harvard undergraduate, studied economics, history, and political science. His senior honors thesis was published. While serving in Congress he received the Pulitzer Prize for his historical biography, *Profiles in Courage*. Three related recent examples should suffice: Secretary of State Henry Kissinger, President Nixon's former National Security Affairs adviser, and his predecessors under Presidents Johnson and Kennedy, Walt Whitman Rostow and McGeorge Bundy. Two political scientists and an economist. It is interesting, that when the Department of Government at Harvard recommended tenure for Bundy, who later became dean, President Conant, a distinguished chemist, noted that the recommendation was made in spite of Bundy's lack of any undergraduate or graduate courses in political science, and sighed in some perplexity, " . . . it couldn't have happened in chemistry" [Halberstam 1973, p. 72]. Will Kissinger return to Harvard? M.I.T. refused to take Rostow back, and he is at the University of Texas. Even Bundy left academia.

Such unique convergences of knowledge and power are not under consideration here. They are alluded to as infrequent events in a larger, more subtle underlying pattern of relationships between intellectuals and the rest of society, governing and nongoverning, which is under consideration here. Justification for inquiring about intellectuals' perceptions of presidential performance rests on certain assumptions and propositions that have to do with the desirability, as well as the possibility, of explaining relationships between governing and nongoverning elites and the masses. They more directly concern the role of intellectuals in shaping the socialization process. In this respect, economists, historians, and political scientists are of special significance because their perceptions and judgments permeate the information exchanges and transactions about politics and the presidency that take place in the formal educational system.

By "transaction" is meant "any process of becoming in which the individual . . . is affected by actions through time when involved as a participant in any ongoing situation" [Cantril 1968, pp. 125–126]. Economists, historians, and political scientists also influence the elite and mass communications media and daily transactions and discourse. The ideas of intellectuals infiltrate the conventional wisdom and remain there, at times intransigently, even after losing credence among the intellectuals themselves.

It is postulated, then, that the place of the presidency in American culture, the intellectual climate about the office, derives in large part from the ideas of these intellectual groups. Further, it is postulated that their ideas have a profound ideological impact on American, and even world, society because they incorporate the assumptions on which perception and understanding are based. This is pointedly true when the ideas are intendedly doctrinal or partisan. But it is equally true when they are intendedly professional, objective, or neutral. Intendedly liberal or conservative, radical or reactionary ideas about the presidency are part of politics and have an obvious ideological impact. So, too, do intendedly Democratic or Republican or other partisan ideas.

But ideas that are intendedly objective, neutral, or even scientific are also ideological in their impact. They are ideological because, while excluding any immediate doctrinal or partisan element, they nonetheless depict only selected features of human institutions and behavior while ignoring others. Hence, men are persuaded to conceive of their past, present, and future in particular ways to the exclusion of others. In this sense, a way of looking at something is ideological because it represents a choice among alternatives. Thus, whether the climate of ideas is intendedly doctrinal and partisan or intendedly objective and neutral, or scientific, it is still ideological. It is in such a climate that the perceptions, understandings, and misunderstandings of citizens and politicians, as well as intellectuals, occur. "What we perceive depends largely on the assumptions we bring to any particular occasion" [Cantril, p. 132]. This is true also of what we understand.

It has long been popular to sort out presidents as strong or weak, active or passive, and try to link these attributes with accomplishments, good, bad, or indifferent [See, for example, Amlund 1964, pp. 309–315; Bailey 1966; Borden 1961, 1971; Burns 1965, ch. 1, 2, 3; Hargrove 1966; Hyman 1958, p. 17ff; Maranell 1970, pp. 104–113; Maranell & Dodder 1970, pp. 415–421; Rossiter 1960, ch. 5; Schlesinger 1948, pp. 65–74 and 1962, p. 12ff.]. Children in school and their parents — indeed, virtually everybody — "knows" that George Washington, Abraham Lincoln, and Franklin D. Roosevelt were our three strongest, most active, and greatest presidents, that they established a new nation, preserved the union, and led us through the greatest depression and war we have ever experienced.[1] In the late Professor Rossiter's felicitous phrase, each of them is "enshrined as a folk hero in the American consciousness" [1960, p. 144]. Equally, but abysmally, it is "known" that Ulysses S. Grant and Warren G. Harding were failures in the presidency, near disasters for the country. It is also "known" that the remaining presidents stretch out from giants leading the presidential parade to pygmies bringing up the rear.

In 1960, an important refinement of this approach was offered with the argument that for a president to accomplish anything depends on his ability to persuade rather than command. Selected successes and failures of Truman and Eisenhower were explained in these terms, measured against a bargaining model of political leadership drawn from the example of Franklin Roosevelt's effectiveness [Neustadt 1960]. More recently, the concept has been added that a president's style consists of his observable ways with words, work, and people. The traditional active-or-passive, strong-or-weak dimension is linked with inferences about an affective dimension of positive-or-negative personality traits to produce a more complex typology of presidential character. Among four possible types, active-positive character, as with Franklin Roosevelt or John Kennedy, is seen as the most effective and beneficial for the nation. It is oriented toward productiveness and persuasiveness and constitutes a generally well-adjusted political personality. Active-negative character, on the other hand, as with Lyndon Johnson or Richard Nixon, is seen as hazardous, if not actually detrimental, for the nation. It is oriented toward personal ambition and constitutes a generally maladjusted, compulsive political personality. The hazard lies in rigidly adhering to failing policies [Barber 1972].

Turning now to our own look at presidential performance, we will confine ourselves to six of the incumbents of the office over the period since World War II: Franklin D. Roosevelt, Harry S Truman, Dwight D. Eisenhower, John F. Kennedy, Lyndon B. Johnson, and Richard M. Nixon. This group includes one general and five politicians.

There are three aspects of presidential performance. One, which will be called "style," looks at the manner of presidents, how they operate. The second, which will be called "accomplishment," looks at what they do and tries to pass some kind of judgment. The third is a kind of summary, overall appraisal related to some or all of the components of the other two. It deals with what Schlesinger called "greatness," and Maranell "prestige."

THE RESEARCH DESIGN

The late historian Arthur Schlesinger, Sr. of Harvard published ratings of U.S. presidents, first by fifty-five and then by seventy-five prominent colleagues [1948, 1962]. It was their consensus that Washington, Lincoln, and Franklin Roosevelt were our three foremost presidents, with Wilson and Jefferson sharing accolades of greatness. In the twentieth century, the Schlesinger panel judged only Theodore Roosevelt and Harry S Truman of sufficient stature to be rated among a half-dozen "near great." Dwight D. Eisenhower, whose second term had just ended, was ranked next to the bottom in a group of twelve that were rated "average." Others, such as Pierce and Buchanan, were rated "below average." Grant and Harding ranked last and were judged failures.

In 1970, a Kansas University sociologist, Gary Maranell, published ratings of the presidents through John F. Kennedy and Lyndon B. Johnson by 571 members of the Organization of American Historians, a usable return of slightly more than 50 percent of his sample of 1,095. His procedures were different, but his results were remarkably similar to Schlesinger's. Lincoln, Washington, and Franklin Roosevelt were again the top three. Jefferson and Theodore Roosevelt edged Wilson out of the top five into sixth place. Truman followed in seventh. Again, Eisenhower was rated relatively low in an "average" group. Buchanan, Pierce, Grant, and Harding again received the lowest ratings. The historians gave Kennedy a relatively high rating, putting him in ninth place. Johnson was pegged a bit above Eisenhower along with Taft and Hoover.

Each respondent was asked to place each of the thirty-three presidents on an eleven-interval Thurstone scale, rather than in one of five categories ranging from "great" to "failure." Rank orderings were then established on the basis of the number of standard deviation units each president was above or below the mean. For Schlesinger's vague criteria Maranell substituted "overall prestige" and five specified dimensions of performance. From his findings it is evident that the historians rated presidents high in overall prestige in relation to their judgment of **1.** accomplishments of great rather than little significance; **2.** strength rather than weakness in directing the government and shaping events; **3.** an active rather than passive approach toward their administration. The historians' ratings of presidential prestige, strength, activism, and accomplishments were all very highly and positively correlated.[2]

My survey is a partial replication for economists and political scientists of Maranell's on historians, but just for the six presidents beginning with Franklin Roosevelt. Being more recent, it includes Nixon's first term. Findings for all three groups of intellectuals are compared, but just for the five contemporary presidents they rated in common. Comparisons are made by looking first at standard deviation scores as the indicator of the president's positions on the various scales, and second at the relationships among the scales as measured by Pearson's r. For reasons to be explained in the next section, most of the statistical analysis in this study differs from Maranell's in that it treats the data as ordinal rather than interval and relies on rank correlations. This survey also differs from Maranell's in an attempt to account for any differences in ratings in relation to doctrinal and political party leanings that are directly sought in the questionnaire.[3] The respondents were asked whether they usually think of themselves as liberal, conservative, or whatever, as well as for their party identifications.

Random samples were drawn of 200 economists and 200 political scientists from the biographical directories of the American Economics Association [1970] and the American Political Science Association [1968]. The economists were selected from those listed as specialists in monetary and fiscal theory, including fiscal policy and public finance. The political scientists were selected from those listed as specialists on the executive. Questionnaires were mailed and returned during the early summer of 1972 before the presidential conventions and campaigns got underway. Complete, usable returns were substantially higher for both groups than for Maranell's historians: 146 economists (73 percent) and 120 political scientists (60 percent). At the time of the survey, Richard Nixon's first term was over, save for a few months, and he was included among six contemporary presidents to be rated. It is important to know his standing at that time,· because all subsequent perceptions and judgments, even of his first term, are adversely affected by the disclosures that ensued from Watergate.

Turning now to the survey results, we will look first at the five contemporary presidents through Johnson as rated by all three groups, then at the ratings that included Nixon by economists and political scientists.

ECONOMIST-POLITICAL SCIENTIST-HISTORIAN PRESIDENTIAL PRESTIGE RANKINGS

On overall prestige, Maranell's historians ranked the top ten presidents from +2.10 for Lincoln first, to +0.61 for Adams tenth. The middle dozen ranged from +0.30 for Polk eleventh, to −0.39 for McKinley twenty-second, the bottom eleven from −0.52 for Arthur twenty-third, to −1.84 for Harding last.

For the contemporary presidents, the historians ranked Franklin Roosevelt third, more than one and one-half standard deviation units above the mean. Truman, ranked seventh, was one unit above the mean. The historians ranked Eisenhower just below Hoover, at −0.29, near the bottom of the middle one-third, Kennedy, at +0.63, was ninth, just after Jackson. Lyndon Johnson, barely above the mean at +0.06, was ranked ahead of Taft and Hoover in the middle of the middle one-third.

Ratings by economists and political scientists just four years later in 1972 are virtually identical with those by the historians for Roosevelt and Truman, as indicated by standard deviation units.

But for the rest of the contemporary presidents they are quite different. At −0.63, Eisenhower drops from the middle into the bottom one-third. Kennedy, at −0.20, drops from the historians' top ten to what would be near the bottom of their middle one-third, just below Hoover. Lyndon Johnson, −0.93, tumbles to the middle of the bottom one-third, between Benjamin Harrison and Zachary Taylor. Nixon, who was not included in the Maranell survey, is rated identically with Johnson on the basis of his first-term performance.

Maranell found that prestige ratings for the thirty-three presidents by historians reflected very similar ratings of strength, activism, and significant accomplishments, and that historians tended to be very similar to one another in their placement of each president in a position on each of these four scales. But the ratings of economists and political scientists of the six contemporary presidents, Roosevelt through Nixon, reveal no statistically significant associations whatever. Among the seven sets of scores, as measured by Pearson's r, the correlations between prestige, strength, activism, and accomplishments, range from +0.11 to +0.52, which on r^2 would at best only account for about one-fourth of the variance. The associations with idealism and flexibility are equally low, as are associations of all six of the dimensions and respondent information. These consistently low correlations indicate that for economists and political scientists, no systematic, statistically identifiable similarity of evaluation exists in the assignment of scale scores. The single exception is a slight inverse relationship between activism and idealism.

These findings will be evaluated in the conclusions, but because they raise questions about whether the interval data are meaningful, the remainder of the statistical analysis treats the scales as ordinal with rank orderings (as determined by standard deviation units above and below the mean) alone compared for the various dimensions of presidential performance.

On this basis then, when we ask about prestige and look at the central tendency of the perceptions of economists and political scientists together with the historians, the results are remarkably congruent. There is complete accord that first, second, and third go to Roosevelt, Truman, and Kennedy. Historians and political scientists concur on Johnson fourth, and Eisenhower fifth. Economists reverse this order, placing Eisenhower fourth and Johnson fifth.[4]

ECONOMIST-POLITICAL SCIENTIST-HISTORIAN PRESIDENTIAL PERFORMANCE RANKINGS: STYLE

In reporting these findings, four dimensions are grouped under presidential style. That is, what is the manner of presidents? How do they operate? These four dimensions are

1. The strong or weak nature of the role each president as an individual played in directing the government and shaping the events of his day.

2. The active or passive nature of the approach each president took toward his administration.

3. The idealistic or practical inclination of the official actions of each president.

4. The flexible or inflexible inclination of the approach each president took to implement his policies.

The economists, historians, and political scientists as groups are in complete accord in the central tendency of their rankings of the five contemporary presidents as to strength of action in directing the government and shaping events. The rank order from strongest to weakest, first through fifth, is Roosevelt, Truman, Johnson, Kennedy, and Eisenhower. Since there is less interdisciplinary harmony on the three other elements of presidential style, the results are summarized in tables 1 through 3. Statistically, the levels of agreement reported are significant, the disagreements are not.[5]

TABLE 1. **Ranking from Active to Passive Approach of Five Postwar Presidents.**

Economists	Political scientists	Historians
1. Roosevelt	1. Roosevelt	1. Roosevelt
2. Truman	2. Truman	2. Johnson
3. Johnson	3. Johnson	3. Truman
4. Kennedy	4. Kennedy	4. Kennedy
5. Eisenhower	5. Eisenhower	5. Eisenhower

TABLE 2. **Ranking on Idealistic or Practical Nature of Official Presidential Actions of Five Postwar Presidents.**

Economists	Political scientists	Historians
1. Kennedy	1. Kennedy	1. Kennedy
2. Eisenhower	2. Eisenhower	2. Eisenhower
3. Roosevelt	3. Johnson	3. Truman
4. Johnson	4. Roosevelt	4. Roosevelt
5. Truman	5. Truman	5. Johnson

TABLE 3. **Ranking of Flexibility of Approach to Implementing Programs of Five Postwar Presidents.**

Economists	Political scientists	Historians
1. Roosevelt	1. Roosevelt	1. Kennedy
2. Kennedy	2. Kennedy	2. Roosevelt
3. Eisenhower	3. Truman	3. Eisenhower
4. Truman	4. Eisenhower	4. Truman
5. Johnson	5. Johnson	5. Johnson

ECONOMIST-POLITICAL SCIENTIST-HISTORIAN PRESIDENTIAL PERFORMANCE RANKINGS: ACCOMPLISHMENTS

In analyzing "accomplishments" we are interested in what the presidents did and what judgments we have of it. The single, specific question used in the surveys was whether the respondents attached great or little significance to the accomplishments of each president.

Here, too, the central tendency of our three groups of intellectuals shows complete agreement: Roosevelt first, Truman second, Johnson third, Kennedy fourth, and Eisenhower fifth. On the statistical measures, this is a perfect level of association that is statistically significant.

It should be noted in passing that on the information variable the level of association between the three groups is low and not statistically significant.[6] Economists, historians, and political scientists have remarkably similar perceptions and judgments of the presidents even though the amount of information they believe they have about particular presidents seems to be highly variable.

ECONOMIST-POLITICAL SCIENTIST PERCEPTIONS OF NIXON'S FIRST-TERM PERFORMANCE

How do 1972 ratings of Nixon's first-term performance fit into the overall picture? This is an important question because everything symbolized by "Watergate" and the Agnew case since then intrudes and colors perceptions of Nixon's presidential performance even for the period before Watergate and the Agnew case. It is also important because of the belief that Nixon's overwhelming reelection margin constituted positive endorsement of his first-term performance rather than disapproval of McGovern and the impact of low voter turnout.

It is all the more interesting, then, that on the prestige dimension, economists rank Nixon fifth, between Eisenhower and Johnson, while political scientists rank him sixth, after Johnson and Eisenhower. In a composite prestige ranking of the six contemporary presidents, drawn from the number of times a president is ranked first, second, third, and so on, Nixon's first-term performance comes out sixth, after Roosevelt first, Truman second, Kennedy third, Eisenhower fourth, and Johnson fifth.

Turning to the four dimensions of presidential style, there is complete accord that on strength Nixon ranks fourth, and that on idealism he ranks last. On activism, economists put him just ahead of Kennedy at fourth. Political scientists put him just after Kennedy at fifth. There is more disagreement as to Nixon's flexibility. Economists rank him high in second place. Political scientists perceive him as more inflexible, ranking him lower in fourth. The composite ranking of the four components of presidential style — strength, activism, idealism, and flexibility — places Nixon in next to last place, just ahead of Eisenhower, but behind Roosevelt, Kennedy, Truman, and Johnson.

Finally, on the significance of Nixon's first-term accomplishments, economists rank him third, just ahead of Johnson. Political scientists rank him fourth, reversing this order. In composite, on significance of accomplishments, Johnson and Nixon are tied, ahead of Kennedy and Eisenhower but behind Roosevelt and Truman.

Apart from these generally low judgments of Nixon's first-term performance, there is already evidence that political scientists at least regard Watergate's impact on the future as very serious. *U.S. News and World Report* [December 3, 1973, pp. 78–82] published a nationwide survey of a structured sample of political scientists drawn by the American Political Science Association to represent geographical and ideological diversity. There was a 66 percent return from 100 mailed questionnaires. On the four questions most relevant to the concerns of this essay, 95 percent think the Watergate scandal created a crisis of confidence; 88 percent believe the Watergate-Agnew cases reduced the power and prestige of the presidency; 77 percent think these cases will help the Democrats, though not decisively, in the 1976 presidential campaign; and 73 percent believe the Watergate revelations will have a souring effect on people's attitudes toward politics.

DOCTRINAL INFLUENCES
IN ELITE PERCEPTIONS
OF PRESIDENTIAL PERFORMANCE

Thus far we have demonstrated substantial agreement in the central tendencies of presidential performance ratings by economists, historians, and political scientists. What disagreements there are among them individually are not reflected at all sharply along purely professional lines. Thus, despite their different professional group status, most economists, historians, and political scientists tend to reach very similar evaluations of presidential prestige, style, and significance of accomplishments.

We now turn to the question of whether differences in their perceptions will be more sharply manifested if we sort them out and look at them on the basis of their doctrinal persuasions. On the questionnaire each respondent was asked: "Do you usually think of yourself as conservative, liberal, or what?" Spaces to be checked were labeled "Conservative," "Liberal," and "Other (specify)." On the basis of the return, and as table 4 shows, it must be said that those who identify themselves as liberals are predominant in these intellectual groups. Thus, it is fair to speculate that the ratings we have already examined reflect the bias of liberal doctrine.

If we further break these doctrinal persuasions down by professional group, we find that liberals are far more numerous among political scientists than among economists.

When the performance ratings are analyzed to determine the influence of liberalism and conservatism there are some interesting similarities as well as differences. The greatest differences are in the ratings of overall prestige. Here conservatives and liberals are in agreement only on rating Truman second. Conservatives put Nixon first and Kennedy last. Liberals put Nixon last and Roosevelt first. Eisenhower ranks third for conservatives, but next to last for liberals. Kennedy, who is last for conservatives, ranks third for liberals.[7]

On the four elements of style — strength, activism, idealism, and flexibility — the findings indicate a mixed pattern of agreement and disagreement as tables 6, 7, 8, and 9 show.

TABLE 4. **Respondents' Self-identification as to Doctrinal Persuasion.**

Doctrinal persuasion	Percentage
Liberal	61
Conservative	16
Other*	23
Total sample: 266 respondents	100

*"Other" included "moderate," "middle-of-the-road," "independent," "pragmatist."

TABLE 5. **Doctrinal Persuasion by Professional Group.**

Doctrinal persuasion	Political scientists	Economists
Liberal	76%	49%
Conservative	7%	23%
Other	17%	28%
Total	100%	100%

TABLE 6. **Conservative and Liberal Ratings of Presidential Idealism.**

Conservatives	Liberals
1. Kennedy	1. Kennedy
2. Eisenhower	2. Eisenhower
3. Roosevelt	3. Roosevelt
4. Johnson	4. Johnson
5. Nixon	5. Truman
6. Truman	6. Nixon

TABLE 7. **Conservative and Liberal Ratings of Presidential Strength.**

Conservatives	Liberals
1. Roosevelt	1. Roosevelt
2. Nixon	2. Truman
3. Johnson	3. Johnson
4. Truman	4. Nixon
5. Kennedy	5. Kennedy
6. Eisenhower	6. Eisenhower

TABLE 8. **Conservative and Liberal Ratings of Presidential Activism.**

Conservatives	Liberals
1. Roosevelt	1. Roosevelt
2. Johnson	2. Truman
3. Nixon	3. Johnson
4. Truman	4. Kennedy
5. Kennedy	5. Nixon
6. Eisenhower	6. Eisenhower

TABLE 9. **Conservative and Liberal Ratings of Presidential Flexibility.**

Conservatives	Liberals
1. Eisenhower	1. Roosevelt
2. Nixon	2. Kennedy
3. Kennedy	3. Truman
4. Roosevelt	4. Nixon
5. Truman	5. Johnson
6. Johnson	6. Eisenhower

Turning finally to the question of doctrinal influence in judgments of presidential accomplishments, we again encounter some agreement.

TABLE 10. **Conservative and Liberal Ratings of Presidential Accomplishments.**

Conservatives	Liberals
1. Roosevelt	1. Roosevelt
2. Truman	2. Truman
3. Nixon	3. Kennedy
4. Eisenhower	4. Johnson
5. Johnson	5. Nixon
6. Kennedy	6. Eisenhower

PARTISAN INFLUENCES
IN ECONOMIST-POLITICAL SCIENTIST
PRESIDENTIAL PERFORMANCE RATINGS

Is political party identification a possible influence in elite perceptions of presidential performance? As in the general populace, economists and political scientists identify with the Democratic rather than the Republican party by more than two to one. There is also a remarkably strong showing by those who regard themselves as independents. But independents have been gaining steadily among the general populace, too. The Democrats have been the majority party in the United States since 1930. They have controlled both houses of the Congress in every session since, except for two years under Truman and two under Eisenhower. Of the six elected presidents in this contemporary period, only Eisenhower and Nixon have been Republicans. Both voter registrations and public opinion polls prove that neither of them could have been elected without the support of both independents and sizable numbers of Democrats who were either defectors or nonvoters. In all of this it is fair to assume Democratic bias in presidential performance ratings among economists and political scientists, and in the country at large.

T A B L E   1 1 .   **Party Affiliation of Economists and Political Scientists Sampled.**

Total sample: N=266

Democrats	39%
Republicans	16%
Independent	43%
Other	2%

T A B L E   1 2 .   **Party Affiliation of Economists and Political Scientists Sampled by Professional Group.**

Economists		*Political scientists*	
Democrats	32%	Democrats	49%
Republicans	18%	Republicans	12%
Independents	48%	Independents	37%
Other	2%	Other	2%
Total	100%	Total	100%

As we look for partisan influence in ratings of presidential prestige, style, and accomplishments, we will try to answer several questions. Are there similarities or differences among Democrats, Republicans, and independents? Do Democrats rate the four Democratic presidents high and Republican presidents low? Do Republicans rate both Republican presidents high and the Democratic presidents low? What about the independents?

How do the partisan ratings compare with those examined previously by liberals and conservatives? Do Democratic ratings tend to be liberal? Do Republican ratings tend to be conservative? Again, what about the independents?

We could postulate that we are not really dealing with discrete sets of variables here, but rather with ones that are highly similar, perhaps identical. We should be able to confirm or refute such postulates from analysis of the findings. We should be able to characterize the increasingly numerous independents. Are they similar to or do they differ from Democrats, Republicans, liberals, and conservatives in their ratings of presidential performance?

We will look first at partisan influence in presidential prestige ratings, second in style ratings, and finally in accomplishment ratings.

T A B L E   1 3 .   **Partisan Influence in Presidential Ratings.**

Democrats	Republicans
1. Roosevelt	1. Roosevelt
2. Truman	2. Truman
3. Kennedy	3. Nixon
4. Johnson	4. Eisenhower
5. Eisenhower	5. Kennedy
6. Nixon	6. Johnson

Because of the agreement on Roosevelt and Truman the low rank order correlation of 0.49 is not statistically significant. However, if we omit them and compare the rankings of the four most recent presidents the correlation is 0.80, which strongly supports the influence of party identification in the ratings. Where do the independents stand in these ratings? Surprisingly, perhaps, identically with the Republicans for a perfect correlation of 1.00. This perfect association, together with the agreement with the Democrats on Roosevelt and Truman, produces for all three groups a statistically significant W of 0.80. How do the partisan rankings compare with the doctrinal rankings? They are identical for Democrats and liberals. Surprisingly, however, there is no statistically significant association between Republican and conservative rankings at all. The correlation here is a low 0.49. Again, it is because Republicans rank Roosevelt at the top in prestige, but conservatives place Nixon there.

If we can say, then, that our Democratic intellectuals tend to be overwhelmingly liberal, we cannot say that their Republican counterparts tend to be overwhelmingly conservative. For both Republicans and independents, doctrinal persuasion is a mixed bag, at least so far as presidential prestige ratings are concerned.

We now turn to strength, activism, idealism, and flexibility — the four elements making up presidential style. On strength, Democrats, Republicans, and independents are in substantial accord. All three groups place Roosevelt first, Kennedy fifth, and Eisenhower sixth. They approach agreement on Truman second and Johnson fourth, but there is no agreement on Nixon. Republicans rank him high, Democrats lower, and independents in between. At 0.94, the overall level of association measured by W among the three groups is very high and statistically significant. Again, as with the prestige rankings, the liberal and Democratic strength rankings are identical. There is no meaningful association here between conservative and Republican rankings, but they are not significantly different from Democrats and liberals.

When we look at presidential activism a similar pattern, but with somewhat less agreement, is apparent. Democrats, Republicans, and independents agree that Roosevelt was the most active, Johnson third, and Eisenhower the sixth or most passive. Truman, Kennedy, and Nixon produce disagreement — especially Nixon. Republicans rank him second, independents fourth, and Democrats fifth. The level of association among the three groups, however, is still fairly high ($W=0.82$), which means that statistically, the agreement on activism is significant, while the disagreement is not. As with strength, the rankings by Democrats and liberals for activism are identical, while the rankings of Republicans and conservatives correlate at 0.90.

On the idealism of presidential actions there is just about as much agreement as on strength and more than on activism. Kennedy, Eisenhower, and Roosevelt are seen as the most idealistic presidents — Truman, Johnson, and Nixon as least. The rankings by Democrats, Republicans, and independents are at a very high level of association, $W = 0.91$. There are no significant partisan or doctrinal differences here.

On the final component of presidential style, flexibility or inflexibility in the implementation of programs and policies, we find the greatest difference in the rankings by Democrats, Republicans, and independents. In general, Democrats rank Roosevelt, Kennedy, and Truman high and flexible, while ranking Eisenhower, Nixon, and Johnson low and inflexible. Republicans, on the other hand, rank Nixon, Roosevelt, and Eisenhower high and flexible, with Kennedy, Truman, and Johnson low and inflexible. The independents tend to agree with the Republicans. All three groups perceive Roosevelt as highly flexible and Johnson as inflexible. These partisan agreements and disagreements, however, are not statistically significant, as $W = 0.63$ is not sufficient for rejection of the null hypothesis.

In summarizing the findings on presidential style, it must be said that with respect to strength, activism, and idealism the levels of agreement are so high that any notion of significant differences of perception attributable to party identification must be rejected. Equally, there is no simple one-to-one differential relationship between Democrats-liberals as against Republicans-conservatives. And, for flexibility, the probability is high that the differences we see could occur by chance.

TABLE 14. **Partisan Ratings of the Accomplishments of the Six Postwar Presidents.**

Democrats	Republicans	Independents
1. Roosevelt	1. Roosevelt	1. Roosevelt
2. Truman	2. Truman	2. Truman
3. Johnson	3. Nixon	3. Nixon
4. Kennedy	4. Eisenhower	4. Kennedy
5. Nixon	5. Johnson	5. Johnson
6. Eisenhower	6. Kennedy	6. Eisenhower

Finally, we turn to the question of whether there are measurable partisan differences in perceptions of the significance of the accomplishments of six of our most recent presidents. The results here are remarkably like those for overall presidential prestige. The overall level of agreement measured by W is high, 0.89; so statistically the apparent partisan differences here are not meaningful. If we exclude Roosevelt and Truman from the analysis, though, as we did when looking at the prestige rankings, the rho correlation between Democrats and Republicans is −0.60 and is strongly suggestive of partisan influence if not of clear-cut statistical significance. One last finding here: on presidential accomplishment ratings, liberals and Democrats are perfectly correlated, as are conservatives and Republicans.

CONCLUSIONS

Americans enjoy the rating game whether they are comparing football teams, basketball teams, television shows, or presidents. Contemporary presidents have assiduously followed their approval ratings in the public opinion polls, sometimes happily, sometimes not. They have been uniformly testy about their standing with their peers among such intellectuals as historians, economists, and political scientists. Nixon read the ratings and grimly asserted that he would be vindicated by history. Johnson remarked that only presidents themselves know how and why they reached particular decisions and the many considerations that affected them because no one else has a president's vantage point. When he was asked to rate the presidents, Kennedy replied: "How the hell can you tell? Only the President himself can know what his real pressures and his real alternatives are. If you don't know that how can you judge performance?" [Schlesinger 1967, p. 619].

Nevertheless, president-rating is a pervasive pastime. It has an especially important role among intellectuals, for in ideologically justifying or attacking the system, or in dreaming up or tearing down utopias and counter-utopias, they pose the questions and terms of reference in which the system is perceived and understood [cf. Wilensky 1967, p. viii]. Perhaps the prevailing terms of presidential reference were best expressed by Rossiter when he said that " . . . the final greatness of the Presidency lies in the truth that it is not just an office of incredible power but a breeding ground of indestructible myth" [1960, p. 108].

We began with assumptions and propositions about the importance of intellectuals as part of a society's nongoverning elite. The notion of the heterogeneity of intellectual opinion was advanced by Bottomore [1964] for testing, with some suggestions as to how it might be explained. Contrary to Bottomore, in the rank order of the contemporary presidents, we found no considerable variety of opinion by economists, historians, or political scientists. On the contrary, so far as rank ordering goes, the shared values and status of economists as opposed to political scientists, or historians, make virtually no measurable difference in perceptions of presidential performance.

But in the actual scale scores assigned, while all three groups agree on very high ratings for Roosevelt and Truman, economists and political scientists rated Eisenhower, Kennedy, Johnson, and Nixon drastically lower than the historians did. These differences may be best explained by changes in perspective between 1968 and 1972, including disillusionment with the continuance of the war and unresolved domestic difficulties.

Within economics and political science we found some explanatory power for different ratings along with dimensions of doctrinal persuasion and political party identification. The few acknowledged conservatives and Republicans do differ from the many liberals and Democrats. But the overall homogeneity of elite perceptions is best explained by widely shared liberal and Democratic commitments.

Rossiter's judgment about incredible power and indestructible myth encapsulates the prevailing elite and mass expectations of the contemporary presidency. Americans have embraced the strong and active style as producing significant accomplishments for the nation and high prestige for such presidents in the national consciousness. The virtual unanimity of historians, economists, and political scientists, of whatever doctrinal persuasion or party identification, that only Franklin Roosevelt and Harry Truman belong in a pantheon of heroes along with Lincoln, Washington, and Jefferson manifests the continuing hold of this presidential ideology on intellectuals.

There are two corollaries to this finding. First is the virtual unanimity of historians, economists, and political scientists that Eisenhower's performance was weak and passive in the presidential role, with no great accomplishments and generally low prestige. The power and myth of the presidential office, then, are not sufficient to assure high ratings for such incumbents as Eisenhower whose performance is found wanting.

Second, the very bottom of the rating scale is reserved for presidents whose performance is perceived as violating public trust. Thus, Grant and Harding are part of indestructible myth because they damaged the presidency and undermined the sense of efficacy of our governing institutions and processes.

Finally, the prevailing liberal and Democratic ideology does not assure high ratings for Kennedy, Johnson, and Nixon, although they are all generally regarded as stronger, more active, and more liberal than Eisenhower. The power of the presidency cannot be judged apart from the purposes for which it is employed. When power fails, as in Indochina, or in coping with other persistent international and domestic problems, it is not so much incredible as finite and limited. When power is abused and public trust is violated, as in a credibility gap, or as in Watergate, the cover up, and all of the related White House horrors, there is no way for an incumbent president to remain unscathed within the protective shelter of myth.

NOTES

1. Mass perceptions are outside the focus of this paper, but see Fred I. Greenstein, "Popular Images of the President," *American Journal of Psychiatry* 122 (November 1965):523–529; Roberta S. Sigel, "Image of the American Presidency: Part II of an Exploration into Popular Views of Presidential Power," *Midwest Journal of Political Science* X (February 1966):123–137; John E. Mueller, "Presidential Popularity from Truman to Johnson," *American Political Science Review* LXIV (March 1970):18–34.

2. As measured by Pearson's r, the lowest correlation found by Maranell was 0.89 and the highest 0.98. (Using r^2, these would account for from 79 percent to 96 percent of the variance. This would indicate that presidential ratings by historians on these four dimensions are very similar.) No remotely comparable correlations were found between these performance dimensions and the other two, idealism and flexibility.

3. Gary M. Maranell and Richard A. Dodder, "Political Orientation and the Evaluation of Presidential Prestige," *Social Science Quarterly* LI (September 1970):415–421, asked their respondents to identify their political party preference in the margin of the questionnaire. Slightly more than 200 professors provided this information. Among those providing this information, liberals outnumbered conservatives nearly 3 to 1 [p. 417]. The findings indicated "that presidential prestige or greatness is associated with different characteristics of perceived presidential attitude among liberal and conservative historians" [p. 421].

4. This level of agreement is statistically significant using Kendall's coefficient of concordance, W and the X^2 test: $W=95$; $X^2=11.46$, $p<0.05$.

5. Using Kendall's W and the X^2 test, the results were as follows:
   1. On strength of role, $W=1.00$, perfect association.
   2. On activism, $W=0.95$; $X^2=11.46$, $p<0.05$.
   3. On idealism, $W=0.82$; $X^2=9.86$, $p<0.05$.
   4. On flexibility, $W=0.91$; $X^2=10.93$, $p<0.05$.

6. $W=0.67$; $X^2=8.00$, $p<0.05$.

7. There are substantially different tendencies here producing a moderately negative rank correlation on Spearman's *rho* of -0.37, but it must be noted that it is not statistically significant. That is, it is not sufficiently high to permit rejection of the null hypothesis.

BIBLIOGRAPHY

Amlund, Curtis A. "President-Ranking: A Criticism." *Midwest Journal of Political Science* 8 (August 1964): 309–315.

Bailey, Thomas A. *Presidential Greatness.* New York: Appleton-Century-Crofts, 1966.

Barber, James David. *The Presidential Character: Predicting Performance in the White House.* Englewood Cliffs, N. J.: Prentice-Hall, 1972.

Biographical Directory of the American Political Science Association. Washington, D. C.: American Political Science Association, 1968.

Borden, Morton. *America's Ten Greatest Presidents.* Skokie, Ill.: Rand McNally, 1971.

Borden, Morton. *America's Eleven Greatest Presidents.* Skokie, Ill. Rand McNally, 1971.

Bottomore, T. B. *Elites and Society.* New York: Basic Books, 1964.

Burns, James MacGregor. *Presidential Government.* Boston: Houghton Mifflin Company, 1965.

Cantril, Hadley. "Some Requirements for a Political Psychology." In *Perspectives in the Study of Politics.* Edited by Malcolm B. Parsons. Skokie, Ill.: Rand McNally, 1968.

Halberstam, David. *The Best and the Brightest.* New York: Fawcett Publications, 1973.

Hargrove, Erwin C. *Presidential Leadership: Personality and Political Style.* London: Collier-MacMillan, 1966.

Hyman, Sidney. "What is the President's True Role?" *The New York Times Magazine,* 7 September 1958, pp. 17ff.

Maranell, Gary M. "The Evaluation of Presidents: An Extension of the Schlesinger Polls." *Journal of American History* LVII (June 1970): 104–113.

Maranell, Gary M. and Dodder, Richard A. "Political Orientation and Evaluation of Presidential Prestige: A Study of American History." *Social Science Quarterly* LI (September 1970): 415–421.

Neustadt, Richard E. *Presidential Power: The Politics of Leadership.* New York: John Wiley & Sons, 1960.

1969 Handbook of the American Economic Association. The American Economic Review LIX (January 1970).

Rossiter, Clinton. *The American Presidency.* New York: Harcourt Brace, 1960.

Schlesinger, Arthur M., Sr. "The U.S. Presidents." *Life*, 1 November 1948, pp. 65–74.

Schlesinger, Arthur M., Sr. "Our Presidents: A Rating by 75 Historians." *The New York Times Magazine*, 29 July 1962, pp. 12ff.

Schlesinger, Arthur M., Jr. *A Thousand Days.* New York: Fawcett Crest, 1967.

Wilensky, Harold L. *Organizational Intelligence.* New York: Basic Books, 1967.

II ☆ DOMESTIC POLICY-MAKING MACHINERY

Are contemporary managerial and technocratic skills compatible with the democratic origins and traditions of the executive branch? Dorothy B. James critically examines the relationship that existed between President Richard M. Nixon and the domestic policy-making apparatus, while Richard Nathan describes the five phases of Nixon's approach to domestic policy making. Both James' and Nathan's assessments reveal the enormous difficulty confronting any contemporary president in governing and managing the bureaucracy.

Dorothy Buckton James, professor and head of the political science department at Virginia Polytechnic and State University, previously was at Lehman College (City University of New York). She has written or edited three books, *The Contemporary Presidency; Poverty, Politics and Change;* and *Outside Looking In: Critiques of American Policies and Institutions.*

Richard P. Nathan, Brookings Institution Senior Fellow, has written *Jobs and Civil Rights,* and *Revenue Sharing and the City.* He has served as assistant director of the Office of Management and Budget; deputy undersecretary of the Department of Health, Education and Welfare; chairman of the 1968–69 Presidential Task Forces on Public Welfare and Intergovernmental Relations; director of Domestic Policy Research for Governor Nelson Rockefeller; and legislative assistant to U. S. Senator Kenneth B. Keating.

3

The Future of
the Institutionalized
Presidency*

DOROTHY BUCKTON JAMES
Virginia Polytechnic Institute and
State University

Wʜᴇɴ GERALD FORD WAS INAU-
gurated as president of the United States, he inherited an office
that had been substantially altered since the 1930s by the twin
trends of routinization and institutionalization. "Routinization" is a shorthand term that indicates the process through
which the innovative actions of individual presidents that provided services for some group or institution have become
routinely expected of all succeeding presidents. That expectation either had been written into law, or become a binding custom that succeeding presidents have ignored at their peril. For
example:

> The president's electoral and press constituencies routinely
> expect live televised press conferences.

*Adapted in part from Dorothy Buckton James, *The Contemporary Presidency* (2nd ed., Bobbs-
Merrill, 1974).

The president's international and electoral constituencies routinely expect summit conferences and ceremonial visiting.

The president's party routinely expects electoral support in midterm elections.

Congress routinely expects to be given an annual legislative agenda with draft bills shortly after the president's State of the Union message.

The Employment Act of 1946 requires that the president routinely watch the state of the nation's economic health and make prescriptions for it at least annually.

The National Environmental Policy Act of 1969 requires similar routine activity on environmental issues.

The Taft-Hartley Act of 1947 routinely involves the president in the settlement of major labor disputes.

The National Security Act of 1947 requires that the president routinely coordinate military and security policy in peace as well as in war.

The Atomic Energy Act of 1946 routinely requires that the president personally approve the use of atomic weapons.

Such customs and laws fit the needs of the president's various constituencies because they reflect changing external conditions that have caused these constituencies to focus increasingly on the president as the major source of initiative in the American political system. At least five major twentieth-century trends seem to have contributed to the accelerating growth of expectation of presidential initiative:

1. In the aftermath of the Great Depression, widespread agreement developed among a majority of Americans in support of economic intervention by the national government. The emphasis on presidential initiative was reflected in such legislation as the Employment Act of 1946, the Taft-Hartley Act of 1947, and the Economic Stabilization Act of 1970.

2. During the mid-twentieth century, war, cold war, and America's emergence as a world leader increased the significance of foreign and military policy for the nation. This enhanced presidential initiative because the president alone has the constitutional mandate to function as chief-of-state and commander-in-chief.

3. Increasing public demand for greater social intervention and centralization (expressed in myriad bills, from Social Security through Medicaid) led to a mammoth growth of federal civilian employment in the bureaucracy, from about 200,000 employees in 1900 to over 2.5 million by 1970. As chief executive the president is constitutionally responsible for administering all of these programs that Congress had passed and for coordinating the bureaucracy that proliferated in response to them.

4. Increasingly through the twentieth century, major areas of public concern (such as civil rights, crime, poverty, and regulation of large-scale business, labor, and agriculture) have transcended state boundaries. For that reason and because of the ineptitude or inadequacy of state and local governments in dealing with them, the public and concerned groups have sought aid from Washington. With its decentralized organization based on the seniority system, Congress has seemed unequal to satisfying the need for coordinated innovation, so public expectation has focused on the president.

5. Technological developments in transportation and communication have also helped to make the president the central focus of American political life because they have enabled him to appeal over Congress' head to its constituents, to set the terms of and dominate public debate, and to dramatize and personalize public events to his advantage. The higher level of public attention to presidential actions and statements than to those of any other individual or group in the society has both reflected and contributed to his advantage.

In short, routinization is the symptom of a pervasive set of economic, technological, social, and international changes that have affected both the presidency and the world during the past few decades. The president has become a more centralizing focus in the American political system as a reflection of external conditions, not as a result of individual "usurpation" (as some writers would have it).

In order to enable the president to provide the services routinely demanded of him, Congress has established such institutions as the White House Office, Council of Economic Advisers, Office of Management and Budget, National Security Council, and the Council on Environmental Quality. Such institutions comprise the contemporary institutionalized presidency — the Executive Office of the President — which has been organized to assist the president in providing the new services that have routinely become expected of him. Accelerating institutionalization of the contemporary presidency reflects accelerating routinization.

The Executive Office of the President differs from the bureaucracy in that it is composed of individuals and institutions designed during the past few decades to assist the president in his continuous, intense, and often unsuccessful struggle to supervise the implementation of national public policy. Only a relatively few individuals at the top of the executive bureaucracy are appointed by the president with the advice and consent of the Senate. Millions of civilian employees in the middle and lower ranges of the eleven executive departments gain their positions in accordance with civil service regulations and can only be dismissed in accordance with those regulations. The bureaucracy also includes independent regulatory agencies and miscellaneous other institutions that enjoy a fair degree of independence from presidential initiative and control. In contrast, the several thousand members of the Executive Office of the President are vastly more amenable to presidential initiative, coordination, and control. They are responsible to him alone, and the key personnel are appointed and may be dismissed by him at will. They are therefore an important presidential asset. Yet, as institutionalization has accelerated they have also become a

serious liability. This mixture of asset and liability makes institutionalization an increasingly awkward dilemma for the contemporary president.

THE DILEMMA OF INSTITUTIONALIZATION

The benefits of institutionalization are obvious. Any president has a paramount need for *information* in his struggle to
supervise the implementation of public policy. He cannot depend on routine channels within the bureaucracy to supply the
information that he wants when he wants it. Because his staff's
loyalties are far less divided (they do not face the same strong
pressures from an outside constituency that his cabinet members
face), they can be more useful to him in providing information,
advice, and ideas for policy initiatives. For example, the Council
of Economic Advisers provides a constant overview of the
economy and information to assist the president in his economic
functions, and they provide them in a manner that is far more
direct and continuous than the reports of the Treasury Department. Furthermore, individual council members may be used on
"spot assignments" to investigate particular questions at the
president's initiative.

The cabinet is also institutionally handicapped by its role in
supervising and controlling the way in which government
policies are carried out, which further enhances the value of the
president's staff. For example, the Office of Management and
Budget's supervisory function over *all* departmental budget requests provides an institutional vantage point that can be useful
to a politically sensitive president. Similarly, personal staff
members of the White House Office can be used as negotiators,
presidential spokesmen, or researchers in areas in which the
president needs help. They release trial balloons, sound out
proposals, and initiate negotiations with congressional,
bureaucratic, party, state, local, or interest group leaders in a
way that does not implicate the president. They can also be used
to carry the "bad" news while he carries the "good." He estab-

lishes their priorities and uses their advice as *he* chooses, but while institutionalization can be a substantial asset for the contemporary president, it poses substantial risks as well.

Obviously, the degree to which presidential influence can permeate the bureaucracy is related to the president's skill in organizing and using his personal staff, his skill as an administrator. Institutionalization can be of little help to a president who lacks the ability to attract an able staff and make good use of the advice he receives.

Yet even an able administrator will find that institutionalization can be a handicap because it absorbs his time and energy, directing his attention toward areas of strong institutionalization and away from others. The increase in the number of individuals within the Executive Office of the President has been accompanied by supervisory problems, which have slowed down the execution and development of policy. Responsibility for supervision of thousands of staff members and advisers must be delegated to others if presidential time is to be freed, but such delegation can only be accomplished at the expense of information. A president needs both *time and information*. The loss of either is costly. But the net result of growing institutionalization has been further isolation of the president since it absorbs presidential time and diminishes the amount and kind of information he receives because of the necessity to delegate authority.

Another problem is posed by the fact that no matter how antagonistic a president and his staff may be to the bureaucracy, they are mutually dependent. Presidents and their staffs may be the primary, or even exclusive, source of *initiation* in the system, but bureaucratic cooperation is needed for *implementation*. The more a president tries to centralize initiation within the Executive Office of the President, the greater the problems he creates for himself in terms of implementation. If he excludes the bureaucracy from the decision-making process, it has no stake in supporting his programs. The bureaucracy's capacity to negate presidential initiatives is a serious limitation on his power. The risks and liabilities of growing institutionalization were amply demonstrated during Richard Nixon's presidency.

CONTROL AND DIVESTMENT:
THE NIXON PARADOX

President Nixon responded in two ways to the assets and liabilities posed by institutionalization. First, he engaged in an active attempt to maximize his control of those policy areas in which he was interested. He did this by greatly increasing and elaborating institutionalization. Second, he pursued an active strategy aimed at divesting himself of responsibility for policy areas in which he lacked interest. Paradoxically, he vastly increased the degree of institutionalization of the presidency at the same time that he attempted to reverse expectations that the president would act in many areas of domestic policy.

Greater Administrative Control in Foreign and Military Policy

Foreign and military policy were always a central interest and concern for President Nixon. He therefore developed a very elaborate staff structure to accomplish this goal.

The chief of staff was Assistant to the President for National Security Affairs Henry A. Kissinger. The NSC secretariat was greatly enlarged to serve Dr. Kissinger. Instead of the heavy focus on operational services of earlier, smaller NSC staffs, the reorganized staff was divided into three functional segments: 1. "operators," who analyzed a mass of departmental data to find items of concern to the president and convey his instructions and reactions to the departments; 2. "planners," who did some original planning but whose primary emphasis was on stimulating more and better planning at the departments of State and Defense; 3. "programmers," who were to ignore the geographic and jurisdictional lines that had divided most policy functions and view policy problems and programs on a global basis [Osborne 1970, pp. 11–13].

Dr. Kissinger was also chairman of a review group of senior departmental planners who reviewed proposals as they came from the departments to the NSC. Interdepartmental regional groups were developed and made responsible to Henry Kissinger, as were a variety of ad hoc committees and groups. In addition, the under secretary of state was given responsibility for a committee of under secretaries to assist in the implementation of policy.

This elaborate system appeared to enable President Nixon to exert greater influence and control over foreign and military policy. However, in the areas in which neither the president nor his adviser showed much personal interest, there was serious disarray (as, for example, the inadequacy of policies for Western Europe, at least until 1974) [The New York Times, January 19, 1971, p. 1]. Furthermore, the comparatively small White House staff was institutionally incapable of coordinating all aspects of foreign policy. Thus, despite the transfer of many foreign policy functions to the White House, the State Department still conducted the great bulk of day-to-day business with the rest of the world. In such areas as Africa and Latin America the State Department made policy simply because the White House was too absorbed with other matters [Smith 1971, p. 1]. This further limited coordination.

Consequently, President Nixon's system widened the gap between initiation and implementation because the State Department had no stake in supporting presidential initiatives on which it had not been consulted. It also led to sharp conflicts between State Department personnel and the White House on such issues as the 1971 Pakistan-India war over Bangladesh independence and the seeming insensitivity of Henry Kissinger to our important ally, Japan [Ball 1972, pp. 10ff.].

Another cost of President Nixon's centralization was the loss of information that it implied for Congress. The Senate Foreign Relations Committee, for example, can request bureaucrats to testify, but members of the White House staff are protected by executive privilege. Therefore, the information on which executive policy was based was not available for legislators.

In recognition of these growing problems, Henry Kissinger was appointed secretary of state in October 1973. However, President Nixon assured himself of greater control over a cabinet member than is customary by having Dr. Kissinger retain his

White House position as advisor on national security questions. Such a dual role was unusual for the contemporary presidency. (President Nixon had previously used it in several domestic instances to maximize his control.)

Continuing to express the president's need to maximize personal control, Secretary Kissinger ran a one-man show in areas of major concern to himself and the president, such as the Arab-Israeli dispute, the international fuel crisis, or policy toward the Soviet Union and China. However, he was not in the country long enough to supervise implementation of the bulk of State Department acts. (Nor was there any indication that his exclusive approach to policy formulation enlisted the personal loyalty of key administrators in the department.) As a result, conflict and the gap between initiative and implementation continued to plague President Nixon.

Similarly, there were high costs for President Nixon's attempt to establish greater presidential control over military policy and appropriations through reorganization and further institutionalization of the Executive Office of the President. Within the National Security Council, Henry Kissinger established a Defense Programs Review Committee under his chairmanship. It was intended to reconcile Defense Department budgetary proposals with the limitations placed by the president on total federal spending. However, they underestimated the capacity of the military bureaucracy to absorb and deflect presidential initiatives. Like all bureaucrats, Pentagon personnel always padded their requests for procurement to take potential presidential and congressional cuts into account. Furthermore, the costs of weapons systems ("cost overruns") had a way of creeping upward once the president had become committed to them. The Pentagon's cost overruns under President Nixon ran at the rate of approximately 30 percent, which in a procurement budget of that size was many billions of dollars [Ognibene 1972, pp. 12–13].

President Nixon's early decision to consolidate authority in the hands of a few individuals in the national security structure and to remain more remote from day-to-day military planning lessened his ability to control military activity in Vietnam. This isolation was reflected in such incidents as the score or more of unauthorized air strikes into North Vietnam that occurred between November 1971 and March 1972 while, at President Nixon's direction, Dr. Kissinger was trying to develop an accord with North Vietnam at the Paris peace talks. Similarly, the Pentagon conceded that on several occasions the Navy had violated the law by engaging in deficit spending without presidential knowledge [*The New York Times*, January 8, 1973, p. 1]. Department of Defense procurement documents disclosed myriad actions taken without the knowledge of the secretary of defense or the president, which arbitrarily increased contract prices to assist companies that the Pentagon deemed "in the national interest" [*The New York Times*, April 30, 1973, p. 1]. President Nixon's isolation did not *cause* such diversion of millions of dollars — diversions had occurred since 1959 — however, his isolation *encouraged* and led to an increased level of such diversions.

When one turns to a consideration of the techniques through which President Nixon attempted to maximize his control in areas of domestic policy, one finds the same pattern with the same results.

Greater Administrative Control in Domestic Areas

President Nixon approached his administrative responsibilities in domestic policy as he did in military and foreign affairs. He reduced the influence of cabinet members and departments as far as possible, and developed the largest, most hierarchical, and most elaborate personal staff ever assembled for peacetime use. In short, to control the traditional bureaucracy, President Nixon increasingly bureaucratized the Executive Office of the President [Udall 1972]. In addition, as the White House staff began to assume the functions previously performed by the cabinet and members of the career civil service, President Nixon blurred the customary distinction between cabinet and staff roles by appointing a few cabinet members to serve also as members of the White House staff.

At the beginning of the Nixon administration, a chief-of-staff system was established for domestic affairs that was intended to function as Kissinger's did in foreign and military affairs. Its unfortunate consequence, however, was to isolate Nixon far more thoroughly than any other contemporary president. President Nixon strongly disliked conflict among his advisers and preferred to make decisions on the basis of staff papers rather than through personal discussions. He therefore preferred to use his chief of staff as an active enforcer of his privacy. Until his resignation in early 1973, H. R. Haldeman functioned vigorously in this role to protect the president from the multiple demands made on his time. He protected the president so thoroughly that key White House and cabinet members felt that there was a "Berlin Wall" around the Oval Office through which few could penetrate for personal contact with the president [Apple 1973, Evans & Novak 1971]. During his first term in office, except for Attorney General John Mitchell (on whom he called for a wide range of advice), President Nixon kept his cabinet members at arm's length [Semple 1970, p. 32]. This was part of an intentional effort to isolate himself from daily details so that he could exercise greater control over areas of personal concern, and it affected all of his personal advisers. Even Henry Kissinger had to receive Haldeman's clearance before he could see the president. Life at the White House began each morning at 8:15 with a briefing session in Haldeman's office for such top aides as Henry Kissinger and John Ehrlichman, whose access to the president was always mediated through Haldeman.

In seeking a chief of staff for domestic policy President Nixon attempted to maximize his personal control by selecting a loyalist who lacked an independent political base. However, the president's antagonism to the press, Congress, and the bureaucracy led him to appoint an individual who was equally insensitive. Previously H. R. Haldeman had done nothing except advertise products and participate in or run a variety of Nixon campaigns for vice president, president, and governor of California. His limited sensitivity to American politics especially hurt the president's relations with Congress, the bureaucracy, and the press because Haldeman organized a homogeneous White House

staff that tended to share his negative attitude toward these institutions [Evans & Novak 1971; Apple 1973]. Had the president
not demanded hierarchy, order, and a shield from the conflict
and controversy that are typical of decision making, he would
have been less isolated. Haldeman simply followed the president's preferences with fierce loyalty.

Furthermore, had Kissinger not been far more knowledge-
able and effective in his sphere than Haldeman was in domestic
concerns, it would have been easier for President Nixon to have
exercised greater administrative control in Kissinger's bailiwick
of military policy. The preeminent position enjoyed by any president as chief of state and commander in chief assures that his
initiatives will always be more effective in those areas. Therefore, President Nixon's hierarchical system seemed to function
fairly well in foreign and military affairs. He was far less successful in developing an effective system for domestic matters. Consequently, he shifted personnel and reorganized his staff system
frequently.

President Nixon's major institutional innovation was the
Domestic Council and its elaborate committee structure. Under
the direction of John D. Ehrlichman, it was intended to formulate
and coordinate domestic policy recommendations for the president and maintain a continuous review of existing programs.
The Council operated through a series of ad hoc project committees that were established to deal with either broad program
areas or specific problems. Cabinet members and bureaucrats
had to touch base with Ehrlichman to get a hearing with the
president.

At the same time, the Bureau of the Budget was renamed the
Office of Management and Budget (OMB) and given expanded
management responsibilities, which included monitoring the
performance of cabinet officials, their departments, and their
programs. Between the Domestic Council and the OMB, the
Executive Office was able to supervise administration more continuously and in a more detailed manner than had any of President Nixon's predecessors. The Domestic Council was primarily
concerned with creation of domestic programs while the Office
of Management and Budget was primarily concerned with

monitoring existing programs and bringing efficiency to the operation of the federal bureaucracy. (In practice there was some overlap of planning and supervisory functions.) In domestic affairs Ehrlichman and the head of the OMB performed the same services that Kissinger performed for foreign policy and defense. They functioned as buffers, sparing President Nixon the role of arbiter between conflicting staff viewpoints. They also provided the "briefs" that he preferred to personal discussion. This gave him time and privacy for decision making.

In a further attempt to centralize control over his administration, President Nixon's 1971 State of the Union Message proposed a sweeping plan to merge seven of the executive departments into four that would absorb many independent agencies. When Congress failed to pass the plan, President Nixon sought ways to accomplish as much reorganization as possible through executive action.

One step was appointment of Secretary of the Treasury George Shultz as an assistant to the president for economic affairs, making him the head of a new cabinet-level Council on Economic Policy while he retained his position as treasury secretary. The function of the new council was to provide overall coordination of the entire decision-making process on both domestic and international economic policy. This included coordination of such departments and agencies as: Treasury, Commerce, Labor, the Council of Economic Advisers, OMB, and the Office of Special Representative for Trade Negotiations. This step enlarged the chief-of-staff system, but President Nixon's primary contacts continued to be with only five trusted aides: H. R. Haldeman, who served as his White House administrator, Henry Kissinger, who coordinated foreign and defense affairs, John Ehrlichman, who coordinated domestic affairs, George Shultz, who coordinated economic affairs, and Roy Ash, who directed the Office of Management and Budget.

Yet another technique for centralizing control was the appointment of many trusted aides to key positions within the bureaucracy. President Nixon also developed an interdepartmental network that was responsive to the White House. This network was based on the assistant secretaries of administration in each department, who were subject to close scrutiny and control by the Office of Management and Budget [*The New York Times*, December 23, 1972, p. 9].

Eventually President Nixon developed a system of "super-secretaries" by consolidating authority in a few Cabinet members whom he made preeminent in the Cabinet by adding to their status as secretaries of departments the status of White House counsellors [*The New York Times*, January 6, 1973, p. 1; January 7, 1973, sec. 4, p. 2]. Secretary of Health, Education, and Welfare Caspar Weinberger was made counsellor for human resources, which gave him responsibility for health, education, manpower development, income security, social services, Indian and native peoples, drug abuse, and consumer protection. These areas were handled by a large number of departments and agencies. Secretary of Housing and Urban Development James Lynn was made counsellor for community development, which gave him responsibility for community institutions, community planning, housing, highways, public transportation, regional development, disaster relief, and national capital affairs. These areas were chiefly handled by the Departments of HUD, Transportation, and Agriculture. Secretary of Agriculture Earl Butz was made counsellor for natural resources, which gave him responsibility for natural resource use, lands and minerals, environment, outdoor recreation, water control, and park and wildlife resources. These areas were chiefly handled by the Agriculture and Interior Departments.

These three new counsellors were directly responsible to John Ehrlichman. Thus President Nixon created a complex system of cabinet members who were responsible to a super cabinet (Weinberger, Lynn, Butz), in turn responsible to one member of a super-super cabinet, John Ehrlichman. This was a clear demonstration of the point that the executive branch of the federal government is "a many splintered thing" [Herbers 1973, p. 1].

While this system might have met President Nixon's need for order and hierarchy, it had serious defects, including the erosion of traditional departments. As has been indicated, the State Department was hardest hit by having Kissinger's staff absorb many of its functions. The Office of Management and

Budget suspended housing subsidy programs without consulting the Department of Housing and Urban Development. Similarly, the Treasury Department's extensive research staff had
traditionally been at the forefront of administrative innovation
on tax legislation, but under the Nixon organization, it was
rarely consulted when high-level White House discussions occurred [Herbers 1973, p.1].

By demoralizing the traditional departments, the Nixon administration isolated itself from sources of information on which
to base policy. Furthermore, although policy may be *initiated* by
the White House staff, it must still be administered by the formal
mechanisms of the departments, because policy *implementation*
demands a substantial organization that the Executive Office of
the President is not equipped to provide. As the president
excluded the bureaucracy from decision making, he decreased
its stake in supporting his initiatives, which widened the gap
between initiative and implementation. The placement of
trusted aides in key bureaucratic positions could increase the
potential for control, but 2.5 million bureaucrats who had little
stake in following presidential initiatives could hardly be "controlled" by a score of aides.

Another consequence of President Nixon's institutionalization was the fact that the spectrum of advice that he received was
very narrow since he increasingly appointed as cabinet members
and aides little-known Nixon loyalists who could be "dismissed
or transferred at will without creating a ripple in public" [Her-
bers]. The work of such individuals was further homogenized as
it was sifted through super cabinet and super-super cabinet
levels before (and if) it ever reached the president. Dissent and
variety had been intentionally removed from the system. The
result was isolation for the president. This isolation was reinforced by the fact that, unlike his predecessors, President Nixon
was reluctant to seek advice outside his institutionalized system,
and intentionally isolated himself from the press.

Staff position papers can rarely indicate the intensity of feeling. Consequently, President Nixon was increasingly surprised
and politically embarrassed by public or congressional reaction
on a variety of issues. For example, he did not receive accurate

assessments of congressional sentiment on the antiballistic missile issue. He clearly underrated public and congressional reaction to the backgrounds of several of his appointees, including two intended justices of the United States Supreme Court and the FBI director. He was taken by surprise at the depth of public opposition to the Cambodia incursion, and to the shooting of students by National Guard troops at Kent State University in 1970. Secretary of the Interior Walter Hickel wrote an extraordinary letter of protest about the administration's reactions to campus unrest following the Kent State incident, complaining that the president was isolating himself from the great mass of American youth, thereby contributing to anarchy and revolt. The letter itself was a symbol of the president's isolation from his own executive departments. The secretary had to *write* because he despaired of breaking through the "Berlin Wall" to *see* the president with whom he had spoken privately only twice in fifteen months [*The New York Times*, May 7, 1970, p. 8]. The prime demonstration of President Nixon's isolation was his complete underestimation of the intensity of public and congressional reaction to the Watergate scandal. This finally destroyed him.

One particular domestic area over which President Nixon tried to exercise greater personal control than had any predecessor was the manner in which the media covered his administration. His concern for and antagonism to the media led him to use a larger group of staff aides for it and develop institutionalization further than had any predecessor in the office. For example, the president established the White House Office of Telecommunications Policy to bring television reporting into line. The Telecommunications Office overlapped the functions of the Federal Communications Commission in such actions as proposing legislation for licensing requirements that would have substantially extended presidential influence had the legislation passed.

In addition, the press secretary, administrative assistants, communications director, and their staffs actively engaged in a campaign to cause the press, television, and radio to present what they perceived to be a more "balanced" picture of the administration. More vulnerable because of its dependence on government licensing, television felt the impact of these actions more heavily than did newspapers. To the degree that the media as a source of alternative viewpoints was limited, the president's policies further contributed to his own isolation.

Divestment of Areas of Responsibility

While institutionalization thus accelerated over those areas in which President Nixon desired to assert greater administrative control, he also engaged in an active campaign to reverse the impact of routine expectations that the president would act in some areas of domestic policy. He hoped thereby to reduce the significance and consequences of a whole series of domestic policy pressures by transferring entire areas of administrative policy responsibility elsewhere. Detailed analysis of these attempts exceeds the scope of an essay on institutionalization, but a brief review may serve to indicate the varied ways in which President Nixon tried to divest his office of some of its domestic policy responsibilities.

His New Federalism took its form because it was an attempt to transfer responsibility for administering many programs from the president to state and local executives. The best examples of this were general and special revenue sharing. Other examples of his divestment strategy include the fact that at his initiative the Post Office was changed from an executive department to a goverment corporation, which ended presidential responsibility for supervising the mammoth postal bureaucracy.

Similarly, he attempted to terminate a wide variety of domestic programs in health, education and welfare that had developed during the previous decade. When Congress voted funds for programs of which he did not approve, or substantially increased funds for programs that would have increased his administrative responsibilities, he took the extraordinary step of impounding those funds. (Previous presidents had used impoundment only rarely for *military* appropriations.)

As yet another example of his divestment strategy, he withdrew the presidency from direct involvement in scientific questions by abolishing the Office of Science and Technology. He also requested abolition of the Office of Economic Opportunity, the Office of Emergency Preparedness, and the National Aeronautics and Space Council.

In addition to his battle to divest his office of some of its responsibilities in domestic affairs, he fought doggedly against accepting new administrative responsibilities that were thrust upon him by congressional, press, public, and interest-group constituencies as a result of the economic and fuel crises. In both of these crises, Nixon absorbed a remarkable amount of political loss before he would function. Even then he acted in the most minimal manner, limiting government involvement as far as possible.

In these crises he aimed to limit presidential involvement because the issues were extremely time consuming, highly resistant to "solution," and would deflect presidential time and energy from areas in which President Nixon had greater interest and influence. It was not simply a matter of preferring "small" to "big" government, because on the issues about which he cared he rapidly increased institutionalization. Rather, it reflected an attempt to select those areas of domestic policy for which he would accept responsibility, thereby countering the twentieth-century trend of routinization. The routine expectation of presidential involvement in economic questions proved irreversible, but he was more successful in divesting himself of other types of domestic responsibility. One development, however, had unforeseen consequences for both his control and divestment strategies — the Watergate scandal.

Watergate's Impact

Most of President Nixon's closest White House aides and advisers were implicated in the Watergate scandal, which included a complex range of covert and questionable political activity including concealed contributions, payoffs, espionage, and sabotage by people working for the Committee to Re-elect the President, and a complicated web of responsibility for attempts at cover-up. Consequently, Nixon's elaborate staff structure crumbled, on the heels of the spring 1973 resignations of Haldeman and Ehrlichman. It became very difficult for the president to handle staffing as many other presidential assistants were implicated, including former Attorney General John Mitchell, Acting FBI Director L. Patrick Gray, Counsel to the President John Wesley Dean III, the president's personal attorney Herbert W. Kalmbach, former Commerce Secretary Maurice Stans, Appointments Secretary Dwight L. Chapin, Chairman of the SEC G. Bradford Cook, and former White House aide Jeb Stuart Magruder. As the stain spread, the major survivor of President Nixon's elaborate institutionalization was Henry Kissinger.

President Nixon's attempts to rebuild his shattered organization were handicapped by his preference for familiar advisers to new people. In consequence, he tried to reshuffle remaining cabinet members and aides rather than bring in new advisers. In this manner he consciously perpetuated his isolation, despite its obvious limitations. Thus, General Alexander M. Haig, Jr. (assistant to Henry Kissinger) became chief of staff, replacing Haldeman. The former secretary of defense, Melvin Laird, replaced Ehrlichman as domestic adviser. A White House aide, Leonard Garment, replaced Dean as White House counsel. Elliot Richardson was moved from secretary of defense to replace Richard Kleindienst as attorney general. James R. Schlesinger moved from CIA director to secretary of defense. Ronald Ziegler continued as press secretary, but also assumed the duties of director of communications, replacing Herbert Klein. When Secretary of State William Rogers resigned, he was replaced by Henry Kissinger who continued to hold his position as assistant to the president for national security affairs.

Nevertheless, try as he would, President Nixon was unable to maintain his preferred staff structure as shifts in personnel and mounting public and congressional pressures related to the Watergate scandal brought change. The president had to abandon his middle-level, super cabinet system (Weinberger, Lynn, and Butz). Furthermore, as the administration came under increasing public and congressional scrutiny and attack, the president's advisers began to act more independently. For example, Attorney General Richardson publicly informed Vice President Spiro Agnew that he was under investigation for committing felonies, and George Shultz and Melvin Laird had a well-publicized dispute over tax policy, as did Henry Kissinger and James Schlesinger about certain foreign policy issues.

Somehow, much of the New Federalism's decentralized structure remained intact. There were, however, far more aggressive attempts on the part of Congress to increase spending for health, education, and welfare issues, and to challenge Nixon's constitutional right to impound funds voted by the legislature. Watergate and related scandals led to a massive loss of public confidence in President Nixon's administration, thereby encouraging the Democratic party, which controlled Congress, to oppose his changes. Increasingly, congressional Republicans had to disassociate themselves from the president in preparation for the 1974 congressional election. Therefore, to cut his losses, President Nixon's last budget attempted to mollify Congress by launching a new series of government initiatives in health and welfare that would have involved the president in a broad range of new administrative responsibilities, but these ameliorative moves were inadequate.

Watergate substantially destroyed Richard Nixon's control structure, interfered with his divestment strategy, and discredited his leadership so thoroughly that he became the first president of the United States ever to resign. What then is likely to be the future of the institutionalized presidency?

The Ford Response and Future Prospects

Gerald Ford's inaugural address pledged an open and more responsive presidency than that of Richard Nixon. President Ford's first day in office began with more sensitivity and responsiveness to press and congressional needs than his predecessor ever displayed. Within his first week he had completely revamped presidential press operations, and although he maintained continuity through early retention of his predecessor's staff, he established two key aides of his own, Robert Hartmann and John Marsh. Furthermore, within his first week in office he announced his intention of returning to reliance on the cabinet and established departments in decision making. Thus, he anticipated a corresponding reduction in the power of the White House staff. His preference for basing decisions on personal discussions rather than memos also indicated a less hierarchical and elaborate staff system than that of his predecessor, and greater presidential accessibility. He also stripped the Office of Management and Budget of the policy-making powers it had acquired under President Nixon.

However, neither President Ford nor his successors will be able to escape the liabilities of institutionalization. There is every indication that the American people will continue to expect the president to be the major source of initiative in our political system. A primary reason is the fact that the trends that were responsible for causing such centralization are likely to continue.

As previously indicated, the first of these trends was a widespread agreement among a majority of Americans in support of economic intervention by the national government. The heavy political losses President Nixon experienced when he tried to avoid action on the economic crisis will be a warning to any successor not to flaunt the expectations for routine action in this area. President Ford's first speech responded to this expectation by indicating that first priority would be given to action dealing with the economic crisis.

The second trend that emphasized presidential initiative was the increasing significance of foreign and military policy. The importance of these concerns is hardly likely to diminish. In fact, it can be argued that they will increase, because the grain and fuel shortage in 1974 were only forerunners of shortages affecting a number of natural resources and foodstuffs for which Americans will have to bid in an increasingly competitive world, a world in which direct American influence has been diminishing. Scarce goods resulting in higher prices, and diminished international influence are likely to increase national frustration and demands for protective action by the president.

The third trend of increasing public demand for greater social interference and centralization continues undiminished in such plans as a national health insurance policy. As chief executive the president's responsibility and initiative will be enhanced by any such demands.

Fourth, the inadequacy of state governments and Congress to deal with major areas of public concern may abate somewhat. For example, state governments have become stronger over the past 20 years through institutional reform. In addition, some of the Great Society and New Federalism issues have strengthened the policy role of state governments. However, the major policy areas of public concern continue to transcend state boundaries. Therefore, it seems likely that innovation by the national government will remain the focus of public demand.

In that regard, in 1974 Congress acted to provide itself with expertise and information to make an independent assessment of presidential budget requests. However, with its decentralized organization, based on the seniority system, Congress remains poorly designed to coordinate innovation. During the height of its antagonism to Richard Nixon there was serious consideration of reorganization, which would have made it an institution better suited to challenging executive initiatives. Unfortunately, however, only the most severe external threat triggers congressional reform. Thus, as the threat diminished in the last year of President Nixon's administration, the Bolling Committee report on reforming the structure of the House of Representatives was defeated, leaving little prospect for significant institutional reform. President Ford's administration is likely to soothe reform instincts even further. Thus, Congress' own limitations are likely to enhance public demand for presidential initiative.

Finally, technological developments in transportation and communication will obviously continue to enable presidents to appeal directly to the public in an unmediated fashion. In addition, the Office of Telecommunications Policy, as developed by President Nixon, was an effective means for absorbing some of the functions of the Federal Communications Commission. In the hands of an equally determined but more skillful and effective president, it could be an even more potent implement for controlling media coverage of an administration.

In short, there is little indication that the president's various constituencies will diminish the demands made on him for innovative action. Consequently, institutionalization is likely to continue with its attendant assets and liabilities for the president. However, President Nixon's example is likely to be a warning to his successors not to isolate themselves behind controlling hierarchies. It is hardly probable that future presidents will share Nixon's deep personal antagonism to the press, Congress, and the bureaucracy. Therefore, they are likely to be more sensitive to sources of information beyond the Executive Office of the President. Future presidents, therefore, are likely to suffer from isolation, but they may be better able to protect themselves through greater organizational skill and political sensitivity from as severe a problem as that which was created by, and which ultimately destroyed, President Nixon.

BIBLIOGRAPHY

Apple, R. W., Jr. "Haldeman the Fierce, Haldeman the Faithful, Haldeman the Fallen." *The New York Times Magazine*, 6 May 1973, pp. 39ff.

Ball, George. "We are Playing a Dangerous Game with Japan." *The New York Times Magazine*, 25 June 1972, pp. 10ff.

Evans, Rowland and Novak, Robert. *Nixon in the White House*. New York: Random House, 1971.

Herbers, John. "Nixon's Presidency: Centralized Control." *The New York Times*, 6 March 1973, pp. 1 & 20.

The New York Times, 1 May 1970, p. 1; 19 January 1971, p. 1; 24 August 1971, p. 26; 23 December 1972, p. 9; 6 January 1973, p.1; 7 January 1973, section 4, p.2; 8 January 1973, p.2; 30 April 1973, p. 6.

Ognibene, Peter J. "The Pentagon's Cost Overruns." *The New Republic*, 2 September 1972, pp. 12–13.

Osborne, John. "Henry's Wonderful Machine." *The New Republic*, 31 January 1970, pp. 11–13.

Semple, Robert B. "Nixon's Executive Style Combines Desire for Order and Solitude." *The New York Times*, 12 January 1970, p. 32.

Smith, Terance. "Foreign Policy: Decision Power Ebbing at the State Department." *The New York Times*, 18 January 1971, p. 1.

Udall, Morris K. *Report on the Growth of the Executive Office of the President: 1955–1972*. Committee on Post Office and Civil Service, House of Representatives. Washington, D. C.: U. S. Government Printing Office, 1972.

4

The President
and the Bureaucracy
in Domestic Affairs

*RICHARD P. NATHAN**
Brookings Institution

T HIS IS NOT THE FIRST TIME IN AMERI-
can history that the office of president has been in difficult
times. Merle Miller's book on Harry S Truman, *Plain Speaking*
[1974], contains a fascinating account of Truman's ideas about
the presidency in the period from 1820 to the Civil War when the
nation had a succession of weak presidents who had many
difficult experiences that President Truman describes well.
Another account of the presidency in difficult times that bears
mention is James S. Young's book, *The Washington Community*
1800–1828 [1966], in which he writes about President Madison
during the War of 1812 when the British burned the city of
Washington. Madison is described by Young as wandering
around in the countryside near Washington looking for a place

---

*This chapter is based on the author's book, *The Plot That Failed: Nixon and the Administrative
Presidency*, Wiley, 1975.

to lodge, all by himself, lonely and confused by the reversals of the period. The American presidency has had hard times before and probably will again.

In the latest era of difficult times, however, there is a new ingredient — the critical relationship between the president and the bureaucracy in domestic affairs. Can the president govern and manage the bureaucracy? Is the bureaucracy capable of being governed and managed? Is a bureaucracy that is incapable of being governed and managed a threat to American democracy? These questions have a significant bearing on the future of the American presidency as well as the American constitutional system. The purpose of this chapter is to address these questions based upon my own experiences as an official in the Nixon Administration during his first term (1969–1973).

THE NEW FEDERALISM: SUBSTANCE AND PROCESS

In considering the relationship between the presidency and the domestic bureaucracy, it is necessary to consider both the *substance* and *process* of government — what the government seeks to achieve and the way it goes about it.

Starting with the substantive side, the domestic agenda of the Nixon Administration can be described under the heading, the New Federalism. The central idea of the New Federalism was that we urgently need to *sort out* responsibilities in American government. Too many different levels and types of governments in contemporary American federalism are doing the same things, creating an unclear idea of who is responsible for getting a particular job done. The result is that public officials cannot be held *accountable*.

The New Federalism sought to identify those functions of domestic government that properly belong within the national government's jurisdiction and those functions that are better handled by states and localities, which according to the theory or rhetoric, however you like it, are "closer to the people."

Working with this basic idea, the Nixon Administration in the early days proposed that we use a new device — revenue

sharing — whereby the national government would return a portion of its income tax revenue to states and localities. In the
future, the New Federalism says that for certain kinds of functions the national government should adopt revenue sharing
policies to provide resources on a broad and basically uncondi-
tional basis to state and local governments so that in these
selected areas of domestic policy they can, to a significantly
greater degree, make their own decisions.

This decentralization reform of the New Federalism needs to
be evaluated along with another important "reform" that was a
major part of the domestic agenda of the Nixon Administration
throughout most of the first term. This second area is welfare
policy, involving both the Family Assistance Plan, which was
rejected by the Congress, and other basic changes in welfare
programs which in many cases were enacted [see Nathan 1975].
The Family Assistance Plan was premised on the theory that
individuals should be allowed, insofar as possible, to make their
own decisions about spending money rather than to have those
decisions made by national government bureaucracies.

Welfare reform and revenue sharing go together. Both of
them say, in effect, that the national government needs to move
away from establishing new programs and new agencies to meet
all kinds of social problems. Instead, we need to rely more heavily on the *community*, through revenue sharing, and on *individuals*, through a welfare-reform strategy, to make choices and
decisions rather than to have the national government make
those decisions for them. In the late 1960s and early 1970s
politicians of both liberal and conservative persuasion, Democratic and Republican labels, were calling for new solutions along
these lines, relying more on individual and community initiative.

The key point is that just as in physics if you want to move
power somewhere, you have to take it away from where it currently resides. In essence what the New Federalism policies involve is moving away from the reliance of an earlier period on
federal government programs and agencies to solve particular
and narrowly defined domestic problems.

But the New Federalism program, by seeking to assign more
responsibility to local governments and individuals, tends to
reduce the relative power of strongly entrenched bureaucracies

of the national government for various domestic programs. How does a president, whose fundamental aim in domestic affairs involves reducing the power of the federal bureaucracy, carry out his purpose?

THE METAMORPHOSIS

Our principal aim here is to assess the metamorphosis of Nixon administration attempts to "get a handle" on the power of national bureaucracies to achieve New Federalism policy changes. Between 1969 and 1973, there were five phases in this metamorphosis.

Phase One: The Balanced-Cabinet Legislative Approach

When the Nixon Administration first came to power, it acted like its most recent predecessors in placing the emphasis on legislative changes to achieve domestic policy aims. Hardly any attention was given to the role of the president as a manager in domestic affairs. Despite Article II, Section 1 of the Constitution, which says that the president is the nation's chief executive, very few presidents (and more than that, very few politicians) are managers either by experience or by orientation. The beginning of the Nixon Administration was no exception. The basic idea was to change direction by presenting new legislation to the Congress, and to concentrate, not on the management of existing programs, but on getting new ones adopted.

Phase Two: Counterbureaucracy

Increasingly, however, the Nixon administration discovered that it is very difficult to get legislation enacted in Congress when your party is in the minority in the House and Senate, because the legislation is fundamentally altered or totally ignored. Thus, the people around Mr. Nixon began to look for other ways to achieve their purposes.

As Mr. Nixon and the men around him learned more about domestic government, they began to be concerned that they could not achieve their major objectives through the legislative route. With the exception of revenue sharing, few bills on the administration's domestic agenda were enacted.

The administration began to take a harder look at the bureaucracy, defined for these purposes in amorphous and quite generalized terms. They discovered something that has become increasingly true of modern government, that is, that frequently *operation is policy*. In other words, what the bureaucracy does day in and day out, in setting regulations and justifying budgets, in approving or disapproving grants, *is* policy-making. With this in mind, the White House establishment began to develop its own "counter-bureaucracy." For example, there was the creation of the Domestic Council and the new Office of Management and Budget (OMB), which had added responsibilities.

The idea of this second phase was to find ways for the White House to *manage* the bureaucracy, to get control over the processes that are part of the everyday routine of administrative tasks in government, in order to achieve policy change through managerial, instead of legislative, actions. Since the role of the federal government has grown so rapidly in the last 40 years and many areas of domestic policy are highly complex, existing laws are therefore vague and discretionary, which left ample room to implement New Federalism ideas by administrative action.

Here was a new concept for the presidency, at least new in the degree to which administrative control was being relied upon and the way in which the task was being undertaken. Despite the fact that the idea of a managerial emphasis made sense, the notion of "running this railroad" from the White House proved to be unsatisfactory because of the difficulty of imposing centralized White House control over the entire bureaucracy [Nathan 1975, ch. 5].

Phase Three: Agency Reorganization

The next phase of domestic strategy was given impetus by the President's Council on Executive Reorganization (also known as the Ash Council since it was chaired by Nixon's long-time friend and advisor Roy L. Ash, who became director of the Office of Management and Budget in 1973). The Council proposed, and the president adopted, a series of formal agency reorganization bills designed to change the structure of the domestic agencies so that Nixon's appointees to the top agency posts would have greater control over the bureaucracy. But as in the case of other domestic legislation, the Congress would have little to do with these legislative proposals. Only one — the bill to establish a new Department of Community Development — got through the hearing stage, but was never reported out of committee. Three other bills, which would have set up new departments for Human Resources, Natural Resources, and Economic Development, never even got a hearing. Failure to obtain approval represented not only partisan divisions between Republicans and Democrats, but also traditional ties between the Congress and departments and agencies who had strong interest-group support.

Phase Four: The Management Strategy

At the end of the first term, right after the president's overwhelming electoral victory and just before Watergate crested, there emerged a fourth stage for creating a new relationship between the president and the domestic bureaucracy.

On the eve of his reelection victory, Nixon made it clear that he was going to have a fundamentally new strategy for domestic government in his second term. He told all of the members of his cabinet that they and their chief subordinates should submit their resignations forthwith. In this case, the instruction was given in a spirit very different from the pro forma tradition of the past. It was made clear that a *new team* would be named for the second term. It would consist of "trusted lieutenants" of the president, men with strong sympathy for his policies and more conservative views than those of their predecessors. Their essential task would be to take charge of the domestic bureaucracies — James Lynn at Housing and Urban Development, Caspar Weinberger at Health, Education, and Welfare, Howard Phillips at the Office of Economic Opportunity, and a second line made up primarily of former White House aides with close ties to John Ehrlichman. The new team would *take on* the Congress and *take over* the bureaucracy. New legislation was to be eschewed in deference to this administrative strategy.

In addition, a new system of super-secretaries was established — Lynn for Community Development, Weinberger for Human Resources, George Shultz for Economic Affairs. Boiled down, the idea was to implement the Ash Council reorganization plan *without legislation.* Greater control for carefully arranged subordinates was spelled out in a series of White House announcements. All of this was quite surprisingly out in the open.

As part of this fourth phase, the White House staff was to be pared down — Haldeman, Ehrlichman, Kissinger, Ash, the new Director of OMB, and Shultz for Economic Affairs were to be the "starting five" among White House aides. Other Executive Office personnel would be cut so that the "trusted lieutenants" appointed as agency heads could have frequent and direct access to the President and his chief aides.

Phase Five: The Ashes of Watergate

All of this was washed away by Watergate. In 1973, other problems came to outweigh the new management strategy. It was abandoned with the resignation of Ehrlichman, its principal designer and tactician. The administration returned to the conventional mode — a balanced cabinet of men who would speak out on their own policy issues, and with little presidential attention to managerial matters.

IMPLICATIONS OF THE MANAGEMENT STRATEGY

Is it wrong for the president to run the government as Nixon was planning to do in his second term in the field of domestic affairs? The fact of the matter is that throughout the history of the executive branch, the president's management authority has been used sparingly. What about an "administrative presidency" such as Nixon was readying for his second term to implement his New Federalism program?

We need to think about the role of bureaucracy in this connection — not just in government — but in industrialized society generally. There has been tremendous growth in specialized and highly technical organizations that control major institutions. The point of Theodore Lowi's impressive book, *The End of Liberalism* [1969], is that we have developed these organizations to the point where a vast amount of the activity of government is controlled, not through the democratic form, but by virtue of the specialized knowledge and expertise of the people who work in particular program areas. Moreover, there are essential differences between control by experts and control by the community through direct democratic or representative political systems. This is the riddle of the American presidency. It reflects the perennial theme of science fiction — the more activities become specialized and centralized, the more limited becomes the influence of the individual. In *The Player Piano* [1952], Kurt Vonnegut wrote about a society in which all activity was controlled by a few specially trained people and their machines. Everyone else had "make-work" activities. The fascination of such writing is that it reflects something hauntingly familiar in our own society.

If it had not been for Watergate, would it have made sense for a president to say, as Nixon did, "I want to take certain types of issues out of the hands of the specialist and put them back in the hands of the *community* and the *individual?*"

THE DILEMMA OF WATERGATE

The dilemma of Watergate, as I see it, is that there were around the president a group of people who were *his* people. They fought for him; they were named by him. In a sense, their careers *were* Nixon. They lost their perspective and erred tragically in the 1972 presidential campaign and its aftermath.

Yet, in order for a president to take over the bureaucracy, he may have to have precisely such a like-minded, closed group working together as a team. This is very different from the customary model in Washington, where even within the cabinet there are checks and balances, because the cabinet includes men with independent reputations and often different viewpoints. There is reason to doubt that with such a pluralistic executive establishment the government can be *managed* by the president. Thus, the management strategy confronts this problem that a like-minded, closed group even in substantive governmental matters could reinforce each other's views in a way that might warp their perspective and produce excesses in policy areas, just as in the case of Watergate, Nixon's political affairs advisors lost their footing to the point where they acted in a manner that was fundamentally at odds with our basic ethical standards.

We are left with a basic question: if the only way the president can achieve changes in certain areas is to exert management control, can we rely on the dedication of his top officials to high standards of public service that would permit such a strategy to be carried out in an even-handed and proper manner? I am not arguing here that one should accept the New Federalism. The point is that if in domestic policy, or some other area, it is concluded that the president should exert strong management influence over established governmental bureaucracies, we need to hope and pray that he and his staff have sufficiently high standards of public service to do this well. This is true because the power and influence of the federal bureaucracy is constantly expanding for many good and legitimate reasons.

BIBLIOGRAPHY

Lowi, Theodore J. *The End of Liberalism*. New York: W. W. Norton & Company, 1969.

Miller, Merle. *Plain Speaking*. New York: Berkeley/Putnam, 1974.

Nathan, Richard P. *Nixon and the Bureaucracy: A Study of the Domestic Government under Richard M. Nixon*. New York: John Wiley & Sons, 1975.

Vonnegut, Kurt. *The Player Piano*. New York: Holt, Rinehart and Winston, 1952.

Young, James S. *The Washington Community: 1800–1828*. New York: Columbia University Press, 1966.

III ☆ FOREIGN AFFAIRS

In this section the focus shifts from the president's role in domestic affairs to his role as world leader. In the first article Marian D. Irish describes and analyzes "The President's Foreign Policy Machine." She contrasts the original constitutional model for the conduct of foreign affairs with the contemporary executive policy-machine model. Focusing on a different area of foreign affairs, Norman Graebner examines the exercise of presidential power in foreign affairs and concludes that there are only two limitations on the president — self-restraint and his personal capacity to control public opinion — since constitutional restraints have generally been proven ineffectual.

Marian D. Irish, Charles O. Lerch Professor of Government Emeritus at American University, has written or edited *The Politics of American Democracy, Twelve Nation States, Continuing Crises in American Government* and *World Pressures and American Foreign Policy.* She has also been Editor of the *Journal of Politics* and a Fellow at the Woodrow Wilson International Center for Scholars.

Norman Graebner, Edward R. Stettinius Professor of History at the University of Virginia, formerly served as chairman of the University of Illinois history department. He has written or edited numerous books, including: *Empire on the Pacific, The New Isolationism, An Uncertain Tradition, Ideas and Diplomacy, The Cold War, Manifest Destiny* and *History of the American People.*

5

The President's Foreign Policy Machine*

MARIAN D. IRISH
American University

T HE U. S. FOREIGN POLICY MACHINE IS
an extremely intricate system of interlocking executive and
legislative components designed to move the nation on pre-
determined courses in external affairs. Every administration has
produced its own policy machine for the conduct of foreign relations. Comparing the successive models is a bit like lining up a
coach and four, a surrey with a fringe on top, a vintage Pierce
Arrow, and Air Force One.

The rapid advance of technology in transportation, communication, and the weapons of war has radically altered the
conduct of foreign policy. The content of foreign policy, however, is as always, the output of human cerebration. The pre-

---

*The research for this essay was done at the Woodrow Wilson International Center for Scholars, 1972–73. © 1975 by Harcourt Brace Jovanovich, Inc.

determined manner in which the policy machine operates depends on the objectives, priorities, and concerns of those who design and control the machine. In the words of the computer programmer, "garbage in, garbage out." Now, as the United States approaches its bicentennial celebration, we are painfully aware that the science of politics (or the art of government) has not kept pace with the technology of the policy machine. Vast and awesome changes have taken place both in the domestic environment where foreign policy is formulated and in the international environment where foreign policy is implemented. But the current foreign policy machine, replete with nearly two centuries of structural improvements and functional accessories, is still operating according to eighteenth-century specifications.

THE ORIGINAL MODEL: THE PRESIDENT AND CONGRESS

The original manual of instructions for the conduct of the nation's foreign affairs — the Constitution of 1787 — is easy to read but difficult to follow. Provisions for the separation, distribution, and sharing of powers between the president and Congress, the president and the Senate, the Senate and House are deliberately ambiguous. The Constitution has always been controversial. It was written amidst acrimonious debates. Those who stayed to the end and signed the final document did so with various reservations and misgivings. And, when the document became the supreme law of the land, it was susceptible to endless interpretation. The meaning of almost every word and phrase has been disputed, even by the Framers when they tried to operate the policy machine in accordance with their own instructions.

The ambiguities of the Constitution reflect the intentions of the Framers. The contrivance of checks and balances may resemble a Rube Goldberg invention, but it performs the functions that the eighteenth-century designers had in mind. It divides the great powers of government among the constituent parts of the machine in a way bound to cause some structural stress and strain; but it also requires accommodation, even consensus, among the constituent parts in the policy process. The Federalist pays homage to the celebrated Montesquieu and his maxim of separate and distinct powers ("an invaluable precept in the science of politics"). But putting theory aside, Madison defended at length the practicality of blending executive and legislative powers so that each department of government would be able to exercise a degree of constitutional control over the others [Federalist Nos. 47–51].

The mechanistic system of checks and balances was a contemporary approach to political science — eighteenth-century Newtonian physics applied to eighteenth-century politics. But the Framers were also of the behavioral persuasion; they knew that in any government "the root is man." In the words of Madison:

> If men were angels, no government would be necessary. But in framing a government which is to be administered by men over men, the great difficulty lies in this, you must first enable the government to control the governed and in the next place oblige it to control itself. A dependence on the people is, no doubt, the primary control on the government; but experience has taught mankind the necessity of auxilliary precautions [Federalist, No. 51].

The continuum of controversy over the conduct and/or content of foreign policy that has marked executive-legislative interactions since the first administration is different from the constitutional battles in the domestic arena. "The Constitution is what the judges say it is," but the judges have said very little about the constitutional side of foreign affairs. Constitutional controversies in foreign policy rarely become cases in court. Rather they involve political issues that are seldom settled, but continuously erupt between the executive and legislative branches of the government.

Since World War II questions of constitutional law in foreign policy have evoked endless great debates in Congress. Could Congress disclaim the presidential agreements made at Yalta or Potsdam? Could Congress prohibit the commander in chief from stationing U. S. military forces in Europe? Could Congress prevent the president from recognizing the People's Republic of China? Did President Truman have the constitutional right to take the nation into the Korean War without prior consultation and consent of Congress? Were the congressional resolutions on Formosa, the Middle East, Berlin, Cuba, and the Gulf of Tonkin tantamount to giving the president war powers? Does the president have the right to commit U. S. military forces, for whatever purpose, without the knowledge or approval of Congress? Does the president have authority to engage in covert operations that involve the use of force against other governments? Does executive privilege mean that the president is within his constitutional right to withhold crucial information from Congress in the arena of national security?

The many different answers to all these questions depend less on constitutional law than on the various standpoints and perspectives (official and personal) of the respondents: the president or Congress, Democrats or Republicans, the party in control of the White House or the majority party in Congress, liberals or conservatives, hawks or doves, the Senate Committee on Foreign Relations or the House Armed Services Committee.

Here we propose to examine three areas in which the Constitution clearly invites both conflict and cooperation in executive-legislative interactions: presidential war powers, national commitments, and foreign economic policy. In all three areas, the president *and* Congress are constituent parts of the policy machine.

"The War Powers"

Article I gives Congress the power to raise and support the armed services and to declare war, but Article II, which designates the president as commander in chief without any stipulated limitations, by implication leaves it up to him to make the crucial decisions: how, when, and where to use the armed forces to implement U. S. foreign policy with or without a congressional declaration of war.

In *The Federalist* Alexander Hamilton made a point of depreciating the significance of the commander-in-chief clause:

> It would amount to nothing more than the supreme command and direction of the military and naval forces, as first general and admiral of the Confederacy; while that of the British king extends to the declaring of war and to the raising and regulating of fleets and armies — all which, by the Constitution under consideration, would appertain to the legislature [No. 69].

George Washington himself believed that it was part of his constitutional obligation as commander in chief to assume personal direction of the armed forces when they were employed in executing the laws of the United States. In full uniform, he led 15,000 militiamen against the embattled farmers of Pennsylvania in the Whiskey Rebellion of 1794.

More significantly for posterity, the first president did not hesitate to issue on his own authority a Proclamation of Neutrality, stating that the United States would not enter into the European wars of the day. Whether such action exceeded the powers that the Framers intended to vest in the president was furiously debated in 1793. Then Secretary of State Thomas Jefferson advised the president that only Congress could declare neutrality because only Congress could declare war. But Alexander Hamilton counselled that neutrality was the only feasible course for a newly developing nation. How then shall we interpret the intentions of the Framers? Washington had presided over the Philadelphia Convention, and Hamilton had taken a leading part in its debates while Jefferson was abroad, serving as minister to France in 1787.

Constitutionally, only the Congress is empowered to declare war. It has done this five times — the War of 1812; the War between the United States and Mexico; the Spanish-American War; and the two world wars — each time at the behest of a president whose conduct of foreign policy had already virtually committed the nation to war. Only once in its history has Congress actually debated whether or not to declare war. In 1812, on the declaration of war reluctantly requested by President Madison, the vote was divided with 19 to 13 in favor in the Senate, 79 to 49 in the House. This split decision prompted the Federalists at the Hartford Convention to demand that not even Congress be permitted to authorize hostilities against a foreign nation unless two-thirds of both houses concurred.

On the other hand, American presidents have on numerous occasions claimed and exercised a constitutional right to dispatch armed forces not only to protect American lives and property but also to pursue broad strategic policies in the conduct of foreign relations. Up to the second half of the twentieth century, however, these were minor operations, confined mainly to the western hemisphere, with quite specific and limited objectives: to protect American lives and property during local political disturbances, to protect American consulates or embassies or to evacuate American citizens in cases of civil disorder, to punish attacks made on American seamen or ships, and to open ports for American commerce. In such instances, solo presidential intervention was justified either because the threat was too trivial to require consultation with Congress or the danger to American lives and property was imminent and the president could not wait for congressional response.[1]

No American president from George Washington to Franklin D. Roosevelt had any inflated notion that he could or should dispatch American military forces on his own authority to help fight other peoples' wars, to win independence, resist aggression, overthrow dictatorship, or contain any ideology. Even Franklin D. Roosevelt, who used his foreign policy powers to turn the United States into an arsenal for democracy, recognized his constitutional limitations as commander in chief. In June 1940, when the Nazi blitzkrieg hit France and Premier Reynaud desperately called for American aid, President Roosevelt replied that the United States would continue to send supplies so long as the French continued to fight, but he also said, "I know that you will understand that these statements carry with them no implication of military commitments. Only the Congress can make such commitments" [Roosevelt 1941, #59, pp. 265–266].

In 1950, at the outbreak of hostilities in Korea, President Truman contemplated a request to Congress for enabling legislation to sanction American intervention, but on advice of his principal foreign policy officers, he decided to go ahead on his own constitutional authority as commander in chief. In retrospect, his secretary of state, Dean Acheson, thought that had the president sought and obtained congressional approval, subsequent reactions of Congress might have been less pejorative, although congressional approval had neither softened nor diverted antiwar criticism leveled against Presidents Lincoln, Wilson, and Franklin D. Roosevelt. It was not the constitutional issue but rather the appalling costs and casualties, as well as the frustrations of limited and inconclusive hostilities that made the Korean War so unpopular at home: that, and the fact that the Republican opposition was able to use "President Truman's War" as a political instrument to end 20 years of Democratic occupancy of the White House [Acheson 1969, pp. 414–415].

The Eisenhower administration almost immediately felt the backlash of the constitutional issues that the Republicans had so zealously revved up in the 1952 presidential campaign. No matter that the Republicans in the first two years controlled both the White House and Congress. Accustomed as they were to opposing foreign policies made in the White House, Congressional Republicans were prepared to play the same role vis-à-vis Eisenhower that they had played for the past 20 years opposite Roosevelt and Truman. A constitutional amendment sponsored by Senator John Bricker (R., Ohio) and cosponsored by nearly two-thirds of the senators, Republicans as well as Democrats, would have severely curtailed executive bargaining power in the conduct of foreign relations; it failed to pass by only one vote.

For 6 of his 8 years in the White House, President Eisenhower had to contend with a Congress controlled by the opposition party. His administration had no alternative but to court congressional cooperation. Mindful of his predecessor's contretemps with Congress over the Korean War, President Eisenhower sought advance congressional approval for whatever use of force he might deem necessary to implement U. S. foreign policy. From the president's standpoint, however, neither the Formosa Resolution of 1954 nor the Mid-East Resolution in 1957 implied that he could not have acted on his own constitutional authority as commander in chief. As he viewed it, "a suitable congressional resolution" was simply a signal of unified and serious intention on the part of the whole American government, the President, the Congress, and the people [Eisenhower 1963, p. 468].

The circumstances under which Lyndon Johnson sought a suitable congressional resolution were somewhat different. In 1964 the country was in the midst of a presidential campaign, and the civil war in Vietnam was already a divisive issue in American politics. In August, when it was reported that U. S. destroyers patrolling the Gulf of Tonkin had been attacked by Communist PT boats, President Johnson immediately ordered a retaliatory air strike against their North Vietnamese bases. But Lyndon Johnson had to play two roles simultaneously, that of presidential candidate seeking reelection as well as that of commander in chief. As a candidate, Johnson made it clear that, in contrast to his "trigger-happy opponent," he had no desire to widen the war in Southeast Asia and was "not about to send American boys nine or ten thousand miles from home to do what Asian boys ought to be doing for themselves." As commander in chief, he asked Congress to support the presidential determination to prevent aggression in Asia and to assist any member of SEATO that asked for American aid to defend its freedom against the aggressor.[2]

The Gulf of Tonkin Resolution, which was rushed through Congress in August 1964, passed by votes of 88–2 in the Senate and 414–0 in the House. Whether or not the resolution was obtained under false pretense and with misinformation (as was later alleged), Congress did understand at the time the full extent of its authorization. "Senator John Sherman Cooper asked the crucial question: 'If the president decided that it was necessary to use such force as could lead us into war, we will give that authority by this resolution?' Senator Fulbright, who was managing the bill, replied in the affirmative, 'That is the way I would interpret it' " [Schlesinger 1973, p. 180]. It was not, however, the way Lyndon Johnson interpreted it. Although later he enjoyed taunting his congressional critics by flourishing a copy of their resolution, like his predecessor, he believed that with or without congressional support he had the right as commander in chief to take whatever measures were required to implement U. S. foreign policy.

In 1965, President Johnson began to escalate the war in Vietnam, turning "their war" into "our war." As Arthur Schlesinger, Jr. points out, there were no serious precedents for this decision. Unlike the Korean War, there was no clear case of aggression in the form of mass invasion across frontiers, and there were no supporting UN resolutions to give the semblance of international sanctions. There was no grave and imminent danger to American security as there had been in the Cuban missile crisis. There were no American civilians to be rescued as there had been in the Dominican Republic. Nevertheless, President Johnson's decision was made with the manifest approval of the American people [Schlesinger, p. 179]. In August 1965, when the Gallup Poll began to ask whether the United States had made a mistake in sending American troops to fight in Vietnam, the replies were 61 percent "No," 24 percent "Yes," and 15 percent "no opinion." It was not until February 1968 that the Gallup Poll showed that less than a majority of Americans favored the intervention. At that point, President Johnson recognized that he was not a viable candidate for reelection to the presidency. On March 31, 1968, in a dramatic televised address to the nation, the president announced the cessation of bombing in North Vietnam and his own resolve not to seek or accept renomination for the presidential office.

No doubt the credibility gap had something to do with waning popular support for the Vietnam war, but President Johnson was neither the first nor the last commander in chief whose credibility could be questioned. Compare, for example, Franklin D. Roosevelt's campaign promise in 1940 — "your boys are not going to be sent into any foreign war" — with his subsequent policies that led to America's entry into World War II. Remember how the Eisenhower Administration got caught in a cover story for the U-2 reconnaissance plane that was downed inside the USSR — a story that, when exposed by the Kremlin, caused the cancellation of what President Eisenhower had hoped would be the high point of his foreign policy, the summit meeting in Paris with Chairman Khrushchev. Remember also the deliberate deception and misinformation from the Kennedy White House with respect both to the aborted Bay of Pigs invasion and the Cuban missile crisis. Thus Johnson, like Truman with the Korean War, suffered neither from a debate over constitutional issues nor from the lack of credibility of the administration but rather from the terrible costs of fighting a losing war that demoralized public opinion and weakened the presidential position.

Ironically, congressional reaction to "the President's War" in Vietnam did not peak under the Johnson administration, which had continuously escalated the military operations in Southeast Asia, but rather under the Nixon administration, which was withdrawing the American troops on schedule. The sharpest expressions of congressional disapproval followed immediately upon President Nixon's April 30, 1970 announcement that he had sent troops into Cambodia in order to protect troop withdrawals from Vietnam. Senators John Sherman Cooper (R., Ky.) and Frank Church (D., Idaho) introduced an amendment to pending legislation on military sales to bar the use of any funds to support U. S. military forces in Cambodia. During the 7 weeks debate on the Cooper-Church Amendment, almost as an aside to the main issue, the Senate repealed the Gulf of Tonkin Resolution that the Johnson Administration had once treated as tantamount to a congressional declaration of war in Vietnam. The Senate voted its approval of the Cooper-Church Amendment on the very day that President Nixon announced that all U. S. troops had been pulled out of Cambodia.

The Senate Committee on Foreign Relations opened its hearings on war power legislation in March 1971 — "for the purposes of clarifying and defining the proper division of the war power between Congress and the President" [War Powers Legislation 1972, p. 179]. Not until well into 1973, however, was the Congress in a strategic position to limit presidential war powers. By then the Vietnam war was officially ended and the American prisoners of war had been brought home on terms arranged by the president without consulting the Congress. By then also, the president was in serious personal and political difficulties emanating from Watergate. Moreover, continued bombing of Cambodia, without further pretence that such operations were related to the safety of American forces in Vietnam, aroused the ire of many congressmen who felt that the president was flagrantly ignoring congressional signals to terminate all military operations in Southeast Asia. In June 1973, Congress moved to cut off all funds for combat activities in Cambodia by August 15, 1973. In effect, this put a deadline on the presidential policy of bombing Cambodia while negotiating for a cease fire.

In the meantime, Congress went to work in earnest on legislation that would require the president — any president — to obtain congressional authorization for commiting U. S. forces outside the United States. The War Powers Act of 1973 drew the support (and opposition) of an unlikely coalition of Democrats and Republicans, liberals and conservatives, hawks and doves. It passed the House by a vote of 238 to 123 and the Senate 75 to 20. As it now stands, the president must consult at once with congressional leaders in any situation where hostilities appear imminent. If the president orders military operations without a congressional declaration of war, he must report to Congress within 48 hours about the circumstances leading to such action and provide an estimate of the probable scope and duration of hostilities. The president must terminate the use of armed force within 60 days unless Congress in the interim has declared war or specifically authorized the use of force (as in a concurrent resolution). The president may gain a 30-day extension if he certifies to Congress in writing that continued use of force is an "unavoidable necessity" to secure the safety of the United States. At any time within the 60 to 90 days, Congress may direct the president to remove all U. S. forces from hostilities outside the country.

Regarding the war powers legislation as "both unconstitutional and dangerous to the best interests of the nation," President Nixon vetoed it. In his veto message he said such legislation "could seriously undermine the nation's ability to act decisively and convincingly in times of international crisis." Nevertheless, during the Arab-Israeli October War, Congress overrode the veto. The Senate vote was expected: 75 to 18, Democrats 50 and Republicans 25, in all, 13 more than the necessary two-thirds. The House vote was more surprising, for the House traditionally supports the president's foreign policy; but there 86 Republicans joined 198 Democrats to override the president's veto, 4 more than necessary for a two-thirds majority. It was a dramatic decision but . . . .

The War Powers Act of 1973 remains as controversial as the constitutional issue it was supposed to clarify. Senator Jacob Javits (R., N.Y.), who pushed for the legislation, claims that it reflects the determination of Congress to recapture "the awesome power to make war," that it warns the incumbent and his successors that Congress will brook no more wars initiated and carried on by a president who lacks congressional approval. Senator Thomas Eagleton (D., Mo.), who opposed the weakened version that came out of the Conference Committee, now says that the act "gives the President and all of his successors in the future a predated 60-day unilateral war-making authority." Merlo Pusey, a long-time student of the presidency, considered it "a rather feeble reassertion of congressional power . . . an effort to restore the historic roles of the executive and legislative branches with a minimum of restraints and formalities [1973]. Barry Goldwater, Sr. (R., Ariz.), who once aspired to the presidency himself, replied "this 'feeble resolution' is destructive of America's credibility in any future crisis, both among our enemies and allies . . . . What the War Powers Resolution would restore is a discredited vestige of the Continental Congress and the Articles of Confederation, the very weakness the Constitution was designed to correct" [1973]. Unfortunately, we shall not be able to know which view is more realistic until this president or one of his successors feels impelled to use armed forces yet again in pursuit of U. S. foreign policy.

National Commitments

The United States emerged from World War II as the single most powerful nation in the world. It could well afford to expend vast sums to extend its commitments: to deter the aggressor, to contain communism, to aid in the economic recovery of Western Europe and Japan, to extend security and development assistance to friendly Third World nations. Its policy makers were in a strategic position to rebuild the free world in the American image. But the price of global foreign policy was higher than its makers bargained for. Year after year American taxpayers were asked to pay ever escalating costs for international security, viewed as an extension of national security. Defense expenditures were accorded top priority in allocating the nation's resources to the detriment of such other great national needs as health care, education, urban development, housing, transportation, conservation of natural resources, crime reduction, and environmental controls. Reaction to the Vietnam War brought to a head demands for a review of U. S. national commitments and a reordering of priorities.

In the 1940s and 1950s the United States had created a network of national commitments for the maintenance of national and international security. But as the 1960s came to an end, the whole international setting was changing. Pragmatic power alignments were replacing the ideological concept of the 1950s, the free world versus the communist world. Bipolarization was fraying at both ends, the Soviet bloc had split, and the Atlantic community was also coming apart. The reentry of the People's Republic of China into the international system was creating new triangular structures with the United States at the base (or apex?): Western Europe, the United States, and Japan; China, the United States, the Soviet Union. Japan and Western Europe were giving the United States tough competition in the free world economy. Countries in the Third World were becoming more nationalistic, more independent, and less influenced by either the Soviet or American way. The rapid rise of multinational corporations and changing patterns of foreign investments were restructuring a world economy in which the United States was no longer predominant. It was a time for reassessing national priorities and international commitments everywhere in the world.

National commitments are made under the authority of the United States ambiguously vested in the president-and-

Congress. Article II gives the president power to make treaties, but it requires him to obtain concurrence of two-thirds of the senators. The Constitution does not specify at what point in diplomatic negotiations the president should seek senatorial advice and consent. When the first president attempted to consult with the Senate on a treaty pending with the Indians, he received a sharp rebuff for violating the separation of powers. On the other hand, when he failed to ascertain the sense of the Senate before initiating the Jay Treaty (and later refused to disclose his instructions to Jay), he was threatened with impeachment for ignoring shared powers. No president since Washington has tried to meet formally with the Senate on treaty negotiations in progress, but from time to time presidents have found it good politics to sound out congressional opinion in advance, particularly when appropriations were needed for implementation.

The Constitution makes no mention of international agreements that do not follow the treaty-making route. Nevertheless every president from Washington to Ford has asserted his constitutional right to make executive agreements on his own authority. Such executive agreements have covered the whole gamut of international obligations, some of them of far-reaching import. The agreements that Franklin D. Roosevelt made at Yalta and Harry Truman at Potsdam changed the face of the postwar world without any prior consultation with, or subsequent approval by, Congress.

Since 1945 the presidents have negotiated and the Senate approved several major multinational and bilateral treaties that commit the nation to the defense of forty-three foreign countries, including the Rio Pact (1947), the NATO Treaty (1949), the ANZUS Treaty (1951), the SEATO Treaty (1954), the Mutual Defense Treaties with the Philippines (1951), Taiwan (1954), and Japan (1960). Hundreds of executive agreements amplify and provide the specifics of implementation under these treaties. Senate committees, or key members of the Senate, have sometimes been informed confidentially as to the nature of "classified" agreements. In other instances, Congress has been given no inkling of agreements in the making or already made that are binding upon the nation. Congress itself, however, has assisted

in building up presidential power through a succession of concurrent resolutions authorizing the president to use armed force
if necessary to defend specific countries or areas vital to American national security: Formosa (1955) to protect Taiwan and the
Pescadores against attack by Communist China; the Mideast
(1957) to protect Mideast countries against aggression from any
country controlled by international communism; Cuba (1962) to
defend Latin America against Cuban aggression or subversion;
Berlin (1962) to defend West Berlin against attack and to insure
western access to the city; Gulf of Tonkin (1964) to defend any
SEATO member or protocol state (including Vietnam) requesting U. S. assistance.

Despite the increasing frequency of American military in-
terventions in foreign nations, Congress was not impelled to
check the escalation of national commitments until the Vietnam
War began to provoke massive public demonstrations of disapproval. In 1967 the Senate Foreign Relations Committee reported
out a National Commitments Resolution declaring it the sense of
the Senate that no future commitments could be made by the
United States without affirmative action by Congress. The year
1967 was not, however, a propitious time to push the public
debate. The nation was at war, and Congress was reluctant to
take any stand that might impair the authority of the commander
in chief. Moreover, with the 1968 presidential election in the
offing, Democrats in Congress were not about to take any action
that the electorate might interpret as an official rebuke of their
party chief.

A more auspicious year to review U. S. commitments overseas was 1969. The newly elected Congress was prepared to lay
down guidelines in a future context so as neither to cast asper-
sions on the previous administration nor to presage confrontation with the new administration. A sense-of-the-Senate resolution was passed in June 1969 declaring that a national commitment results " . . . only from affirmative action taken by the
executive and legislative branches of the United States government by means of a treaty, statute, or concurrent resolution of
both Houses of Congress specifically providing for such commitments." As with the War Powers Act, opinion is divided as to

whether the National Commitments Resolution actually curtails presidential power. To begin with, the 1969 resolution does not apply to commitments already in existence (of which there are hundreds). Further, the resolution does not apply to all future commitments but only to those that involve a promise or pledge to assist a foreign country by use of armed forces or financial resources under certain circumstances. And finally, most important, a sense-of-the-Senate resolution is not legally binding on presidential policy making.

Recognizing the inherent weakness of the National Commitments Resolution, a subcommittee of the Senate Foreign Relations Committee (chaired by Stuart Symington, D., Mo.) undertook a detailed study of existing U. S. security agreements and their impact on U. S. foreign policy. The deeper the Symington Committee probed, the more concerned it became about the extent of secret agreements, de facto understandings, covert activities, and paramilitary operations authorized by the executive without congressional knowledge or approval. In country after country, it found that one secret agreement led to another until the degree of American involvement was far greater than was originally intended and certainly much more extensive than the American public had been led to believe. The subcommittee found in case after case that the executive practice was to maximize U. S. commitments in secret discussion with foreign governments and to minimize their import at home.

In its final report [*U. S. Security Agreements and Commitments Abroad* 1971] the Symington Committee recommended that Congress insist on approving all agreements, formal and implicit, made by the executive and to take a long hard look at the authority of the president to station U. S. forces anywhere in the world without specific prior approval of the Congress. But even in its own investigations of agreements already made, the subcommittee came up against a wall of executive secrecy and classified information, especially with respect to relationships that exist between the United States and those host countries where the United States has deployed nuclear tactical weapons.

Meanwhile, the newly elected president, also sensing the changing mood of America —"no more Vietnams" — was promising a "new approach to foreign policy, to match a new era of international relations." Thus, at Guam, in November 1969, he enunciated what he modestly called "the Nixon Doctrine."

> Its central thesis is that the United States will participate in the defense and development of allies and friends, but that America cannot — and will not — conceive all the plans, design all the programs, execute all the decisions and undertake all the defense of the free nations of the world. We will help where it makes a real difference and is considered in our interest.

> It is misleading, moreover, to pose the fundamental question so largely in terms of commitments. Our objective, in the first instance, is to support our interests over the long run with a sound foreign policy. The more that policy is based on a realistic assessment of our and others' interests, the more effective our role in the world can be. We are not involved in the world because we have commitments; we have commitments because we are involved. Our interests must shape our commitments, rather than the other way around.

While the Nixon Doctrine appeared to promise a retrenchment in world affairs, it also expressed a firm intent to keep all existing treaty commitments; to provide a shield wherever any nuclear power threatened any nation allied to the United States or whose survival was considered vital to American security; and in other types of aggression to furnish military and economic assistance when requested and as appropriate. There was and is nothing small or narrow about the Nixon Doctrine.

Neither the National Commitments Resolution nor the Nixon Doctrine give us a clear reading on the shaping of national commitments for the 1970s. For nearly the entire period since World War II, considerations of national and international security dominated U.S. foreign policy. American leadership of the free world generated global reliance upon the United States for peacekeeping operations and mutual defense programs. United States' commitments, for the most part, were tied to strategic interests viewed from political and military perspectives. Given the awesome technology of nuclear weaponry and the constant fear of nuclear war, the president's foreign policy machine was specially designed to provide the expertise and intelligence needed to deal promptly and decisively with recurrent crises. Congress was disposed to grant the president whatever powers he requested to cope with specific emergencies. This skewing of the tandem relationship between the president and the Congress was generally acceptable as long as the American people under presidential leadership were able to get what they wanted in the world outside. But as the power position of the United States moved from virtual omnipotence at the beginning of the 1950s, to one of increasing vulnerability in the late 1960s, public confidence in the president's ability to handle foreign policy problems on his own began to wane. As the prevailing winds of public opinion began to shift, Congress, as the representative body of the people, began to reassert its constitutional initiatives in policy formulation, especially with respect to foreign economic policy.

Foreign Economic Policy

In his foreign policy message of 1972 (the year he journeyed to Peking and Moscow), the president produced a "new economic policy" as a counterpart to the Nixon Doctrine in national security policy:

> America has entered a new era in its economic relations with the rest of the world.
>
> For a quarter of a century now, since the end of World War II, America has borne the principal burden of free world defense, of foreign aid, of helping old nations back on their feet and new nations to take their first, sometimes faltering steps. We have laid out nearly $150 billion in foreign aid, economic and military. We have fought two costly and grueling wars. We have undergone deep strains at home, as we have sought to reconcile our responsibilities abroad without reference to our own needs here in America . . . .
>
> But the time has also come to give a new attention to America's own interests.

To put it more bluntly, the United States is no longer either willing or able to pay the price for leadership of the free world. Foreign policies programmed to contain communism, to deter aggression, and to counter subversion on a global scale threatened to bankrupt the nation. The United States emerged from the Vietnam War with its domestic economy assailed by problems of inflation and unemployment, and its status in the world economy sharply threatened in the arenas of trade and finance.

What constitutes "America's own interests" in the international economy has always been a matter of concern and controversy to U. S. policy makers. A major motivation in calling the Philadelphia Convention in 1787 was to give the national government power to regulate foreign commerce, commerce among the states, and trade with the Indians. Article I of the Constitution clearly assigns this power to Congress along with the power to levy taxes on imports and to regulate the value of foreign coin. The president, however, also acquires power over such matters through his role in treaty making and his suspensory veto over legislation. Further, Article II requires him to recommend to Congress such measures as he judges necessary and expedient, a requirement that in effect gives him the initiative in formulating economic policy.

Justice Holmes once observed, "a Constitution is not intended to embody a particular economic theory" [*Lochner* v. *New York,* 198 U. S. 45]. Certainly, we do not find in the Constitution any of the verbalisms that are popularly associated with the "American way": private enterprise, freedom of contract, freedom of competition, or the separation of government and business. In the original instructions there is no mention of government controls over profits, prices, or wages, or any guarantees of income security or consumer protection. The Constitution as amended, however, specifically prohibits both the national government and the states from taking life, liberty, or property without due process of law, or from seizing property for public use without just compensation. The Constitution does not ban a socialist government, but it does make nationalization of the economy a prohibitively expensive policy.

The conventional wisdom of eighteenth-century agrarian America was based on notions of natural law: "that government is best that governs least" and "every man works best in his own interest." In the second half of the twentieth century, U. S. policy makers still find it useful to hark back to the traditional ideology, albeit tempered by modern concepts of government-in-business and business-in-government. Immediately after World War II, time and circumstances were joined to restructure international economics in the American way, "to make the world safe for capitalism," and thereby to further "America's own interests" in the new world economy. Specifically, the objectives of U. S. postwar foreign economic policy were to obtain at lowest costs natural resources from anywhere in the world for military and/or industrial purposes in the United States; to export the American ideology of private property rights and its concomitant of just compensation for the taking of property as a counter-policy to nationalization in developing countries; to secure unrestricted markets for American-made goods and to promote American private investments and corporate enterprise throughout the free world.

In the first decade after World War II, aggressive Soviet policies in Eastern Europe, motivated by the ideology of communism and backed by nuclear power as well as by conventional armed forces, appeared to pose a serious threat to the fulfillment of American plans. It is an overstatement to claim (as do some recent revisionist historians) that the Truman Doctrine, the Marshall Plan, the policy of containment, the whole network of mutual defense treaties, and all the foreign assistance programs — military, economic, technical — were primarily designed to advance America's own interests in the world [J. & G. Kolko 1972]. But certainly there has been an inextricable commingling of national security policies and foreign economic policies, not only in the first decade, but throughout the period from Presidents Truman to Ford.

The early decision of the U.S.S.R. not to participate in the International Monetary Fund and the International Bank of Reconstruction and Development meant that these institutions became instruments of the free world, largely under the aegis of the

United States. Thus ideology served as a useful tool to link the industrial world with the Third World in the framework of international finance and capital investments.

Ideology was also used to justify controls on trade with communist countries. The Export Control Act of 1949 imposed severe restrictions on U. S. exports to the Soviet Union and the countries of Eastern Europe. President Truman invoked the 1917 Trade-with-the-Enemy Act to embargo all trade with Communist China and North Korea following Chinese intervention in the Korean War in 1950. In the same year, Congress enacted the Battle Act prohibiting U. S. assistance to any country shipping strategic goods to communist countries, leaving it to the discretion of the president to determine whether suspension of aid programs in specific cases was actually in the national interest. In 1954, President Eisenhower extended the embargo to North Vietnam, and Congress, in turn, banned the extension of aid, credit guarantees, and food-for-peace programs to any communist country. In 1960, President Eisenhower declared an embargo on commerce with Cuba.

Ideology as an instrument of foreign policy is useful only if it accords with objective reality. As long as U. S. allies in NATO really feared the possibility of communist aggression from Eastern Europe, they went along with U. S. policy to restrict East-West trade. But as they regained their own strength and waxed prosperous, they began to deprecate ideological barriers and to press for resumption of lucrative East-West trade patterns. Similarly, in the United States, when the balance of payments became a critical issue in the early 1960s, the Kennedy administration was persuaded by international business interests to reassess the American embargo on trade with Eastern Europe. President Kennedy was able to override congressional opposition to credit guarantees for heavy sales of wheat to the Soviet government in 1963–64. Congress, however, repeatedly rejected presidential requests in both the Kennedy and Johnson administrations to relax the embargo on industrial goods for East-West trade. Not until 1969, when the Export Control Act was up for termination or renewal, was Congress ready to reconsider the issue of trade with communist countries. By then, the position and condition of the United States in the world economy had so changed that new economic policies more in line with new realities than with the old rhetoric had become the order of the day. Thus the Nixon administration was prepared to accept the end of ideologic barriers and come to terms with Peking and Moscow (though not with Hanoi or Havana) on a purely pragmatic basis.

Early in his first administration, President Nixon went to Congress for trade legislation that would give his administration bargaining powers in international negotiations. He pointed out that intense international competition, new and growing markets, changes in cost levels, technological developments in both agriculture and industry, and large-scale exports of capital were so changing the character of the international economy that U. S. policy makers could no longer think about trade policies "in the old simple terms of liberalism or protectionism." In a letter to Wilbur Mills, the president described the proposed Trade Act of 1970 as "modest in scope but significant in impact" and asked the Congress to authorize funding for U. S. participation in the upcoming international trade negotiations sponsored by General Agreement on Tariffs and Trade (GATT) [*Tariff and Trade Proposals* 1970]. To give him an effective bargaining position in negotiating with U. S. trading partners, the president asked for authority to raise or lower specific tariff barriers. To gain support in the domestic economy, he asked for technical improvements in the adjustment assistance provisions to compensate industry for any injuries "truly caused" by changing U. S. trade policies.

On August 15, 1971 President Nixon appeared on television to announce to the world at large, "the most comprehensive new economic policy to be undertaken by this nation in four decades." Most of the new economic policy was directed toward shoring up the sagging domestic economy, but domestic and foreign economic policies are intermeshed in any industrial nation. In the context of an international financial crisis, the president served notice that the United States was about to press for "an urgently needed new international monetary system. This action will not win us any friends among the international money traders. But our primary concern is with the American workers and with fair competition around the world." On the same day, the president also proclaimed a 10 percent temporary surcharge on imported goods and by executive order imposed a 90-day wage-price freeze. As a further temporary measure to protect American labor and to remove the "unfair edge" of foreign competition, the president freed the U. S. dollar from its historic $35-an-ounce gold price in the world market.

Over the past 25 years the United States had provided $143 billion to the major industrial nations of Europe and Asia "to help them get on their feet and to protect their freedom." But now that they had regained their vitality and had become strong competitors not only in the world markets but also in the American economy, the president gave them fair warning; henceforth they must be prepared to compete as equals and also to pay their full share of "the burden of defending freedom around the world." Stripped of its rhetoric, the new economic policy of 1971 was designed to promote American competition in the industrial world rather than American leadership of the free world. The cold war, viewed as foreign economic policy, was over.

In May 1972, Richard Nixon made his dramatic journey to Moscow, the first American president ever to visit the Kremlin in an official capacity. At a working summit meeting, Soviet and American policy makers at the highest level concluded a series of agreements aimed at limiting strategic nuclear arms and improving cultural and commercial relations between the two nations. Later in the year, representatives of the United States and the Soviet Union negotiated a comprehensive trade agreement that stipulates the framework within which private American firms can participate in Soviet trade and Soviet agencies can place orders in the United States for machinery, industrial products, agricultural products, and consumer goods. Further, to facilitate trade relations, the United States promised most-favored-nation status to the Soviet Union, and the president signed a determination making the Soviet Union eligible for credits from the Export-Import Bank of the United States.

The politics of American pluralism as well as constitutional issues had, however, put a crimp in Nixon's new economic policy. On April 10, 1973, the president sent Congress his Message on Trade, a complicated package of interrelated proposals dealing with different facets of his foreign economic policies. The president asserted that the proposed Trade Reform Act of 1973 called for "the most important changes in more than a decade in America's approach to world trade." He reminded the Congress that the United States was already committed to another round of negotiations with its major trading partners to achieve a more equitable trading system. Therefore, asking the Congress for more powers than it had ever granted any president, he requested the authority to eliminate, reduce, or increase customs duties in the context of negotiated agreements over a five-year period. He also requested a congressional resolution favoring negotiations and agreements for the reciprocal reduction of non-tariff barriers in order to enhance the negotiating authority of the executive. "It is important that America speak authoritatively and with a single voice at the international bargaining table."

But there's the rub! In national security policy, there is a single overriding concern, the common defense, that calls for unified command and decisive action. But "America's own interests" in foreign economic policy are pluralistic and particularistic. Texas cattlemen, Nebraska wheat growers, textile manufacturers in South Carolina, auto workers in Detroit, consumers with a yen for Japanese cameras or small cars, grape growers in California, brewers in Milwaukee and St. Louis, investment bankers in New York, oil producers in Texas and Oklahoma, globe-trotting Americans and their hosts abroad, the Hiltons, the Sheratons, and the Holiday Inn people — all these and many others have varying stakes in the foreign economic policy of the United States. There is no "single voice" to bespeak the general will of the American people in economic policy. In the constitutional model — the president-and-Congress — the balance of power tilted toward the executive on war powers and national commitments to insure prompt and resolute responses. In foreign economic policy, following the same logic, the balance of power tends to shift towards the Congress, which is designed to represent diverse constituencies and to reach consensus out of conflict through a process of debating and accommodating.

President Nixon's failure to win congressional support for

his Trade Reform Act of 1973 was, however, largely a matter of timing and peculiar circumstances. Normally, a president just beginning his second term with a landslide vote of public confidence is in a prime position to move the nation. But 1973 was the first full year of Watergate. The Ervin Committee was on television almost daily, uncovering the misbehavior that had originated in the White House during the campaign to reelect the president: breaking and entering, burglary, bugging, bribery, cover up, and perjury. Some of the president's closest advisers were under indictment; some had already been convicted; and the president himself was invoking executive privilege to buck further investigation. It was also a year of head-on confrontation between the president and Congress over constitutional prerogatives with respect to shared economic powers. Congress was asserting its power of the purse to authorize and appropriate for governmental functions according to its collective perception of national priorities. The president was using his executive powers to veto appropriations that exceeded the guide lines laid down in his budget and to impound funds that did not fit into his plans for the economy. All in all, it was not a propitious time for the president to ask Congress for an unprecedented grant of economic powers.

The president's difficulties with Congress in 1973 were confounded by his own determination to make détente and expansion of East-West trade a part of his new world trade policy. Again the timing was unfortunate. In 1973, the Soviet Union was becoming more repressive toward dissidence within its own political system; and American liberals began to question the end of ideology as a policy tool in Soviet-American relations. The hawks in Congress were charging that the SALT agreements, which the president had accepted at the Kremlin along with the trade and cultural agreements, had given the Soviet Union an appalling advantage in nuclear power relationships. And many American Jews, often an influential interest group in national politics, were asking the United States to use its bargaining power in foreign economic policy to exert pressure on the U. S. S. R. to end its restrictive policy toward Jewish emigration. The outbreak of the October Mideast war, the Arab embargo on oil to the United States, Moscow's support of the Arabs, all this fanned anti-Russian sentiment. By the end of the year, the administration was forced to capitulate on the issue of the most-favored-nation status for the Soviet Union.

THE EXECUTIVE POLICY MACHINE

The constitutional model for formulating and implementing foreign policy is the president-and-Congress. But in the three areas that we have singled out for discussion — war powers, national commitments, and foreign economic policies — the original functional design has been considerably altered by the assembly in the executive machinery of new parts designed to keep the president in central control of the policy process.

Article II of the Constitution refers to the executive simply in the third person singular: "The Executive power shall be vested in a President . . . . He . . ." What "he" does in office depends upon the time and circumstances of his entering office; upon his own perception of national interests, presidential authority, and executive privilege. It also depends on how "he" uses the executive machinery, especially those parts assembled in the Executive Office of the President.

The Principal Officers

The Constitution specifies that the president may require the opinion in writing of the principal officer in each of the executive departments upon any subject relating to his official duties. Article II gives the president power to choose his principal officers, subject to confirmation by the Senate. In national security and foreign policy, the appointive power that the president shares with the Senate extends to the entire diplomatic service, from ambassadors plenipotentiary to foreign service officers of the lowest grade. It extends to all the cabinet secretaries (Defense, State, Treasury, Commerce, and so on), and to many, but not all, of the top positions in the bureaucracies (undersecretaries, assistant secretaries).

Article II further provides that Congress may vest the appointment of inferior officers in the president alone, or in the heads of departments. The distinction between principal officers and inferior officers today rests on historical precedents and contemporary politics. Thus the Senate passes upon presidential appointments of plebes to the Naval Academy, second lieutenants in the army, and junior foreign service officers; but it has no say in the selection of the assistant to the president for National Security Affairs. Moreover, recent attempts on the part of Congress to put senatorial confirmations on a modern functional basis have so far met with presidential vetoes.

Officially, the secretary of state has the lead position in the presidential foreign policy machine. Traditionally, he is described as the principal foreign policy adviser to the president. He is the first-ranking member of the president's cabinet, a statutory member of the National Security Council, and also of the Council on International Economic Policy. In all public relations pictures, he sits at the right of the president. The secretary represents the United States at international meetings of foreign ministers, and in the protocol of diplomacy, all visiting dignitaries make their first call at his office. Actually, the role played by the secretary of state in policy making depends on the individual incumbent and on his interpersonal relations with the president and other principal officers in the administration.

The president's principal officers and advisers who make up the executive policy machine number in the hundreds. Just as we look at the personal factors that explain why a president acts as he does in a given situation, so we must also consider what personal idiosyncrasies influence the official decision of cabinet secretaries, presidential assistants, and others at the policy level in national security and foreign affairs.

In the first term of the Nixon administration, the president chose for his secretary of state William P. Rogers, a long-time friend who had served as attorney general in the Eisenhower administration. Rogers appeared content to take a back seat in the foreign policy machine and to leave the driving to the president's assistant for National Security Affairs. Meantime, Rogers not only enjoyed the protocol privileges of the office but also managed to smooth over executive-legislative interactions on Capitol Hill, which had been sorely strained by presidential war powers in the latter days of Dean Rusk at State. In the second term, with the appointment of Henry Kissinger in the dual role of secretary of state and the president's assistant for National Security Affairs, the bureaucracy at the State Department hoped to provide more inputs for the foreign policy machine than they had been able to do under Secretary Rogers. Kissinger's own influence in the policy machine, however, was derived principally from his strategic post in the Executive Office rather than from his prestigious position at State.

Ironically, because of its traditional role in diplomacy, the State Department has come to be regarded more as a spokesman for foreign viewpoints than for national interests. Most of the cabinet secretaries — Defense, Treasury, Commerce, Agriculture, Labor — head departments with special and vested interests in the domestic setting, as well as in international affairs. Because the State Department has no significant political base at home and dwindling operations abroad, the secretary finds it increasingly difficult to pull rank on his fellow cabinet members. In the National Security Council, for example — flanked by the Joint Chiefs and also representing the industrial interests in the defense establishment — the secretary of defense is likely to have more political clout than the secretary of state. News stories in 1974 indicated that Secretary of Defense James Schlesinger was assuming an active role in foreign policy matters, especially in U. S.-USSR relationships; his hard line on defense expenditures did not jibe too well with Kissinger's soft line on détente. Undoubtedly, Kissinger's frequent absences from the capital in pursuit of negotiated peace put him at a disadvantage in interagency politics at the cabinet level. Theodore Sorensen (White House assistant in the Kennedy administration) observes, "Congressional relations in particular require constant Cabinet-level handholding . . . . An absentee Secretary cannot get the trade bill or IDA appropriation he needs; and congressional blockage of most-favored nation treatment and export credits for Moscow may slow down détente far more than another Kissinger visit can speed it up" [Washington Post, March 7, 1974].

The role that the secretary of defense plays in the foreign policy machine depends on the inclinations and capabilities of the incumbent as well as upon interpersonal and interinstitutional relationships. Melvin Laird, whom President Nixon chose to be his first secretary of defense, was a different kind of secretary than Robert McNamara had been in the Kennedy and Johnson administrations. Secretary Laird came to the post after years of service in Congress on the House Armed Services Committee, while McNamara's previous experience had been in private enterprise in the managerial hierarchy of the Ford Motor Company. A skillful politician, Laird knew the importance of personal ties and political contacts in the intermeshing of national security policy, foreign policy, and economic policy. As secretary of defense he was an indefatigable go-between for the president, the president's assistant for national security affairs, the Joint Chiefs of Staff, the foreign policy planners in International Security Affairs, the congressional committees (especially the Armed Services committees), and the Republican party leadership.

During the Nixon administration's first term, mounting concern for the position of the United States in the international economy gave new status to the Treasury and Commerce departments. The secretary of the Treasury is the president's principal adviser in the formulation of foreign economic policy. Whoever holds the office serves on the board of governors of the International Monetary Fund, the World Bank, the Inter-American Development Bank, and the Asian Development Bank. Moreover, these are not merely ex officio assignments. The U. S. secretary of the Treasury is expected to play a leading role in these international financial institutions, not only as a spokesman for American national interests but also as an exponent of worldwide stability in financial and trading relationships. How well the role is played depends on the personality and outlook of the incumbent, the backstopping he gets from the experts in his own bureaucracy, and the nature of his instructions from the president. When President Nixon chose John Connally to replace David Kennedy as secretary of the Treasury in 1971, Connally was asked to assume major responsibility for launching the President's new economic policy at home and abroad. A renegade Democrat from Texas, with limited experience in banking and finance, but with a flair for dramatic political performance, Connally made the whole world take notice of America's new course in foreign trade and international finance for the 1970s.

Responsibility for U. S. foreign economic policy is parceled out among some sixty different units in the executive policy machine. An important feature of President Nixon's managerial revolution was the coordination of all these different parts under the direction of the secretary of the Treasury, who also served as the president's assistant for Economic Affairs. President Nixon's first choice for the dual assignment was George Shultz, who had previously served as secretary of Labor, then as director of the Office of Management and Budget. Like his counterpart, Henry Kissinger, in the national security policy machine, Shultz was initially recruited from the academic community. His designation as "Economic Czar" was somewhat anomalous, for his own economic convictions were deeply rooted in private enterprise and laissez-faire government. Given a different set of convictions, his successors may carry out the assignment quite differently both as to style and substance.

The Department of Commerce is charged with promoting the nation's economy at home and abroad. Most of its international programs have been of a service character to encourage foreign interest in American business or to assist American business in its reach for foreign markets or investment opportunities. In the 1960s, the Commerce Department began to step up its activities in the international arena as it became apparent that American business would have to establish new trade patterns and find new trading partners in the highly competitive global economy. Not until the Nixon administration, however, did the Commerce Department become an important component in the foreign policy machine. The function of the department in promoting American business interests abroad was upgraded by the appointment of a succession of assertive and enterprising secretaries who made a point of stimulating East-West trade. Maurice Stans, an investment banker who had also served the Eisenhower White House, was Nixon's first secretary of Com-

merce. During his time in office, the United States began to remove the trade barriers with communist countries that had long
been part of the cold war strategy. In 1971, the Commerce Department permitted export of nonstrategic goods to the People's
Republic of China under "general license." In 1971, Stans, along
with other top officials of the Commerce Department, toured six
countries in Eastern Europe on a mission to stimulate East-West
trade. Peter Peterson, who succeeded Stans as secretary (when
Stans made the fateful decision to join the Committee to Re-elect
the President), continued to build commercial bridges between
East and West. It was Peterson who signed the much vaunted
trade agreement with the Soviet Union in 1972, the same treaty
that slowed up congressional action on the Trade Reform Act.

In addition to his duties in the Commerce Department, the
secretary, who is ex officio a member of the Domestic Council,
the Council on International Economic Policy, the Council on
Economic Affairs, and other presidential committees on specific
economic problems, counts on the staff work of his own
bureaucracy to enhance the departmental role — and hence his
own prestige — in interagency policy making.

We must also keep in mind that interpersonal relations stir
multiple interactions. To get a true picture of the role and function of the secretary of defense in the foreign policy process, one
needs a wide-angle lens to show his official and personal relations with the president, the president's assistant for National
Security Affairs, the director of the Office of Management and
Budget, the Joint Chiefs of Staff, the secretary of state, the director of the Central Intelligence Agency, the secretary of the Treasury, the chairmen of the House and Senate committees on Armed
Services, Appropriations, Foreign Relations, and Foreign Affairs, let alone with the career officers in his own bailiwick. Given
the frequent turnover and continuous replacement of principal
officers, the task of assessing power relationships in the policy
process is infinitely complicated. Even so, we must recognize
that no policy maker, not even the most isolated of presidents,
can perform his role and functions except in relationship to the
various parts of the policy machine.

How a president chooses his principal officers — whom he

appoints and to what offices, their personal qualifications, their private concerns, their public stances — signals how he expects to shape the style of his administration. But how to direct and control the permanent bureaucracy that backstops government operations while political executives come and go is a problem that appears to stymie every president. Heads of operating agencies, even though they hold presidential appointments, tend to be guided in policy decisions by the expertise immediately available to them in their own agencies. Career officers tend even more to identify their interests and the interests of their own organizations with the national interest. Because the substance of foreign policy is fragmented among many different agencies — State, Defense, Treasury, Agriculture, Commerce, AID, CIA, USIA, etc. — interagency policy making is bound to involve a great deal of jockeying for position and infighting to protect and promote the various missions. Every president from Franklin D. Roosevelt to Richard M. Nixon has tried to solve the problem of bureaucratic rivalries and conflicts with plans for structural reorganization and functional management, none with notable success.

President Nixon in his first term proposed a sweeping reorganization of the entire executive branch on a functional basis. Congress virtually ignored the proposals, but following his landslide victory in November 1972, the president made another determined effort to extend his personal influence and power in policy making across departmental lines. His immediate strategy was to move many of his own men out of the White House into key positions in the operating agencies. Second-term appointments would be made on the twin bases of personal loyalty to the president and managerial skills, rather than according to political qualifications. A more complicated scheme was the construction of a "super cabinet" in which a small number of presidential counselors would hold dual appointments as heads of departments. Although the debacle of Watergate put a crimp overall in the "managerial revolution," partial achievement was obtained in national security affairs and foreign economic policy. Henry Kissinger, serving as secretary of State and the president's assistant for National Security Affairs, dominated national security and foreign affairs in all their ramifications. Similarly, George Shultz as secretary of the Treasury and the president's assistant for Economic Affairs exercised wide authority, not only over his own department but over the whole range of agencies involved in economic policy.

The Executive Office of the President

In his now classic study of *Presidential Power*, Richard Neustadt points out that the most compelling problem of the man on top of any political system is how to be on top in fact as well as name. "The search for personal influence is at the center of the job of being President" [1960, p. vii]. The Executive Office of the President is the institutional answer. It gives him the managerial tools and communication lines that he needs to control and coordinate all the various parts of the executive policy machine. It is also designed to curb his personal and partisan predilections by furnishing him with the kind of counsel and expertise that is required for making rational decisions at the highest level of policy determination.

Established in 1939, in the second term of Franklin D. Roosevelt, the Executive Office of the President has been constructed and reconstructed to suit the personal style and political concerns of each incumbent. At the outset, the Executive Office comprised only two units: the Bureau of the Budget, moved from the Treasury Department, and the White House Office, a small corps of personal assistants designed to help the president keep track of the burgeoning New Deal agencies. The inputs of the Truman Administration included the Council of Economic Advisers to implement the Employment Act of 1946 and the Office of Emergency Preparedness and the National Security Council to implement the National Security Act of 1947. President Eisenhower created the National Aeronautics and Space Council in response to Soviet achievements in space weapons and explorations. President Kennedy added the Office of Science and Technology in 1962 and the Office of Special Representative for Trade Negotiations in 1963 to point up the new frontiers of his administration. President Johnson established the Office of Economic Opportunity as the command post for his war against poverty.

President Nixon added and abolished more units in the Executive Office than any one of his predecessors. He established the Domestic Council in 1970 to counterbalance the National Security Council and to emphasize his concern for both domestic and foreign policy. He added the Council on International Economic Policy in 1972 to show his special interest in international economic problems, and the Council on Economic Policy in 1973 to demonstrate his equal interest in domestic and international economic problems. In 1973, as part of his projected managerial revolution, he abolished the Office of Emergency Preparedness, the National Aeronautics and Space Council, and the Office of Science and Technology. Also in 1973 he created the Energy Policy Office, soon replaced by the Federal Energy Office, to cope with what was fast becoming the most serious foreign and domestic economic problem of his administration.

The White House Office

The White House Office, as Franklin D. Roosevelt envisaged it, comprised a small number of personal assistants "with a passion for anonymity" to help the president oversee the bureaucracies. Roosevelt preferred to handle problems of foreign policy on his own since they were too important to be left to White House assistants.

Harry Truman, overwhelmed by his sudden accession to high office, found the presidency too tremendous for one man to manage. His answer was to have people around him whose opinions he respected, to whom he could talk freely, and on whom he could count not to arrogate presidential authority. Truman expanded the White House Office, organized it more tightly, and met with top members of the staff to give out daily instructions. He depended on the staff to brief him on policy matters and to provide him with a range of arguments that might affect his decisions. But Truman's White House Office was just that; staff members never presumed to act as policy makers. Harry Truman made his own decisions. His most innovative contribution to the presidency was the creation of the National Security Council, which he used both vigorously and shrewdly as an instrument for extending his personal influence over the entire national security establishment. In the formulation of foreign policy, however, he relied principally on the judgment of his secretary of state, Dean Acheson, who also acted as his chief of staff for the conduct of foreign affairs.

General Eisenhower, accustomed to an efficient military staff, reorganized the White House Office on a functional basis under a chief of staff. Like his predecessor, however, Eisenhower did not expect his White House staff to assume authority on matters involving substantive policy. For matters of foreign policy, he depended largely, but not entirely, on the advice of his secretary of state, John Foster Dulles. Eisenhower participated regularly in the meetings of the National Security Council, which he regarded as the primary instrument of foreign policy in his administration. The position of assistant for National Security Affairs, created in the Eisenhower administration, was essentially a staff position. Robert Cutler, the first appointee to the office, acted as chief communicator, but never as a policy maker, in the highly sophisticated national security policy machine.

President Kennedy wanted a smaller staff than his predecessor (but the size actually increased). Unlike Eisenhower, Kennedy recognized no chief of staff and authorized no staff meetings. Theoretically, all of Kennedy's special assistants enjoyed equal status and had direct access to his office to discuss their respective assignments. In foreign policy, however, despite his lack of experience, Kennedy was inclined to act as his own secretary of state; Dean Rusk was definitely "Number Two" [Halberstam 1972, p. 32]. McGeorge Bundy, Kennedy's assistant for National Security Affairs, had less machinery to coordinate but certainly more input into the policy process than his predecessors in the office. No one, however, thought of describing McGeorge Bundy as John F. Kennedy's alter ego in national security affairs.

Lyndon Johnson was personally more concerned about building a Great Society in the United States than in developing new nations or combatting communism through counterinsurgencies in the Third World. Thus, at the outset of his administration, Johnson was apt to leave the problems of foreign policy to the principal officers who were holdovers from the Kennedy administration. Secretary of State Dean Rusk, Secretary of Defense Robert McNamara, and Special Assistant McGeorge Bundy, individually and as a troika, became much more powerful in the Johnson administration than they had been under Kennedy. But, following his own resounding victory at the polls in 1964, Johnson decided to assume personal control over the foreign policy machine. He instituted the Tuesday Lunch, a weekly meeting with his secretaries of state and defense and his assistant for National Security Affairs. The Tuesday Lunch, however, which was in the nature of a personal consultation between the president and his principal officers, did little to strengthen liaison between the White House staff and career officers in the operating agency, despite the projection of an elaborate interdepartmental apparatus.

In the first term of the Nixon administration, the White House Office emerged as the single most powerful unit in the national government. In the second term, a restructured White House Office was to have acted as a highly centralized control mechanism, cutting across departmental lines and assuring unified policy direction in all areas. But in the wake of Watergate, the White House Office as an instrument of presidential influence over the operating agencies was virtually cut off from the rest of the political system, except in those areas where the president's assistants were accorded cabinet rank, as in the case of Henry Kissinger for national security affairs and George Shultz for economic affairs.

The Office of Management and Budget

The single most important managerial unit of the president's policy machine is the Office of Management and Budget (OMB). Reconstituted in 1970 by executive order, the OMB was given extensive powers not only to help the president prepare *The Budget of the United States Government* but also to assist him in coordinating all departmental proposals, plans, and programs within his responsibility as chief executive. No agency in the national government may plead its special concerns to Congress directly; all requests for legislative authorizations or appropriations must be cleared by the OMB and must carry with them a stamp of presidential approval.

Budgetary allocations for international affairs have been comparatively small in all presidential budgets. This may be attributed in part to the nature of foreign policy, which, in the main, does not require huge outlays for operations. The conduct of diplomatic and consular business is mostly a matter of covering salaries and representation allowances. Hence, the State Department's activities can be carried on with a relatively small budget. A presidential decision to make new approaches to China and the Soviet Union or to acquiesce in the normalization of relations between the Federal Republic of Germany and its eastern neighbors may represent significant shifts in U. S. foreign policy, but such shifts do not entail any great change in budget estimates.

Nevertheless, how much *The Budget of the United States Government* allocates to various programs in international affairs has a great deal to do with the content of U. S. foreign policy. The president's sense of national values and policy priorities, as they are expressed in the budget, are crucial to such foreign operations as educational and cultural exchanges, overseas information services, economic and technical assistance to developing countries, participation in international financial institutions, humanitarian assistance to international refugees or victims of natural disaster, military assistance, covert intelligence operations, and government insurance for private investments in the Third World.

It is in the linkage of national security policy to foreign policy that the budget assumes paramount importance. Every president from Roosevelt to Ford has accorded the highest priority to defense expenditures, which are justified in terms of foreign policy decisions. Estimates for defense expenditures mount when national security is equated with international security. Among the tremendously expensive policy decisions are those concerning the maintenance of American forces in Europe and Asia, the provision of a nuclear shield to our allies in NATO, the provision of military and economic assistance to more than two score allies, the containment of communism and deterrence of Soviet aggression with nuclear weapons that ring China and the USSR.

Policy decisions in the area of national security call for political and economic, as well as military, assessments. Who are our friends and who are our foes, now, and in the decades to come? Power relations are bound to change in the 1970s, as they did in the 1960s, and in the 1950s. What are our adversaries now doing, or planning to do? What are the capabilities of our allies, and how much can we expect them to contribute to the costs of mutual security? What forces are needed, not only to repel the invader from our shores, but also to meet our commitments elsewhere in the world? What exactly are these national commitments that may involve the use of American armed forces overseas? What is a realistic strategy for nuclear deterrence? What weapons should we now deploy? What new weapons should we now fund for research and development? What progress is likely to be made in negotiating arms limitations? When the president prepares the budget for Congress, these are the prime questions his administration must be prepared to answer as justifications for estimated expenditures. In the performance of this responsibility the president counts principally on the OMB, through which all executive agencies for national security and foreign affairs must clear their plans, programs, and budgets.

The National Security Council

As he prepares his various communications to the Congress — the Budget, the State of the Union, the Report on the National Economy, and the Foreign Policy Message — the president's recommendations begin in his own mind, with his own perceptions of the national interest, his own political and economic predilections. But every president is also influenced by the continuous advice that he gets from persons — official and nonofficial — who have direct access to his office. National security, linked as it is to foreign policy, is much too technical and complex to be left to personal judgment. The president needs help. He needs systematic intelligence, as well as political, economic, and military advice of the highest order to support his own opinions. And he needs a coordinating mechanism to reach into the operating agencies and to secure the best expertise available in formulating policy, the highest skill in implementing programs. Every president from Harry Truman to Gerald Ford, each in his own way, has trusted the National Security Council (NSC) to further this function.

The National Security Council meets at the behest of the president, who may at his pleasure and discretion invite other than the statutory members to attend and participate in discussion. A popular pastime among Washington bureaucrats is to scan successive pictures of the National Security Council in session and to calculate the current status of their own chief in relation to other chiefs. Who is sitting at the table, next to whom? Who is no longer in the picture? The NSC and its components have gone through many vicissitudes under differing presidential styles.

President Eisenhower used the NSC most systematically. An elaborate interdepartmental mechanism was devised to assist the council both in planning and in carrying out policy recommendations. Most of this mechanism was scrapped by the Kennedy administration, which preferred a more flexible pool of policy advisers with ad hoc task forces concentrating on crisis situations.

In his first Foreign Policy Report [1970], President Nixon promised "a basic restructuring of the process by which policy is made . . . new methods of planning and a more rigorous and systematic process of policy making." At the outset he directed that the NSC be reestablished as "the principal forum for presidential consideration of foreign policy issues." So that the "revitalized" NSC could better carry out its function, a new interdepartmental substructure was created, paying lip-service to the primacy of State. A Senior Review Group, chaired by the president's assistant for National Security Affairs, was to review policy studies prepared by the interdepartmental groups and to see to it that such studies "present the facts, the issues, the arguments, and the range of choice, before the studies are turned over to the President and the National Security Council." A high-level Washington Special Action Group was created to deal specifically with crisis situations.

As in previous reorganizations, however, restructuring the policy process did not work out exactly as projected. The NSC, which began by meeting frequently and regularly, was called together less and less often by President Nixon. As the NSC staff under Kissinger doubled in size, it took over more and more of the staff work originally assigned to the staff of the interdepartmental groups. The military incursion into Cambodia, the president's journeys to Peking and Moscow, the top secret negotiations with North Vietnam in Paris, the massive bombing of North Vietnam when the negotiations failed, the halt of the bombings to secure more secret negotiations, the alert of U. S. nuclear forces during the October 1973 Mideast War — apparently none of these momentous decisions moved through that "restructured process" that President Nixon had claimed was basic to his national security system.

Oriented toward old-world diplomacy and balance-of-power politics, Henry Kissinger has had his own concept of foreign policy and how it should be conducted. His forte has been personal diplomacy; that he has used it effectively is attested to by his efforts to achieve "peace with honor" in Vietnam, his skillful negotiations toward détente with Peking and Moscow, and more recently his success in bringing about a cease-fire and peace talks in the Mideast. Kissinger has been, however, a stellar performer. While serving under President Nixon, he became dissatisfied with the kind of intelligence furnished him by the CIA and with the slow motion of the state department. He preferred to use his own staff at the White House not only for formulating but also for implementing his master plan for keeping the United States "Number One" among the great powers of the world. But his distrust of bureaucrats in general resulted in closed decision making to such an extent that the defense department was alleged to have resorted to rather primitive spying within the NSC staff to gain in advance clues to Kissinger's solo diplomatic moves.

Kissinger's approach to national security and foreign policy stems largely from his perception of political and military power relationships. In this context his handling of the Mideast crisis was a brilliant tour de force. At the same time, however, his failure to grasp the implications of "oil as a weapon" in international economic warfare proved to be nothing short of a national disaster. Partly because Kissinger's NSC system was not able to cope with foreign economic problems, President Nixon found it necessary to create the Council of International Economic Policy in 1970 and the Federal Energy Office in 1973.

The Economic Councils and the Federal Energy Office

By 1970, the position of the United States in the international economy was rapidly deteriorating. The remarkable resurgence of Western Europe and Japan had radically altered the balance of economic power in the world, and the United States was forced to readjust its policies and programs in an international environment in which its former protegés had become formidable rivals. In 1971, for the first time in this century, the American trade balance had turned into a deficit. The situation was aggravated by long-term balance-of-payments problems, expensive foreign-aid programs, zooming defense expenditures, the long and costly war in Indochina, American tourism on an unprecedented scale, and increasing overseas investment of private U. S. capital.

The state of the economy — national and international — has always been a major concern of U. S. policy makers. It was not happenstance that the first addition to the Executive Office of the President after World War II was the Council of Economic Advisers (CEA). Congress recognized that the policy machine required economic expertise as the nation moved from a wartime to a peacetime economy. As defined by statute, the principal function of the CEA is to help the president prepare an annual report to the Congress on the state of the economy, together with recommendations for promoting employment, production, and purchasing power. In practice, the CEA, which rarely meets (except for public relations photographs), is essentially a staff operation to provide the president with position papers on specific economic problems.

Because the CEA is more concerned with domestic economic problems, President Nixon in 1972 created the Council on International Economic Policy (CIEP). Under President Nixon, the CIEP, like most of the councils that Nixon set up, had little or no conciliar function. Rather, it was a staff device that worked through interagency groups to give the president personal influence and central control over international economic policies.

The way in which the CIEP tackled President Nixon's Trade Reform Act of 1973 illustrates the intermeshing of domestic and foreign policy, political and economic interests, and national security concerns in the Executive Office of the President. Peter Flanigan, as executive director of the CIEP (and the assistant to the president for International Economic Affairs) brought together two interagency groups, one to work on pending trade negotiations, the other on proposed trade legislation, in accord with White House guidelines on overall policy. The working staff included representation from the operating agencies: State, Treasury, Labor, Commerce, and Agriculture; and from the Executive Office; OMB, NSC, CEA, and the Office of the President's Special Representative for Trade Negotiations. The proposed Trade Reform Act of 1973 that emerged from the CIEP apparatus was a masterpiece of interagency accommodation to White House leadership. But, as we suggested earlier, unified direction is not always the most successful ploy in fashioning policy for a pluralistic economy, certainly not with respect to trade legislation that affects a whole spectrum of special interests in the domestic setting. At any rate, Congress, responding to diverse constituencies, continued to debate the Trade Reform Act of 1973 in 1974.

In 1973, the national economy was suddenly confronted by

an energy crisis that threatened massive repercussions in domestic and foreign policy. As early as April 1973, President Nixon had informed the Congress that the administration was anticipating energy shortages and increases in energy prices. He urged the Congress to take action on the reorganization proposals he had made two years earlier to establish a single Department of Energy and Natural Resources that could bring together some 64 different units in the national government involved with some aspect of energy policy. At that time, the president was thinking more about how to increase energy supplies than how to regulate energy use. To this end he terminated the 14-year-old restrictions on oil imports that were designed originally to protect domestic oil producers.

In June 1973, the president again warned the Congress that unless it acted swiftly and effectively, the nation would face a genuine energy crisis. Since Congress had not moved on his proposals to centralize the adminstration of energy policies, the president, on his own authority, established an Energy Policy Office (EPO) in the Executive Office to be responsible for "the formulation and coordination of energy policies at the presidential level." Governor John Love (R., Colo.) was recruited as an assistant to the president for Energy Matters and to head the newly created EPO. Love became just one of many persons to be "energy czar" in a fast-moving game of musical chairs that continued in the Ford Administration. His job was to develop comprehensive plans for energy development and to coordinate the widely fragmented programs in energy policy. Again the president asked Congress to establish a cabinet-level Department of Energy and Natural Resources and also an Energy Research and Development Administration to explore and develop new sources of energy including nuclear power.

By the fall of 1973, the energy crisis was no longer a possibility in the offing; it had arrived with a vengeance. The Arab embargo on oil shipments to the United States in retaliation for U. S. leanings toward Israel in the Mideast War had gravely aggravated the situation. Certainly U. S. foreign policy in the Mideast was not the only factor in the critical escalation of energy shortages in the United States; less than 10 percent of

U. S. oil supplies come from the Arab countries. Nevertheless, it was one of the more obvious causes; hence the frantic efforts of the president's assistant for National Security Affairs to act as mediator between the Arabs and the Israelis. Obviously, a cut-off of oil supplies not only jeopardized the national security of the United States, but also threatened economic recession in the industrial world, especially in Japan and Western Europe, both of which count much more than the United States upon oil from the Mideast.

President Ford's signature on the so-called "Energy Bill" (October 11, 1974) paved the way for creation of a temporary Energy Resources Council in the White House to coordinate federal energy agencies. In addition, the bill led to the establishment of an Energy Research and Development Administration. Although providing more organizational structure to energy policy making, it remains to be seen whether this approach will end the game of musical chairs for "energy czars."

Like most economic policies, energy policy has many different advocates, many different critics. Who's to blame for the energy crunch? Arab countries that have turned oil into a strategic weapon? Oil producing countries that seek to increase their gross national product by raising the price of oil on the world market? The multinational oil companies that have made enormous profits out of America's great demand? The automobile manufacturers of America that mass produce the biggest gas-guzzling cars in the world? Architects who design and builders who construct high-rise, air-conditioned buildings? American housewives whose way of life calls for electric washers, dryers, dishwashers, vacuums, and the family station wagon? What's to blame for rising unemployment in businesses directly affected by the energy shortage; for truck strikes; closed gas pumps — too many fingers in the policy pie? Sixty-four different agencies in Washington dealing in some aspect of energy policy? Too much bureaucratic in-fighting? Too much partisan politics? Executive-legislative rivalries? Conflicts of committee jurisdiction in the Congress? Whatever the answers, it is clear that energy is in critically short supply and that allocation and regulation have been neither adequate nor well conceived.

CONCLUSION

Several years ago, in lengthy testimony before the Senate Foreign Relations Committee, William P. Rogers expounded upon the institutional advantages of the presidency: the unity of office, its capacity for secrecy and dispatch, and its superior sources of information. From his vantage point as secretary of State, Rogers thought these advantages were particularly germane to foreign affairs:

> The heightened pace, complexity, and hazards of contemporary events often require rapid and clear decisions. The nation must be able to act flexibly and, in certain cases, without prior publicity. Unlike the Presidency, the institutional characteristics of Congress have not lent themselves as well to the requirements of speed and secrecy in times of recurrent crises and rapid change. The composition of Congress with its numerous members and their diverse constituencies, the resultant complexity of the decision making process, and Congress' constitutional tasks of debate, discussion, and authorization inevitably make it a more deliberative, public, and diffuse body [United States Foreign Policy, 1971, p. 503].

Secretary Rogers' arguments are persuasive if one accepts as a maxim that prompt decisive action is the prime necessity in national security and foreign policy. At this point, one is bound to add, especially in the nuclear age. One shudders, of course, at the notion of Congress debating a declaration of war while the intercontinental missiles are already hurtling toward us. But from my vantage point as a professor in international relations, I cannot recall a single instance in the history of American foreign policy where the national interests were better served by speed and secrecy than by debate and deliberation.

The hierarchical pattern of decision making in the bureaucracies, the coordinating and central control mechanisms in the Executive Office, the president at the apex of power in the executive policy machine — these are institutional advantages that allow the president to speak authoritatively and to act swiftly.

But the fact that he is the sole spokesman and ultimate policy maker in his administration does not mean that he always expresses the general will (that is, the will for the general good). Even in matters of national security, where there is common concern, there is still much room for debate and dispute before consensus can be reached on what is to be secured, how, and at what cost.

The collegial pattern of decision making in Congress, "535 divergent characters" as Mike Mansfield, the Senate majority leader, has described it, each one speaking his own piece and casting his own vote on behalf of his own constituents, the bicameral organization, the partisan committee system, the fragmented process of authorizing and appropriating — these are institutional disadvantages that tend to give the public a poor image of their representatives in Congress. But, on economic and political issues where different sections of the country and different sectors of the population hold very different opinions, there are advantages to the slow movement of the legislative process toward enactment of public policy. After the lengthy hearings, the debating and filibustering, the bargaining and compromising, what emerges is likely to be accepted as legitimate for the very reason that it has survived the whole legislative process. Public opinion polls tell us that the public holds both the president and Congress in low esteem. But, perhaps because I am a renegade professor of Constitutional Law, I still have enormous respect for the original model, the president-and-Congress, replete with eighteenth-century checks and balances, as well as modern functional accessories.

NOTES

1. There are many different lists on the use of American armed forces abroad. The number of instances reported vary from list to list. See *War Powers Legislation. Hearings Before the Committee on Foreign Relations, U. S. Senate, 92nd Congress, 1st Sess.* (Washington, D. C.: Government Printing Office, 1972), pp. 298–316, 375–406.

2. For a brief account of the Vietnam issue in the 1964 presidential campaign see *Congress and the Nation 1945–64* (Congressional Quarterly, 1965), pp. 52–59. For a more diffuse and interpretative discussion, see Theodore White, *The Making of the President——1964* (New York: Atheneum Publishers, 1965).

BIBLIOGRAPHY

Acheson, Dean. *Present at the Creation*. New York: W. W. Norton & Company, 1969.

Congress and the Nation 1945–1964. Washington, D. C.: Congressional Quarterly, 1965.

Eisenhower, Dwight D. *Mandate for Change*. New York: Doubleday & Company, 1963.

The Federalist. Edited by Edward Mead Earl. New York: Modern Library, 1937.

Goldwater, Barry. Letter to the editor in reply to Pusey. *The Washington Post*, 6 December 1973.

Halberstam, David. *The Best and the Brightest*. New York: Random House, 1972.

Kolko, Joyce and Gabriel. *The Limits of Power: The World and United States Foreign Policy, 1945 – 54*. New York: Harper & Row, 1972.

Neustadt, Richard. *Presidential Power*. New York: John Wiley & Sons, 1960.

Roosevelt, Franklin D. *The Public Papers and Addresses of Franklin D. Roosevelt*. Edited by Samuel Rosenman. New York: The Macmillan Company, 1941.

Pusey, Merlo. "A Warning to the President." *The Washington Post*, 19 November 1973.

Schlesinger, Arthur M. Jr., *The Imperial Presidency*. Boston: Houghton Mifflin Company, 1973.

Sorenson, Theodore. Quoted in *The Washington Post*, 7 March 1974.

Tariff and Trade Proposals. Hearings Before the Committee on Ways and Means of the House of Representatives, 91st Congress, 2nd Sess. Washington, D. C. : Government Printing Office, 1970, part 1, p. 65.

United States Foreign Policy, 1971. A Report of the Secretary of State. Washington, D. C.: Government Printing Office, 1972.

United States Security Agreements and Commitments Abroad. Hearings before the Subcommittee on U. S. Security Agreements and Commitments Abroad of the Committee on Foreign Relations. 2 vols. Washington, D. C.: Government Printing Office, 1971.

War Powers Legislation. Hearings before the Committee on Foreign Relations, U. S. Senate, 92nd Congress, 1st Sess. Washington, D. C.: Government Printing Office, 1972.

White, Theodore. *The Making of the President — 1964.* New York: Atheneum Publishers, 1965.

6

Presidential Power and Foreign Affairs

NORMAN A. GRAEBNER
University of Virginia

HISTORICALLY EVERY SUSTAINED criticism of United States foreign policy has centered ultimately on the question of presidential power. President Richard M. Nixon's decisions to order American forces into Cambodia and to intensify the bombing of North Vietnam and Cambodia, without any consultation with Congress, merely carried this traditional controversy to new levels of intensity and bitterness. Writers charged that Nixon, through his unprecedented concentration of war-making authority in the White House, circumvented the Constitution and enlarged on practices always regarded as questionable. Speaking at Oxford University shortly after his defeat in the 1972 presidential race, Senator George McGovern declared characteristically, "I am convinced that the United States is closer to one-man rule than at any time in our history — and this paradoxically by a President who is not popular" [*Washington Post* January 28, 1973]. Similarly, historian Arthur M. Schlesinger, Jr. wrote that on matters of war and peace the president of the United States had become, with the possible exception of Mao Tse-tung, the most absolute ruler among the major leaders of the world [January 7, 1973, p. 12]. Apparently the whole system of federal checks and balances had disintegrated under the impact of a strong and active presidency. Still the nature of those checks, as well as the cause and extent of their failure, remained elusive.

Through practice, if not through constitutional fiat, the executive branch of the United States government had gained almost unchallenged primacy in foreign policy formulation long before the twentieth century. Under the principle of separation of powers, the Founding Fathers in 1787 had sought to compel any future president to share with Congress his control over external affairs. The Constitution, it is true, granted the executive primacy in treaty-making and war-making decisions, as well as in matters of recognition and appointments. Article II assigned to the president the role of "Commander-in-Chief of the Army and Navy of the United States." But Article I granted to Congress the power to declare war. The House of Representatives gained control over the purse, while the Senate held the right to approve or reject treaties and presidential appointments. The Constitution, moreover, ordered the president to secure the Senate's "advice and consent" on questions of foreign policy. Despite such constitutional limitations on presidential authority, however, the executive, as official spokesman of the nation, as commander in chief of the armed forces, and as head of the nation's entire bureaucratic structure, commanded from the beginning both the authority and the special knowledge required to dominate the decision-making process in the entire field of foreign affairs.

In practice two circumstances could contribute to the president's war-making power: one where the threat was too trivial to require congressional approval; the other where the threat was too immediate to allow time for congressional consent. Nineteenth-century presidents, on many occasions, used the armed forces against pirates, Indians, border ruffians, and rioters without asking the approval of Congress. When the British attacked Washington in 1814, President James Madison had no time to call Congress into session to determine a proper American response. In the twentieth century, too, in such extreme conditions, the president's war-making power is beyond challenge. But between these extremes two bodies of constitutional power came into conflict — the president's authority as commander in chief as opposed to Congress's right to determine the course of a conflict by exercising its power to declare war and to set the level of expenditure. Normally the refusal of Congress to declare war would be sufficient either to terminate an engagement or to prevent it altogether.

As the United States' undeclared war in Vietnam faced ever-increasing opposition in Congress, administration spokesmen insisted that the president's command of the armed forces eliminated the need for congressional approval of the war. "There can be no question in present circumstances," declared Leonard C. Meeker, legal adviser to the State Department, in March 1966, "of the President's authority to commit U.S. forces to the defense of South Vietnam. The grant of authority to the President in Article II of the Constitution extends to the actions of the United States currently undertaken in Vietnam" [*Department of State Bulletin* LIV: 484]. Arguing for presidential primacy in matters of war, Under Secretary of State Nicholas Katzenbach informed the Senate Foreign Relations Committee in August 1967 that "the expression of declaring war is one that has become outmoded in the international arena." Under modern conditions, he said, it was for the president alone to determine when and how the armed forces of the United States should be used. President Lyndon Johnson made even greater claims for executive authority when he informed a news conference in August 1967 that the administration did not require congressional authorization to commit armed forces, but had asked for the Gulf of Tonkin Resolution in 1964 because, he added, "if we were going to ask them to stay the whole route . . . we ought to ask them to be there at the take-off" [*New York Times*, August 19, 1967].

Such claims to executive primacy over matters of war and peace continued in Nixon's presidency. When the Senate in 1969, by a vote of 70 to 16, passed the National Commitments Resolution, which was designed to limit national commitments to actions taken by both the executive and legislative branches, the adminstration replied, "As Commander-in-Chief the President has the sole authority to command our armed forces, whether they are in or outside the United States. And, although reasonable men may differ as to the circumstances in which he should do so, the President has the constitutional power to send U.S. military forces abroad without specific Congressional approval" [quoted in Robinson 1973, p. 11]. In denying that he required any congressional authorization for his invasion of Cambodia in 1970, President Nixon declared that he was meeting ". . . his responsibility as Commander-in-Chief of our armed forces to take the action I consider necessary to defend the security of our American men" [Reston, March 19, 1973].

Throughout the Vietnam war, executive branch lawyers stressed the vagueness of the Constitution on questions of foreign policy and war powers; they insisted that the question of authority to act or to restrain be left to the requirements of the moment, according, as Katzenbach expressed it, to "the instinct of the nation and its leaders for political responsibility . . . ." In practice, those who viewed the Constitution as imprecise argued that the president must be left unencumbered to use the armed forces and to commit the United States as he saw fit, seeking congressional approval only when it appeared useful or convenient. Still, the Constitution was rather specific on the matter of executive control of the war-making power. By declaring that Congress must declare war, the Constitution gave Congress the power to authorize its initiation and continuance. The president, as commander in chief, was to repel attack and conduct any war that Congress approved. Alexander Hamilton in *Federalist* Number 69 insisted that the right of raising and regulating the armed forces, as well as declaring war, belonged to the legislative branch. Professor Richard B. Morris of Columbia University has argued that the war-making power of the president, according to the debates on ratification and the *Federalist*, was little more than the power to defend against imminent invasion when Congress was not in session.

THE MYTH OF CONSTITUTIONAL LIMITATIONS

Whatever the validity of any constitutional argument, presidential control of the country's external relations never rested on the Constitution or on the special complexity of international affairs. Abraham Lincoln saw this clearly when, near the end of the Mexican War, he wrote to his friend William H. Herndon,

> Allow the President to invade a neighboring nation, whenever he shall deem it necessary to repel an invasion, and you allow him to do so, *whenever he may choose to say* he deems it necessary for such purpose — and you allow him to make war at pleasure. Study to see if you can fix *any limit* to his power in this respect . . . . If, to-day, he should choose to say he thinks it necessary to invade Canada, to prevent the British from invading us, how could you stop him? You may say to him, "I see no probability of the British invading us" but he will say to you "be silent; I see it, if you don't" [1953, I:451].

The decisions of two presidents on Vietnam seemed to substantiate Lincoln's fears that any presidential commitment of forces to repel an attack regarded by the president as dangerous to the United States would destroy all limits to presidential power. Johnson and Nixon, without formal congressional approval, ordered air and ground action of increasing magnitude and destructiveness. To those who saw no danger to the security of the United States in North Vietnamese behavior, the presidents and their advisers, indeed, replied that the danger was clear to them. In confronting Congress, the executive claimed superior knowledge, much of it kept secret. This gave both presidents a sharp advantage over their critics, enabling them to ignore countering arguments and to exploit the willingness of most Americans to accept executive judgment as valid. Neither

Johnson nor Nixon had the power to silence Congress: yet their power to send troops into combat seemed to have no visible limits.

The reason is clear. The essence of their power lay less in the Constitution or in their role as commander in chief than in their successful management of public and congressional opinion. With public support the executive can make almost any demand on Congress, because the arguments that capture the public will capture much of Congress as well. Thus in supporting presidential policy congressmen, in large measure, vote their convictions rather than their fears of public retribution. But whatever the motives of Congressmen, it is in essence their willingness to support executive decisions, and this alone, that as Lincoln said, grants virtually unlimited presidential power. With access to television at prime time, with the power to control press conferences, and with batteries of speech writers, a president can make words accomplish almost impossible feats. The executive with its enormous resources has the power, in the absence of any historical consensus that might tell the President how to act, to dominate the public and congressional mind [War Powers Legislation, 1972, p. 580]. In their book, Presidential Television, Newton H. Minow, John Bartlow Martin, and Lee M. Mitchell [1973] insist that presidential television threatens to tilt the constitutional balance of power in favor of the executive. Indeed, the ultimate limits on presidential power are the president's own self-restraint and the extent of his capacity to control the public.

After 1969 it was Nixon's control of public opinion, not his control of the armed forces, that permitted him to defy his critics in Congress and his spokesmen to trample on congressional committees at will. This relationship of the president to Congress explains why the great debates on executive power are never simple executive-congressional confrontations. A congressional majority underwrote the war in Vietnam from 1961 to 1973 through its power of the purse. The war always belonged to Congress as much as to the president. They fought it together. Not even Nixon's bombing of North Vietnam from early 1971 until the end of 1972 and his subsequent bombing of Cambodian targets belonged to him alone. These policies were sustained by congressional majorities and by those Americans outside Congress who supported the bombing, or at least had no interest in voicing their disapproval. The central question, therefore, was not the executive's limitless power over foreign affairs but why Congress refused to exert its authority to limit executive action, for Congress's power of the purse is far greater than the president's power as commander in chief of the armed forces. When the majority of Congress after June 1973 opposed presidential policy in Southeast Asia, that policy ceased to exist. Yet nowhere did congressional action infringe on the president's power as commander in chief.

Many writers have argued that Congress cannot command or compel the president to change an established course. It would be far more accurate to say that a divided Congress, or one whose majority is under presidential control, cannot compel the president to change his course. A united Congress can command any policy through its control of the purse and its power to pass legislation over a presidential veto. What gave presidents Johnson and Nixon control over Vietnam policy was not their destruction of congressional power but their control of the congressional mind. Perhaps Congress cannot control and should not control the State Department, but it has great powers of resistance. It can approve appointments, and it commands the budgets of both the State Department and the armed forces. It cannot match the executive branch in staff work, but it can question decisions based on faulty staff work or on no staff work at all, especially when such decisions fail to result in constructive policies.

Senator J. William Fulbright saw more clearly than most why the White House enjoyed almost unchallenged control of United States foreign policy. What sustained the control, he said, was the lingering mood of national insecurity and the concomitant demand for victory, all underwritten after Korea by the perennial refrain that any additional Communist gain would lead to war and global disaster. That insecurity, sustained by war, posed for Fulbright a threat to the American system. "Neither constitutional government nor democratic freedom," he declared in April 1971, "can survive indefinitely in a country chronically at war, as America has been for the last three decades" [New York Times, April 4, 1971]. Two years later the senator repeated this theme. Fulbright said, "One of the main reasons for the inability of Congress to resume its proper role, is the existence of the war. When you have a Congress and a country dominated by this war fever, the feeling that our men are on the front lines — It's an atmosphere almost impossible to overcome . . . . We've been in a forty-year crisis. This is the fundamental reason for the deterioration of Congress. There's nothing you can do until you can get over the feeling that there is impending disaster . . . . " [quoted in Yergin 1973, p. 13]. To silence the majority under such circumstances an administration had merely to warn Congress that any interference with its containment policies — from bombing in Southeast Asia to requesting a defense appropriation — would produce disaster.

As long as the country maintained a large standing army, extensive air power, a vast network of alliances, and a multitude of other commitments, and as long as its leaders sustained an atmosphere that convinced most Americans that such instruments were necessary, Congress had no chance to oppose successfully any decisions or requests defended in the name of national security. It was not strange, therefore, that no prominent Republican conservative opposed Nixon's claims to executive primacy in foreign affairs, although the conservative Republican tradition had favored congressional control. The conservatives simply endorsed the president's policies. To challenge the President's authority to bomb in Southeast Asia, Senator Barry Goldwater, Sr. wrote to The New York Times in March 1973, would destroy the president's peace efforts. "Acting as Commander-in-Chief . . . ," the senator added, "the President possesses full constitutional authority to judge that the terms of the armistice which he negotiated have not been met by the enemy and that our actual state of war continues there that carries with it his power and duty to enforce that settlement." For Goldwater the president possessed authority independent of Congress in the areas of foreign affairs and national defense [Reston, March 29, 1973; Wicker, January 14, 1973]. Still if the Supreme Court had decided in Orlando v. Laird that Congress had indeed collaborated in the war, Congress, it seemed, had the right to disengage itself from the war by withdrawing its sanctions and appropriations.

It was the president's command of majority opinion and the resulting divisions in Congress that encouraged him, in defense of his policies, to demonstrate an unprecedented arrogance toward an increasingly rebellious minority during the winter of 1972–1973. James Reston charged in his column of December 28, 1972, that the president was "using power without pity, and without consultation and without any personal explanation." His policy had become, wrote Reston, "war by tantrum." Two weeks later conservative columnist James J. Kilpatrick complained that "The President has failed (and we have to assume the failure is deliberate) to make even the most minimal gestures of political accommodation to the Congress. These are matters of grace, of form, of politesse. Mr. Nixon has spurned them. . . . Relations with the press, always bad, have grown worse" [January 16, 1973]. When Congress sought information on foreign policy during April 1973, administration spokesmen laid claims to executive privilege that were unprecedented in American history. The president, said Attorney General Richard G. Kleindienst, had the power to withhold from Congress any information, documents, or witnesses belonging to the executive branch. The president himself made clear his intention to carry on the war in Southeast Asia, if necessary, with money appropriated for other purposes [Ripley 1973; Commager 1973]. A divided Congress had no power to challenge such claims to executive power over the country's external relations.

Writers stressed the point that Nixon, unlike Franklin D. Roosevelt and Harry Truman, failed to involve Congress in the country's foreign policy decisions. It is true that his decisions were personal, usually formulated and sometimes carried out in secret, and usually initiated without consultation and announcement. But at issue was not the president's accountability to the American people or the counsel he received from Congress or experts outside of government, but the support that his policies received from the public. As long as 55 percent of the nation's citizens supported his bombing policies, the silent majority in Congress would assure him the necessary votes. Congressional support was often assumed rather than sought, but it was no less real. Whether the president withdrew from the public, his cabinet, or even his advisory staff was immaterial as long as such men as Representative Gerald Ford maintained the necessary pro-Nixon majority in the House on matters of Vietnam and Cambodia. The Democratic party, standing as a unit in Congress, could have curtailed the president's power. But as long as large numbers of Democrats agreed with his decisions, the president's rejection of the normal bipartisan techniques were of little consequence, except to his critics.

Those who opposed the president assumed that other procedures would have produced other, more acceptable policies; that greater attention to other voices would have created doubts regarding the wisdom of executive decisions. It is not known whom the president consulted before any of his dramatic actions beginning with the Cambodian invasion of 1970 and ending with the Cambodian bombing in 1973. But if the president did not use wide-ranging sources of opinion available to him, the reason is clear. Almost without exception that advice would have challenged him. Thus, although the president scorned his critics in Congress and the press, he did not scorn the public. His speeches on the war were not designed to convince his critics but to maintain control of his silent majority. If Nixon's policies were justified, then the Vietnam war indeed represented a vast triumph for the American political system. If they were wrong, the failure lay in the vulnerability of the American people to presidential formulation of policy. The problem lay not in the Constitution but in the public mind. The Constitution of the United States cannot protect the American people from erroneous assumptions and the pursuit of illusory goals in the realm of external affairs.

LIMITS ON PRESIDENTIAL POWER

In practice executive power rests on the capacity of a president to define the enemy in terms that will establish the minimum objectives of policy and simultaneously define the means that will promise victory at the least possible cost to the American people. Those who would attack such a policy, once established, by arguing for reduced commitments, must face the charge that they endanger the country in the face of the executive's superior knowledge. Those who would increase the means of achieving victory will stand accused of impatience, unnecessary risk-taking, or a willingness to waste human and material treasure needlessly. This explains why successive presidents have faced little difficulty in outmaneuvering their critics. Once an administration has put across the notion that established policy is essential to the country's security, that policy can scarcely be challenged. The American people want their security, and they are willing to pay for it. Thus every twentieth-century American president who faced crises abroad defended his policies by stressing the disasters that would flow from alternative choices and by assuring the nation that it could achieve its essential goals at lower cost by supporting presidential decisions.

The task of explaining and defending those decisions that first led to the Americanization of the Vietnam war fell to President Johnson. His capacity to solidify his administration and to capture the support of Congress and the public rested in large measure on the rhetoric of the previous fifteen years in which dire consequences had been predicted from any further communist gains in Asia and which had guaranteed successful containment through either Saigon's political triumph over North Vietnam or the military capabilities of SEATO. When both defenses collapsed, the Johnson administration kept its critics in line by holding fast to its minimum goal of self-determination for South Vietnam, a goal that carried the burden of both this country's democratic mission and its quest for security. At the same time, the administration assured the public that each new increment of power would bring the needed victory. As each successive prediction proved erroneous, the administration faced an escalation of both the costs of the war and the volume of public and congressional criticism.

To justify the escalating costs, the Johnson administration enlarged the consequences of victory and defeat. Never had any such body of argument assigned so much of the burden of the world's future to so limited a struggle. Asserting the validity of the Munich analogy — that any backward step would lead to repeated concessions and finally to world war — the administration predicted that the successful halting of aggression in Vietnam would prevent not only the loss of all Southeast Asia but also the outbreak of another general war. The president assured the American people in 1967, "I am convinced that by seeing this struggle through now we are greatly reducing the chances of a much larger war — perhaps a nuclear war." Walt W. Rostow declared with even greater optimism that if the United States could "get on with the job, the struggle in Vietnam might be the last confrontation of the postwar era." Victory in Vietnam would demonstrate at last that aggression could not succeed and would also assure the success of self-determination for the people of Vietnam. Finally, Hanoi's defeat would terminate the Communist effort to expand its sphere of influence through wars of national liberation. In short, the Johnson administration promised to contain Communist expansion everywhere by fighting in Vietnam. Despite the importance assigned to it, the war remained undeclared. The administration based its right to conduct the war without direct congressional approval on the Gulf of Tonkin Resolution and on U. S. commitments to SEATO, although that alliance itself never made any decision to enter the war in concert.

Having escalated the war in direct defiance of his critics, Johnson was compelled to anchor his policies to rhetoric that conveyed both the high promise of success and the dire consequences of failure, for nowhere in Vietnam was there anybody of clearly recognizable circumstances, such as those Hitler posed for Europe after 1939, that carried their own convictions and recommended their own responses. Countless Americans, but not a majority, simply refused to take the rhetoric seriously. To defend his Vietnam intervention, President Johnson exaggerated the importance of that region to the United States and the rest of the world. Eventually the Vietnam war demanded an exorbitant price in terms of the alienation of much of the nation's best-informed youth as well as its intellectuals; the expenditure of resources desperately needed at home; the neglect of Europe and Latin America; the disintegration of the war on poverty; the devastating surge of inflation, which undermined an otherwise superb economic record; the increasing opposition in Congress; and, finally, the near-collapse of a political machine that had kept Democrats in the White House for twenty-eight of the previous thirty-six years. Still the president ignored the advice of the critics. Ultimately, he found it easier to retire than to change an established foreign policy.

President Nixon's ability to control the nation's attitudes toward Vietnam through four more years was perhaps the most successful experience in presidential public relations in the history of the American presidency. During his first weeks in office Nixon outlined a program for Vietnam that assured him the support of the American people. Upon his return from Saigon in March 1969, Secretary of Defense Melvin Laird informed Congress that the United States would soon increase the fighting capacity of the South Vietnamese army beyond the levels contemplated by the Johnson administration. Secretary of Defense Clark Clifford, in 1968, had limited his goals to a South Vietnamese combat capability sufficient only to permit Saigon to cope with internal insurgency after the establishment of peace. Laird, on the other hand, ordered the creation of a South Vietnamese combat force capable of replacing Americans in the continuing war. Not until the South Vietnamese had achieved complete self-sufficiency, however, would there be a complete American withdrawal from Vietnam. By promising both victory and the eventual de-Americanization of war, Laird had created the foundations of a Republican Vietnam policy.

Critics argued that Vietnamization, designed to guarantee a Saigon victory, would produce not a peace through negotiation, but a continuation of the war with United States support. Those who challenged the president's policy agreed generally that no amount of military pressure would modify Hanoi's demands. Six Rand Corporation analysts warned in early October 1969: "Even if a new strategy should produce military successes in Vietnam, substantially reduce U. S. costs and dampen domestic opposition, Hanoi could not be induced to make any concessions — so long as they implied recognition of the authority of the Saigon government." Throughout the autumn of 1969 the antiwar movement centered on the campuses, where student activists prepared for the nationwide moratorium of October 15. Hundreds of rallies that day, some attended by many thousands of persons, comprised the largest demonstration of antiwar sentiment during four years of war [For a full account of the moratorium, see *New York Times*, October 16, 1969]. Student leaders, facing determined opposition from the White House, now planned the giant march on Washington, set for November 15.

Nixon met the student challenge head-on with a nationally televised speech on election eve, November 3. Following months of continued polarization of American opinion, the president's speech comprised his first massive effort to win popular support for his Vietnam program. His arguments were as simple as they were effective. The nation, he began, had two choices if it would end the war — either "a precipitate withdrawal of all Americans from Vietnam without regard to the effects of that action" or a "search for a just peace through a negotiated settlement if possible, or through continued implementation of our plan for Vietnamization if necessary . . . . " The president quickly disposed of the first alternative, for, he warned, "the precipitate withdrawal of all American forces from Vietnam would be a disaster not only for South Vietnam but for the United States and for the cause of peace." For the South Vietnamese it would mean additional massacres; for the United States, the nation's first defeat and "a collapse of confidence in American leadership, not only in Asia but throughout the world." No nation, he explained, that betrayed its allies and its friends could be great. "Our defeat and humiliation in South Vietnam," the president continued, "would . . . spark violence wherever our commitments help maintain peace — in the Middle East, in Berlin, eventually even in the Western Hemisphere." Such rhetoric reestablished the minimum goal of victory.

Vietnamization combined with the gradual withdrawal of American forces, the president promised, would bring the war to a successful conclusion whether the peace negotiations in Paris succeeded or not. But a fixed timetable would remove any incentive for the enemy to negotiate an agreement, discount the importance of Vietnamization, and ignore the level of enemy activity. Offering no concessions, he threatened Hanoi with reescalation. "If I conclude that increased enemy action jeopardizes our remaining forces in Vietnam, I shall not hesitate to take strong and effective measures . . . . " Having made a serious bid for time and patience by assuring the nation that he had a workable program in operation, he called on the "silent majority" of Americans to support him. Turning finally on his domestic detractors, the president concluded: "The more support I can have from the American people, the sooner that pledge [to win the peace] can be redeemed . . . . Let us be united for peace. Let us also be united against defeat. Because let us understand: North Vietnam cannot defeat or humiliate the United States. Only Americans can do that" [New York Times, November 4, 1969]. By posing two alternatives, one promising victory and peace, the other presaging humiliation and disaster, the president aroused the overwhelming support of the silent majority. Again he managed to skirt the alternatives posed by the war's critics — a modification of the Saigon regime or a war without foreseeable end. Not without reason, South Vietnam's president declared the speech "the greatest and most brilliant I have known a United States President to make."

Nixon had effectively blocked the antiwar appeal to the nation's silent majority and guaranteed himself the continued support of Congress. Seven months later the president ran the risk of losing that support with his Cambodian venture. His rationalization did not convince his critics, but it kept the silent majority in line. The movement of North Vietnamese men and supplies into Cambodia, he said, gave the United States no choice but " . . . to go to the heart of the trouble. That means cleaning out major North Vietnamese and Vietcong occupied sanctuaries which serve as bases for attacks on both Cambodia and American and South Vietnamese forces in South Vietnam." As he continued his direct appeal to the nation, he stated, "A majority of the American people are for the withdrawal of our forces from Vietnam. The action I have taken tonight is indispensable for the continuing success of that withdrawal program." His decision would keep American casualties to an absolute minimum and end the war in Vietnam with a just peace. Finally, the president moved to protect American prestige. The United States, he declared, dared not behave like a "pitiful, helpless giant." Again at stake in Cambodia was the credibility of United States power to defend free institutions everywhere from the forces of totalitarianism and anarchy. "It is not," he said, "our power but our will and character that is being tested tonight . . . . If we fail to meet this challenge all other nations will be on notice that despite its overwhelming power the United States, when a real crisis comes, will be found wanting."

Long before his reelection campaign in 1972, Nixon had eliminated Vietnam as a troublesome political issue. If the war raged on, the president's Vietnamization program had shifted the burden of American involvement from the ground to the air. Indeed, beginning in early 1971, the administration had unleashed on Vietnam the heaviest air war in history. This permitted extensive troop withdrawals and a precipitous reduction in American casualties. By early 1972, the United States had less than 200,000 troops in Vietnam — a decrease of almost 400,000 from the Johnson years. The president promised to continue troop withdrawals until he reached the goal of a residual force of some 30,000 [Osnos 1971; New York Times, November 7, 1971]. Secretary Laird assured the country in November 1971 that the Nixon policies had given the Saigon regime a reasonable chance to survive, provided that this country continued to retain sufficient ground forces in Vietnam to guarantee the success of the bombing campaign. Having proclaimed Vietnamization a success, President Nixon offered to terminate all United States war activity in Vietnam and to withdraw all American troops in four months if Hanoi agreed to an internationally supervised cease-fire and the release of all American prisoners [Newsweek, January 17, 1972, p. 45].

Nixon's Vietnam strategy rendered the Democratic leadership vulnerable on the war issue. In 1972, Americans rejected any policy that threatened the existence of the Saigon government. Stewart Alsop attacked the bipartisan maneuver in Congress to cut aid to South Vietnam. "To force those who have fought on our side to surrender," he wrote, "would be a terrible betrayal, an act of gross immorality" [Newsweek, November 8, 1971, p. 122]. George McGovern's long-standing opposition to the war comprised no threat. But when Edmund Muskie, in February, unveiled his peace plan for Vietnam, the administration responded fiercely with the charge that the leading Democratic presidential candidate was undermining the government's peace strategy in Paris. Muskie's warning to Saigon that the United States would not support the war indefinitely, exposed him to accusations that he was prepared to accept defeat in Southeast Asia. Clearly the president still had full command of the Vietnam issue [Apple 1972; Newsweek, February 14, 1972, p. 100; Washington Post, January 16, 1972].

CONGRESS, THE COURTS, AND FOREIGN AFFAIRS

Twice during the 92nd Congress the Senate passed amendments that would have eliminated funds for the Vietnam war and compelled the president to withdraw American forces. The House refused to go along on the ground that such restrictions were an improper abridgement of the president's authority to conduct foreign policy [New York Times, October 22, 1972]. During January 1973, House Democrats, by a vote of 154 to 75, and Senate Democrats, by a vote of 36 to 12, resolved to pass legislation that would end the Indochinese involvement [Washington Post, January 7, 1973, editorial]. Still the Democrats in Congress faced the widespread notion, encouraged by the president, that any such move would undermine the negotiations in Paris. It was not clear that any confrontation with the president could succeed. If the cease-fire negotiations failed, the administration's critics would carry the responsibility. If the negotiations succeeded, their warnings that the cease-fire would not result in a genuine settlement mattered little, for any agreement that negotiated a return of all United States prisoners and extricated the United States from the war would be overwhelmingly acceptable to the American people [Newsweek, January 15,

1973, p. 76]. On January 27, 1973, the four Vietnam belligerents signed the cease-fire agreement for Indochina that provided for the return of all American prisoners and the withdrawal of all United States military personnel in 60 days. Nixon could scarcely conceal his resentment toward those editors and congressmen who refused to praise his "peace with honor." But the critics could see little honor in the 10-year American involvement. Nor would they agree with the president that American withdrawal from the war was synonymous with peace. The war, they predicted, would continue.

After January 1973, Nixon's purpose in Cambodia was the negotiation of a cease-fire between the Lon Nol government in Phnom Penh and its enemies. By April the cease-fire was still nonexistent and the level of fighting around the capital had increased. The president responded to the continued insurgency with another massive air offensive, although administration spokesmen admitted that bombing targets were scarce. By late April the United States had carpet-bombed the Cambodian countryside for over 50 successive days. Early in May, Secretary of State William P. Rogers, addressing the Senate Foreign Relations Committee, justified the bombing by arguing that the Vietnam cease-fire agreement permitted bombing as long as the communists, including Hanoi, refused to sign a special cease-fire for Cambodia. Rogers linked the North Vietnamese presence in Cambodia with the survival of the Saigon regime [Johnston 1973]. What disturbed some members of Congress even more was Secretary of Defense Elliot Richardson's assertion that the administration would continue the bombing whether Congress authorized the expenditure or not. The president, he said, would reduce troop levels in Europe, if necessary, to cover the cost of the Cambodian operation.

Convinced that the administration's war in Cambodia had no constitutional support, Senate leaders, Republicans and Democrats alike, introduced measures to cut off funds for any military action in Cambodia that was not specifically approved by Congress. One central proposal, backed by the overwhelming majority of the Senate, would have permitted executive military action against an immediate threat to national security for 30 days without congressional approval. Meanwhile, the House examined the Senate war-powers bill as well as various versions of its own. During May a Gallup Poll revealed that almost 60 percent of the American people disapproved of the Cambodian bombing and that over 75 percent believed that the president should seek congressional approval before carrying out any additional military action in Southeast Asia [New York Times, May 13, 1973]. Clearly the president's policy in Cambodia was now doomed.

Republican leaders in the House hoped to head off a vote that would curtail the president's authority, but in mid-May the House voted 219 to 188 to prevent the Pentagon from using funds that had been previously appropriated to carry on the bombing. Then by a vote of 224 to 172, it forbade the use of any money in a $2.9 billion supplemental appropriation bill to be used anywhere in the vicinity of Cambodia [Newsweek, May 21, 1973, pp. 37–38]. Early in June the Senate attached a restrictive rider to a $3.4 billion supplemental appropriation bill that, its backers believed, the president dared not veto. The House passed the measure and then attached it to the even more vital appropriation bill for funding the operations of government. The president vetoed the first bill, declaring that it would undo his work in obtaining an honorable peace in Indochina. "We are now involved," he warned, "in concluding the last element of that settlement. It would be nothing short of tragic if this great accomplishment, bought with the blood of so many Asians and Americans, were to be undone now by Congressional action." It was this argument that had sustained his control of Congress and the public through four years. But this time it failed. Congress moved rapidly toward a showdown with the president. It began to attach riders restricting the use of federal funds in Cambodia to increasingly essential financial legislation until the administration had either to capitulate or see the whole government grind to a halt. Finally the House and Senate agreed to the president's proposal of a cutoff on August 15 [Newsweek, July 9, 1973, pp. 26–27].

Unwilling to accept the August 15 deadline, Representative Elizabeth Holtzman, Democrat of New York, and three Air Force officers brought suit before Judge Orrin G. Judd of the U. S. District Court in New York. The judge, on July 25, ruled that the president had no authority to conduct an executive war without the approval of Congress. The United States attorney for the Eastern District of New York immediately filed a notice of appeal. In the past Judd had held that congressional appropriations constituted approval of executive policy, but he argued that Congress in no way had upheld the continuation of the American action in Southeast Asia after the January cease-fire. The president had agreed to the August 15 deadline, but Judd believed that the bombing should stop immediately to save Cambodian lives. The president had made clear his intention to bomb up to the deadline. On July 27 the United States Court of Appeals of the Second Circuit issued a stay of the Judd decision. Immediately Representative Holtzman appealed the stay to Justice William O. Douglas of the United States Supreme Court [New York Times, August 5, 1973]. On August 5, Justice Douglas upheld the injunction ordered by the federal court in Brooklyn. He did not argue the constitutionality of the war, but he insisted that the bombing was a capital case in which some were bound to die and that the United States was not in danger. Therefore, the possible victims should have the defense of the court. But the remainder of the Court, polled by Justice Thurgood Marshall, overruled Douglas and upheld the administration's right to continue the bombing up to the August 15 deadline. The Court's majority agreed that it had no precedent for halting a war through judicial action.

THE PRESIDENT AND THE PUBLIC MIND

Many who criticized the Congress for its failure to restrain the president found a solution in organizational reform. Some writers favored new laws, such as the War Powers Act, that would compel the president to consult members of Congress. One advocate of formal controls on executive action wrote: "Major decisions would come to be taken in consultation. The fundamental danger of rash or corrupting decisions taken by a lone President, communing only with God and his own sycophantic subordinates, would be reduced" [Sundquist, November 11, 1973]. Similarly D. L. Robinson of Smith College, writing in *Worldview* [1973], argued for the reorganization of Congress. He noted, "There can be no effective resurgence of legislative authority in the American system until Congress reconstitutes itself. No other authority on earth, save the constituents themselves, can do that job." Even *The New York Times* editorialized, "Until Congress can improve its own committee and seniority systems, modernize its appropriations process and bring the foreign policy, military and intelligence establishments more effectively under its supervision and review, its intermittent battles with the White House are likely to be inconclusive at best and futile at worst" [August 5, 1973].

Members of Congress hoped to spur public interest in Congress's plight. But it was clear, as Senator Robert A. Taft, Jr., (R., Ohio) observed, that the weakness of Congress lay less in its organization than in the fact that it did not stand as an effective policy-making body. Its membership, he charged, tended to pursue parochial and individualistic interests and seemed unwilling to seek positions based on party unity. To deal effectively with the president, warned Taft, Congress needed "centralized and identifiable party and legislative responsibility" [Broder 1972]. This required stronger party caucuses, party policy committees, and party leadership. Writers on presidential power seemed to agree. James MacGregor Burns [1973], for example, argued that the answer to congressional weakness did not lay in a mindless attack on the presidency, the only instrument available for giving direction to federal policy. Rather, he said, the answer lay in the rejection of unquestioning bipartisanship (anchored to the assumption that politics should stop at the water's edge) and in reasonable party debate and electoral competition.

In large part the successive war powers measures, including the one that Congress passed over the president's veto in November 1973, carried the burden of the perennial move to limit the executive's war-making authority. What these measures, beginning with Senator Jacob Javits' first war-powers bill in June 1970, sought to accomplish was the restoration of balance between the president's control of the armed forces and the right of Congress to declare war. The various bills sought to differentiate between the circumstances in which the president could act unilaterally and those in which he required the prior authority of Congress. Under these measures, even the use of armed forces under emergency conditions required congressional approval within 30 (later extended to 90) days. Perhaps it would be naive, as James L. Sundquist [1973] wrote, to assume that the effective power to declare war can be wielded by a 535-man deliberative body such as Congress. But if the president, after as little as 30 days of fighting, could not convince a solid congressional majority of the validity of his policies, those policies would already have laid the foundation for a major uprising within the American populace and would be floundering militarily or morally along the battle fronts. In practice the war powers measure would not limit presidential power at all if in future crises the executive could establish its dominance over congressional and public opinion as easily as it had in the Vietnam war. Indeed, even as Congress passed the War Powers Act over the president's veto, the White House warned that it "seriously undermines this nation's ability to act decisively in times of international crisis" [Reston, November 10, 1973].

Thus in the design and conduct of successful foreign relations the level of public understanding is crucial. If Congress would strengthen its role, especially when that role appears vital for the proper performance of the country's external relations, it has no choice but to discover some effective means to challenge the president's control of the public mind. The judgment that any congressman or citizen makes about specific displays of presidential authority depends solely upon the broader intellectual and emotional responses to the policies pursued. The critical issue in the perennial congressional-executive struggle for control of policy, therefore, is less that of presidential power than that of the quality of the policies for which that power is employed and the merit of the executive arguments used to sustain them.

Ultimately, the only check on the misuse of presidential power rests in a more sophisticated concept of national interest and a more general awareness of the limits of national will than the American people displayed in supporting the Vietnam war. Above all, these requirements demand that the nation desert the perennial militarism that underwrote its beliefs and objectives. The abuse of the war-making power was more the effect than the cause of the country's refusal to accept failure in war or diplomacy. Thus the foreign policy crises of the early 1970s were intellectual and emotional, not constitutional. President Nixon never operated outside the framework of the law in the Vietnam War. He gave the people what they wanted. What was unique in his largely unprecedented claims to executive authority was the nature of the war, which permitted a maximum of presidential control over military strategy and a minimum of direct congressional involvement. And what made a fundamentally intellectual crisis appear to be constitutional was the equally unprecedented condition wherein the president's critics gradually dominated almost every platform of American public discourse — Congress, the press, television, and the campuses — while his supporters were indeed the silent majority of Congress and the Gallup Polls.

BIBLIOGRAPHY

Alsop, Stewart. *Newsweek,* 8 November 1971.

Apple, Jr., R. W. *The New York Times,* 16 January 1972.

Broder, David S. *The Washington Post,* 10 December 1972.

Burns, James MacGregor. *The New York Times,* 8 April 1973.

Commager, Henry Steele. *The Washington Post,* 27 May 1973.

Johnston, Oswald. *The Charlottesville Daily Progress,* 16 January 1973.

Kilpatrick, James J. *The Charlottesville Daily Progress,* 16 January 1973.

Lincoln, Abraham. "Letter to Herndon." *The Collected Works of Abraham Lincoln.* Edited by Roy P. Basler. New Brunswick, N. J.: Rutgers University Press, 1953, I:451.

Minow, Newton H.; Martin, John Bartlow; and Mitchell, Lee. *Presidential Television: A Twentieth-Century Fund Report.* New York: Basic Books, 1973.

Newsweek, 8 November 1971, p. 122; 17 January 1972, p. 45; 14 February 1972, p. 100; 15 January 1973, p. 76; 21 May 1973, pp. 37–38; 9 July 1973, pp. 26–27.

The New York Times, 19 August 1967; 16 October 1969; 4 November 1969; 4 April 1971; 7 November 1971; 22 October 1972; 13 May 1973; 5 August 1973, editorial.

Osnos, Peter. *The Washington Post,* 7 November 1971.

Reston, James. *The Charlottesville Daily Progress,* 28 December 1972; 19 March 1973; 29 March 1973; 10 November 1973.

Ripley, Anthony. *The New York Times,* 15 April 1973.

Robinson, D. L. "Presidential Autocracy and the Rule of Law." *Worldview* 16 (March 1973):11.

Schlesinger, Jr., Arthur M. "Presidential War: 'See if you can fix any limit to his power.' " *The New York Times Magazine*, 7 January 1973, pp. 12ff.

Sundquist, James L. *The Washington Post*, 11 November 1973.

War Powers Legislation: Hearings before the Committee on Foreign Relations, U. S. Senate, 92nd Congress, 1st Sess. Washington, D.C.: Government Printing Office, 1972.

The Washington Post, 16 January 1972; 7 January 1973, editorial; 28 January 1973.

Wicker, Tom. *The New York Times*, 14 January 1973.

Yergin, Daniel. "Fulbright's Circle." *Worldview* 16 (February 1973): 13.

IV ☆ CONGRESSIONAL PERSPECTIVES

Two acknowledged leaders in the U. S. House of Representatives, both scholars in their own right, Republican John B. Anderson (Illinois) and Democrat Morris K. Udall (Arizona), have similar perspectives on the nature of congressional-presidential problems, but offer substantially different prescriptions for their cure. Their respective conservative and liberal instincts seem to be reflected in their prescriptions. While Anderson limits his to congressional "in-house" improvements and some statutory changes, Udall proposes that the Constitution be amended to allow the Congress to use the parliamentary system's vote-of-no-confidence provision.

John B. Anderson, a Republican leader in the U. S. House of Representatives from Illinois, is a Phi Beta Kappa graduate of the University of Illinois with law degrees from both Illinois and Harvard. He is the author of two books, *Between Two Worlds: A Congressman's Choice* and *Congress and Conscience.*

Morris K. Udall, a Democratic leader in the U. S. House of Representatives from Arizona, has written articles for the *Reader's Digest, Progressive,* and *New Republic* in addition to writing *The Job of the Congressman* and *The Education of a Congressman.*

7

A Republican Looks at the Presidency

JOHN B. ANDERSON
Member of Congress

Perhaps no better time in the twentieth century could have been chosen for an analysis of the future of the American presidency, for no other reason than we are now engaged in a national cathartic examination of the Nixon administration, and by extension, of course, the presidency. My observations will surely indicate my belief that such an examination is overdue, and that imbalances presently exist in the federal government as a result.

A note about my topic, "A Republican Looks at the Presidency," is necessary at the outset. Throughout my essay will run a thread of tension more between the presidency and Congress than between Republicans and Democrats; and I shall discuss partisan politics only insofar as the two-party system affects the presidency. I expect nonetheless that having been a Republican so long that I have developed biases that could, however, be interpreted by some as a "Republican" point of view.

My theme has three parts. First, the genesis of the contemporary presidency as the overwhelmingly powerful institution in the federal structure can be attributed to presidential and congressional reaction to three periods of national emergency—the New Deal, World War II, and the cold war. The seemingly successful executive leadership in these crises led to and fed rising expectations about the potential for executive leadership. Second, it is my belief that we arrived at the apogee of presidential power in the early 1960s, with an excessively inflated idea about what foreign and domestic ills could be cured by dynamic executive leadership. Third, a combination of misguided presidential leadership in Vietnam and the failure of the Great Society to achieve so many of its objectives provoked a disenchantment with the presidency. It is my feeling now, as a result of Watergate and related revelations of the outrageous misuse of presidential power, that we must guard against distrusting in the extreme the institution that we once embraced in the extreme.

THE NEW DEAL

My contention that the modern presidency began with the New Deal should not be construed as suggesting that before Franklin Roosevelt the presidency was a weak or vestigial organ of the federal power triangle [see Milton 1944]. At each phase in the previous growth of presidential leadership there had been presidents who, as James MacGregor Burns has written "extracted every morsel of executive power from the Constitution," and in the case of the Republican Theodore Roosevelt had "gone on to wield power beyond the letter of the Constitution." Capsulizing his view of the presidency, Theodore Roosevelt wrote the following to Sir Otto Trevelyan in June 1908, a few months before leaving office.

> While President I have been President, emphatically; I have used every ounce of power there was in the office and I have not cared a rap for the criticisms of those who spoke of my "usurpation of

power"; for I know that the talk has been all nonsense and that there had been no usurpation. I believe that the efficiency of this Government depends upon it possessing a strong central executive, and whenever I could establish a precedent for strength in the executive, as I did for instance as regards external affairs in the case of sending the fleet around the world, taking Panama, settling affairs of Santo Domingo, and Cuba; or as I did in internal affairs in settling the anthracite coal strike, in keeping order in Nevada . . . or as I have done in bringing the big corporations to book . . . in all these cases I have felt not merely that my action was right in itself, but that in showing the strength of, or in giving strength to, the executive, I was establishing a precedent of value. I believe in a strong executive; I believe in power; but I believe that responsibility should go with power, and that it is not well that the strong executive should be a perpetual executive [Bishop 1920, II:94].

It might be said that when a particularly forceful intellect or personality becomes president, there is an unsurprising, predictable presidential imperative to squeeze as much power out of the office as possible.

Opposition to this view of the presidency was expressed by Roosevelt's former secretary of war (1905–1908), and his successor as chief executive, William Howard Taft. According to the twenty-seventh president:

The true view of the Executive functions is, as I conceive it, that the President can exercise no power which cannot be fairly and reasonably traced to some specific grant of power or justly implied and included within such express grant as proper and necessary to its exercise. Such specific grant must be either in the Federal Constitution or in an act of Congress passed in pursuance thereof. There is no undefined residuum of power which he can exercise because it seems to him to be in the public interest, and there is nothing in the Neagle case [In re Neagle, 135 U. S. 1 (1890)] and its definition of a law of the United States, or in other precedents, warranting such an inference. The grants of Executive power are necessary in general terms in order not to embarrass the Executive within the field of action plainly marked for him, but his jurisdiction must be justified and vindicated by affirmative constitutional or statutory provision, or it does not exist. There have not been wanting, however, eminent men in high public office holding a different view and who have insisted upon the necessity for an undefined residuum of Executive power in the public interest. They have not been confined to the present generation [Taft 1916, pp. 139–140].

It should not be surprising that when an individual of particularly strong intellect and personality takes office he gets his bearings, takes his cue, and justifies his assertiveness by the actions of his strongest predecessors. In Franklin Roosevelt's experience the two previous presidents who fit into that category were his cousin Theodore Roosevelt and Woodrow Wilson, who in their different ways had dominated the Executive Branch, the Congress, and their parties. As he took office, their influence on FDR became clear. "Theodore Roosevelt and Wilson," he said on the eve of his first inauguration, "were moral leaders, each in his own way and for his own time, who used the Presidency as a pulpit." The presidency, he said, "is preeminently a place of moral leadership. All our great Presidents were leaders of thought at times when certain historic ideas in the life of the nation had to be clarified."

What the nation could not have known, and what perhaps FDR himself could not have known, was just how well he could not only preach from the pulpit, but also wield the power of the presidency. Rather than cite examples, I shall quote a conclusion drawn by Richard Neustadt after he had completed his study of *Presidential Power*. He wrote of FDR and power:

> No President in this century has had a sharper sense of personal power, a sense of what it is and where it comes from; none has had more hunger for it, few have had more use for it, and only one or two could match his faith in his own competence to use it. Perception and desire and self-confidence, combined, produced their own reward. No modern President has been more nearly master in the White House [1960, p. 161].

Considering Franklin Roosevelt's character, the state of the Union in 1932, and the will of Congress, it is difficult to imagine a set of circumstances that could have made the expansion of executive power more inevitable. President Roosevelt was assured that the presidency ought to be the nation's source of leadership, regardless of national circumstances, and furthermore, felt personal doubt neither about his ability to master the power of the presidency nor to employ it in pursuit of what was right. The nature of presidential supremacy must surely have been reinforced by the calamitous effects of the Great Depression, which at the time of the inauguration had one-third of the nation's work force unemployed. And, to cap this short review of the circumstances surrounding the first FDR inauguration, there was little reason to expect any more forceful leadership from the Congress than had been forthcoming in the previous 4 years [see Scharz 1970, p. 281].

"This is a day of national consecration," Roosevelt said in his first inaugural. "We must move as a trained and loyal army willing to sacrifice for the good of a common discipline . . . . We are, I know, ready and willing to submit our lives and our property to such discipline, because it makes possible a leadership which aims at a larger good." Then he lay down the gauntlet. Unless Congress acted, he promised he would demand of them, "the one remaining instrument to meet the crisis — broad executive power to wage a war against the emergency, as great as the power that would be given to me if we were in fact invaded by a foreign foe" [U. S. Congress, House 1965, pp. 235–239].

One cannot help but admire the personal strength and ingenuity in confronting so decisively the unprecedented nonmilitary threat; and in the absence of congressional ability to pick up the gauntlet and to propose its own initiatives, one must concede Mr. Roosevelt great credit for providing desperately needed leadership. But far less sanguine conclusions can be drawn about the effect of these measures on the structure of our government.

In his first major official act, for example, he proclaimed a National Bank Holiday on the basis of the 1917 Trading With the Enemy Act — a statute designed by its authors to meet only wartime exigencies. What developed from this and similar acts by Roosevelt and subsequent presidents is a disturbing, frequently employed modus operandi that can be stated this way: in time of crisis the president should utilize any statutory authority at hand, with little regard for its original purpose, and with the expectation of ex post facto Congressional imprimatur.

If this is a potentially injurious methodology, and I believe it is, let me be clear that it is less the result of Democratic or Republican tendencies (the two most accomplished previous practitioners were Republican Presidents Theodore Roosevelt and Abraham Lincoln), and more the result of institutional imperatives. John Locke, the English political philosopher who greatly influenced the authors of the Constitution, argued, for example, that the threat of a national crisis — unforeseen, sudden, and potentially catastrophic — required the creation of broad emergency powers to be exercised by the chief executive where the legislative body had not provided a means or procedure of remedy. Specifically, Locke said it was the "prerogative" of the executive because lawmaking bodies tend to have their power diffused greatly, tend to be slow to act, and further, find it impossible to "foresee and so by laws to provide for all accidents and necessities" [1924, p. 200].

In the American experience, moreover, the utilization of emergency powers by the chief executive evolves from the incumbent's view of his office. According to one authority,

> Emergency powers are not solely derived from legal sources. The extent of their invocation and use is also contingent upon the personal conception which the incumbent of the presidential office has of the Presidency and the premises upon which he interprets his legal powers. In the last analysis, the authority of a President is largely determined by the President himself. Presidential interpretations throughout the decades have fixed the standards and limits of executive competence [Sturm 1949, p. 121].

During the period of the New Deal the courts appeared willing to legitimize executive actions that seemed justified in terms of the existing national emergency. Taking cognizance of Justice Louis Brandeis's words in 1932 that the Depression constituted "an emergency more serious than war,"

> New Deal lawyers festooned early legislation with "emergency clauses." When the Court in January, 1934, in a 5–4 decision written by Chief Justice Hughes, upheld a Minnesota moratorium on

mortgages, it indicated it might be receptive to such a view of the depression. "While emergency does not create power," Hughes states, "emergency may furnish the occasion for the exercise of power" [*Home Building and Loan Association v. Blaisdell*, et al., 290 U. S. 426 (1934)] [Leuchtenberg 1963, p. 143].*

Perhaps even more disturbing than the extent to which the Congress initially acquiesces in granting emergency powers to the president, however, is the tendency for Congress to allow those powers to remain on the books, alive in statute, long after the precipitating emergency has subsided.[1] I believe most Americans may find it an unexpected legacy of the New Deal that the open-ended emergency powers granted to President Roosevelt in the Emergency Banking Act of 1933 remain in effect today [*Statutes at Large*, vol. 48, part 1, sec. s, 1, 1933]. Under that statute, during any period of national emergency declared by the president he may "investigate, regulate, or prohibit, any transactions in foreign exchange, transfers of credit or payments between, by, through, or to any banking institution . . ." Thus, it is not difficult to imagine that a law written more than 40 years ago, which excludes Congress from a significant role, could be employed by the executive in an attempt to solve some future crisis.

If the Great Depression had been the only crisis the nation had to face in the 1930s, some kind of equilibrium might have developed between the president and Congress for that period, and the acquisition of presidential power might have been stemmed by an increasingly observant Congress. But the nation was trying to climb out of the Depression at the same time it was unknowingly taking the first steps toward World War II. That combination of incredible circumstances, unpredictable and beyond the control of the president or the Congress foreordained the continuation of the developing pattern: an executive that demands extraordinary discretionary powers during periods of crisis, a passive, acquiescent Congress that responds for the most part uncritically, and with little or no subsequent review on the

---

*This and subsequent quotations from William Leuchtenberg's *Franklin D. Roosevelt and the New Deal*, 1963, are reprinted with permission of the publisher, Harper & Row.

part of Congress of the powers it has granted. Furthermore, implicit in this pattern is the executive as initiator and Congress as the legitimator.

THE BURGEONING WHITE HOUSE BUREAUCRACY

Following the Great Depression another innovation occurred in the development of the modern presidency — the enlargement of the chief executive's staff and family of official advisers. Under the authority of the Reorganization Act of 1939 (53 Stat. 561), President Roosevelt, in two reorganization plans that became effective on July 1, 1939, established the Executive Office of the President. Designed to contain those staff agencies that would immediately aid the president, the Executive Office was envisioned and proposed by the President's Committee on Administrative Management, chaired by Professor Louis Brownlow, which had submitted its report on these matters to President Roosevelt and Congress in early January 1937. In its recommendations the panel had urged that the President

> ... be given a small number of executive assistants who would be his direct aides in dealing with the managerial agencies and administrative departments of the Government. These assistants, probably not exceeding six in number, would be in addition to his present secretaries, who deal with the public, with the Congress, and with the press and the radio. These aides would have no power to make decisions or issue instructions in their own right. They would not be interposed between the President and the heads of his departments. They would not be assistant presidents in any sense. Their function would be, when any matter was presented to the President for action affecting any part of the administrative work of the Government, to assist him in obtaining quickly and without delay all pertinent information possessed by any of the executive departments so as to guide him in making his responsible decisions; and then when decisions have been made, to assist him in seeing to it that every administrative department and agency affected is promptly informed. Their effectiveness in assisting the President will, we think, be directly proportional to

their ability to discharge their functions with restraint. They would remain in the background, issue no orders, make no decisions, emit no public statements. Men for these positions should be carefully chosen by the President from within and without the Government. They should be men in whom the President has personal confidence and whose character and attitude is such that they would not attempt to exercise power on their own account. They should be possessed of high competence, great physical vigor, and a passion for anonymity. They should be installed in the White House itself, directly accessible to the President. In the selection of these aides the President should be free to call on departments from time to time for the assignment of persons who, after a tour of duty as his aides, might be restored to their old positions [President's Committee on Administrative Management 1937, p. 5].

Since the beginning of the presidency, the chief executive had been allowed the services of one administrative secretary. In 1929 Congress increased the number of aides by providing (45 Stat. 1230) for the addition of two more presidential secretaries and authority for an administrative assistant. With the 1939 reorganization, the chief executive obtained six administrative assistants (still authorized at 3 U.S.C. 105) in addition to three secretaries. After the United States entered World War II, the president began adding more personal staff through appropriation acts that authorized their existence and salary.

The number of aides continued to grow in the aftermath of the war. According to one account,

At the close of President Truman's administration (mid-year 1952) there were three Secretaries, the Assistant to the President, a Special Counsel, six Administrative Assistants, one Administrative Assistant in the President's office, a Social Secretary, a Secretary to the Wife of the President, Military, Naval, and Air Force Aides (one each), a Physician, a Legislative Assistant, and Executive Clerk and a Chief Usher [Hobbs 1954, pp. 87–88].

The number doubled under President Eisenhower and has continued to grow each year.

With this growth two other problems have arisen in presidential staffing arrangements. One troublesome area involves the

misuse of special temporary positions (authorized in 5 U.S.C.
2103) for permanent policy employees. As a report for the House
Post Office and Civil Service Committee recently commented:

> Long ago Congress gave the President authority to employ per-
> sonnel notwithstanding civil service regulations governing qual-
> ifications, pay, etc. These positions have been described or labeled
> as "ungraded." Historically, these jobs have been restricted to, and
> used primarily in, the housekeeping function of the executive res-
> idence. There, many custodial and wage-board type employees are
> required along with an occasional French chef or unusual
> specialist of some kind. The current Administration has made a
> basic policy change in the use of this authority. Now many high-
> level policy employees are being employed without regard to civil
> service regulations [U. S. Congress, House 1972, p. 6].

The number of ungraded positions in the White House
Office jumped from 3 in 1970 to 67 in 1971 and increased to 76
the following year. During this same time the Domestic Council
counted an entire staff of ungraded positions, numbering 52 in
1971, 70 in 1972, and 66 the following year.

The other shift that occurred with the continued growth of
the presidential staff was the assumption of policy roles and
positions of power by White House aides. During the Nixon administration, Dr. Kissinger, as assistant to the president for National Security Council staff, competed with Secretary of State
William Rogers in setting foreign policy. That contest was resolved by the departure of Rogers and the assumption of both
roles by Kissinger.

But the situation was not any different when considering
domestic policy. In a speech given in May 1971 in San Jose,
California, Senator Ernest F. Hollings remarked,

> It used to be that if I had a problem with food stamps, I went over
> to see the Secretary of Agriculture, whose Department had juris-
> diction over that program. Not any more. Now, if I want to learn
> the policy, I must go to the White House and consult John Price.[2]

> If I want the latest on textiles, I won't get it from the Secretary of
> Commerce, who has the authority and responsibility. No, I am
> forced to go to the White House and see Mr. Peter Flanigan. I

shouldn't feel too badly. Secretary Stans has to do the same thing. [Bonafede 1971, p. 1240].

Even officials in the executive departments and agencies became distraught over the growing authority of the White House staff and its assumption of policy functions. A top Commerce Department bureaucrat reflected this attitude in a *New York Times* column, saying " . . . the business community pays no attention to this Department; if you have a policy problem, you go see Peter Flanigan — and he is available."

"Peter Flanigan," the official said with a sigh, "is to the Department of Commerce what Henry Kissinger is to the Department of State" [*New York Times*, March 20, 1972].

Further complicating the problem of growth and authority is the problem of accountability in the dual appointment situation whereby executive branch officials were given a White House office and title in addition to the position for which they are actually compensated. In the Nixon administration Office of Management and Budget Director Roy Ash also was an assistant to the president, as was Secretary of the Treasury George Shultz, as was Secretary of State Kissinger. These dual roles, however, became problematical when the president refused to allow one of these individuals to testify before a congressional committee because of their status as a presidential adviser. Thus, in addition to sheer size and policy-authority issues, presidential dual staff arrangements raise the question of accountability and separation of powers insofar as congressional access to executive branch officials is limited.

WORLD WAR II

Development of a large and powerful White House bureaucracy coincided with the events leading to World War II — the second major crisis of survival out of which even greater presidential power vis-à-vis the Congress flowed. In the prewar period of 1933 to 1939, those who wanted to restrict executive freedom in the conduct of foreign affairs focused upon the issue of neutrality. The question was whether arms should be embargoed against all belligerents, or whether as Roosevelt proposed, only against some at his discretion.

At first the Roosevelt position lost. Notwithstanding the insistence of the chairman of the House Committee on Foreign Affairs that "the Administration's resolution be passed as it was" [Robinson 1967, p. 263], and despite a House vote that endorsed the proposal, the Senate would not concur. Rather than accept the unpalatable Senate blanket embargo, the House Foreign Affairs Committee let the measure die.

The issue recurred, however, and between 1935 and 1939 the Senate predilection prevailed to the extent that congressional stipulations were placed on the sale and shipment of arms to foreign nations. In sum, the Congress, although significantly divided on the issues, for the first time thwarted a major foreign policy initiative of the Roosevelt administration.

In a number of other actions President Roosevelt utilized emergency powers in the emergency situation in Europe and Asia to achieve his foreign and diplomatic policies. In September 1939 Roosevelt issued a proclamation (54 Stat. 2643) of national emergency.

> The President was careful to stress in a press conference that the emergency which he had recognized was a limited one, that it was intended to permit the invocation of only a few statutes which would allow the necessary protective arrangements to be made against a spreading of the crisis. Otherwise, the vast collection of statutes at his disposal would not be used. The emergency was therefore "limited" in the sense that in the opinion of the President it warranted the use of only a few of the many available statutory powers. This description of the emergency originated with the President. There is no basis for it in the statutes. They pertain usually to a "national emergency" without specifying its intensity, whether "limited" or "unlimited." A recognition of an emergency by the President called all of these statutes into play. Mr. Roosevelt was, therefore, entirely free to select the statutes which might be comprehended by his notice of a "limited emergency." Whatever restraint might affect his choice would be self-imposed. His refinement of emergencies appears to have been prompted by a concern with public relations, rather than with any

fine legal distinctions. Mr. Roosevelt felt that ' . . . if one were to issue a Proclamation of National Emergency without any limitation, scare headlines might be justified, because, under that, the Executive could do all kinds of things.' All actions of the government in the emergency which had been recognized would be done, the President declared in his press conference, on a peacetime basis. Neither the defense of the country nor its internal economy would be placed upon a war footing [Robinson, p. 264].*

In organizing to meet the threatening international crisis, FDR, in May 1940, revived the old Council of National Defense, a World War I vestige that had been dormant since the departure of the Wilson administration. The Council's Advisory Commission was the instrument of primary importance to the president as he could place decision-makers on the panel without the requirement of obtaining Senate confirmation. The Council of National Defense itself never met apart from the cabinet under Roosevelt. "The individual members of the Commission had been active in preparing plans for what might be required to meet the possible needs of the future, and had taken initial steps in carrying some of their plans into operations" [Koenig 1944, p. 13].**

The next unit created to direct and coordinate administrative activities related to the pending international exigencies was the Office for Emergency Management. In establishing the components of the Executive Office of the President in 1939, E.O. 8248 made reference to such a body, saying: " . . . in the event of a national emergency, or the threat of a national emergency, such office for emergency management as the President shall determine" was authorized to be created. OEM was set up on the authority of an administrative order in May 1940.

Most, but not all, of the agencies concerned with the defense program became a part of OEM. The organization of the government in crisis proceeded upon the theory that the regular departments

---

*Reprinted with permission from James A. Robinson, *Congress and Foreign Policy-Making.* (Homewood, Ill.: The Dorsey Press, 1967 ©), p. 264.

**This and subsequent quotations from Louis W. Koenig's *The Presidency and Crisis* reprinted with the permission of the author and the publisher, King's Crown Press of the Columbia University Press, New York, New York.

and agencies should dispose of crisis matters insofar as they were capable. Otherwise, the matters should be handled by new agencies created especially for the crisis. The new agencies might be a part of the Executive Office of the President or they might be independent of it. The allocation of the new agencies was determined by the belief of Mr. Roosevelt that direct operating duties should be brought into the Executive Office under either of two circumstances. First, when the attitude of an existing agency toward defense problems is hostile and a change in personnel of the agency cannot otherwise be justified. Second, when the activity is peculiarly related to the crisis and is of such importance that it must be brought under the President's control [Wann 1968, p. 140].

At present both the Council of National Defense and the Office for Emergency Management are dormant but available as instrumentalities which a president might utilize in organizing for and managing an emergency. Under their umbrella of authority a number of subordinate units were created to act upon a threatening exigency. In activating either or both of these units, a chief executive might hire staff, delegate authority for them to exercise, and commit funds assigned to a program not having a specified administrative organization attached to it.

It was also in this twilight period between the invasion of Poland and the bombing of Pearl Harbor that President Roosevelt engaged in a series of questionable but congressionally unchecked actions. Although the United States professed a policy of neutrality, FDR transferred fifty retired American destroyers to Great Britain in exchange for American defense bases in British territories located in the Caribbean. In his message to Congress informing the legislators of this agreement, the chief executive referred to the arrangement as "the most important action in the reinforcement of our national defense that has been taken since the Louisiana Purchase."

The parallel to Jefferson and Louisiana was less than perfect. While the response to the disclosure of the transfer was generally enthusiastic — even the Chicago Tribune approved it — many were disturbed by the method Roosevelt had chosen. Critics charged that he had flouted the authority of Congress, whose rights in the matter he had previously conceded; that he had acted without taking the people into his confidence; and that he had transgressed international law. At a time when Britain faced annihilation, Roosevelt and his supporters had little patience with animadversions based on Edwardian conventions of international law. To his admirers, the transaction was a magnificent stroke of daring statesmanship. They rejoiced in the abandonment of traditional neutrality and the fusion of British and American interests. Henceforth, as Churchill told the Commons, the United States and Great Britain would be "somewhat mixed up together" [Koenig 1944, p. 82].

Some eight months after the announcement of this agreement with the British, the president proclaimed a condition of unlimited national emergency and thereby removed any self-imposed restrictions upon his authority to deal with the mounting international exigency. And what might the chief executive do under this proclamation?

[H]e might increase the strength of the armed forces and order reserves and retired officers to active duty; he might regulate transactions in foreign exchange, transactions by Federal Reserve banks, and waive or modify monthly apportionment of appropriations; he might take over power houses, dams, conduits and reservoirs for the manufacture of munitions or any purpose involving the safety of the United States; he might suspend the eight-hour day for persons engaged in work covered by government contracts; he might suspend or amend regulations governing radio and wire communications; he might direct preferences and priorities in transportation; he might requisition any American vessel, terminate charters of Maritime Commission vessels, suspend provisions relating to the citizenship of officers or crews, and regulate the movement of all vessels in territorial waters [Leuchtenburg 1963, pp. 305–306].

The president next negotiated a series of defense agreements that were highly questionable in view of the avowed neutrality policy. In August 1940, it was announced that the U. S. Navy would police the Canadian and American coasts, providing mutual defense to both nation's borders. Canadian seamen would, of course, be released by this action to aid the British Navy.

In April 1941, an agreement was reached with the Danish minister whereby Greenland would be protected by American military and naval personnel.

> Mr. Roosevelt was unconfiding to Congress on the Greenland situation. He did not favor Congress with a communication on the subject, however important it was in the strategy of defense for the Western Hemisphere. Congress could become informed only by the diligence of its members in reading the newspapers, or by the skill of its committees in questioning executive officers. Those members who enjoyed the confidence of knowledgeable persons in the Administration might through them gain further insights. But there was no formal contact between Mr. Roosevelt and Congress. It was kept completely in the dark, even after the agreement had been completed and whatever inhibitions of secrecy there may once have been were now removed [Koenig 1944, pp. 12–13].

By November 1941, an agreement had been reached with the Dutch government allowing American troops to occupy Dutch Guiana. "The President did not communicate with Congress concerning Dutch Guiana either before or after the occupation. The only illumination given by the President was contained in a White House Statement" [Koenig, pp. 26–27].

> The occupation of Iceland follows much the same pattern. It was facilitated by an agreement with the Danish minister at Washington which subsequently was disclaimed by the government in Denmark. The President acted without first consulting Congress. He did, however, make a report to Congress after the occupation had been completed. His action had been of tremendous importance. By sending American troops to the territory of a nation at war with Germany, the President had taken steps which were tantamount to placing the United States itself at war. Our troops were occupying territory which Germany might be expected to claim by force of arms [Koenig, pp. 46–47].

The prewar independence demonstrated by the Senate in urging an arms embargo diminished significantly as hostilities intensified and Congress considered the Lend-Lease Act. Compared to the earlier congressional posture, adoption of this law could be described accurately as a flip-flop. It authorized the president to exchange, sell, transfer, lease, lend, or otherwise provide any defense article to any country whose defense he determined essential to United States security.

Because our purpose here is to discuss the growth of the American presidency, and not the need in 1941 to assist the defense of Europe, I will not discuss the pros and cons of the act as foreign policy — it was an overwhelming success. More important for our discussion though, is what role the executive and Congress played in developing the act and implementing it. First, the act originated in the executive. It was written at the Treasury Department. The legislation was passed substantially as the executive wanted, and the president was given a free hand in its implementation. In short, the Congress made legitimate the policy presented to it by the executive and made modifications that, in comparison to the powers it granted, were modest.

Furthermore, the Congress had embarked on a pattern of legitimizing executive initiatives and granting executive blanket discretion in the conduct of the war. It did so in making Lend-Lease materials available to the Soviet Union in 1941; only a half-dozen representatives and senators knew the purpose of the appropriation that Congress passed to build the atomic bomb; the first legislative overhaul of the foreign service was undertaken at the behest of the State Department in legislation the department authored and that the Congress passed with minor changes. The pattern continued immediately after the war with the Truman Doctrine in 1947, the Marshall Plan in 1948, the Berlin airlift in 1948, the Vandenberg Resolution of 1948, and subsequent U. S. participation in the North Atlantic Treaty.

This list certainly is not inclusive, and exceptions to the pattern of executive initiative endorsed by Congress can surely be cited. In addition, it could be argued persuasively that the reason Congress so thoroughly accepted these executive proposals was their essential wisdom. Nonetheless, one cannot escape the disturbing conclusion that Congress had adopted a passive role for itself in the development of these major foreign policy initiatives, and in so doing abetted the impression that the presidency was the place to look for effective policy and programs.

THE COLD WAR

It is difficult to point to the time when most Americans began to feel that the postwar difficulties we faced with communism represented not just the threat of another war, but a vast fundamental and enduring conflict between the West and East, Democracy and Communism. But the "cold war," stretching from its first flashpoint in the 1948 Berlin airlift through the decision in 1964 to commit U. S. ground troops in Vietnam, represents the entrenchment of presidential dominance of foreign policy.

It has been argued that in the two major conflagrations — the decision to commit troops to Korea and Vietnam — the requisite speed in making the decision precluded thorough congressional involvement. The need to act with "dispatch," it has been argued, generally excludes the more "deliberative" body from active consultation and places the responsibility with the more responsive, decisive executive. I suggest, first that this belief, which was widely held by the end of World War II, became more of a justification on the part of the executive to ignore or bamboozle the Congress than an accurate description of the institutional imperative. It must also be said that a large portion of Congress believed it as well, with the result that Congress rarely took advantage of opportunities to act.

Though not the focus of American attention, for example, the appropriate committees of the Congress were well aware more than a year in advance of the Korean War that Korea was a trouble spot; the 38th-parallel division had been hastily drawn up at the end of World War II to facilitate Japanese surrender to U. S. and Soviet forces. It belabors the obvious here to say that a Congress, fulfilling an aggressive oversight role through its committees, would have been almost as aware of developments in Korea — at least on a month-to-month, and probably week-to-week basis — as the executive. Furthermore, it should be remembered that notification of the Communist invasion of South Korea came to official Washington on June 24, 1950, nearly six days before the decision was made to engage U. S. troops. In short, given the development of a national emergency, the Congress had time to assess the situation, and at a minimum, receive administrative proposals with a critical eye.

In fact, however, congressional leaders played no part in the preliminary decisions to deploy the Seventh Fleet to protect Formosa and to inhibit Formosa from attacking mainland China, nor did they play a role in the decision to accelerate American aid to the Philippines and to the French in Indochina. They were notified of the decision just moments before the press. And finally, when the president had made his decision to commit the U. S. to war, he summoned fifteen congressional leaders to the White House and announced his decision. It is reported that the Senate Floor Leader, Republican Senator Kenneth Wherry, said he thought Congress should have been consulted prior to ordering U. S. troops into action. President Truman, however, justified the decision by discussing the disastrous events of previous hours. As before, announcements of the president's decision were released to the press during the meeting.

Thus, though an active Congress might have played the role of constructive critic or ally, it acted to ratify a decision in which it had not participated. For the most part the Congress, like the nation, cheered the decision. In the House, members applauded as the ranking Republican on the Foreign Affairs Committee said, "We've got a rattlesnake by the tail and the sooner we pound its damn head in, the better." But by the summer of the next year the commander in the field, General MacArthur, said the war was at a stalemate, and by the 1952 elections, voters turned not to Congress but to another president for a solution.

In the literal sense, the Korean War — insofar as it bolstered executive power — remains today. The proclamation of national emergency by which President Truman summoned the nation to war and strengthened the armed forces, is still technically in existence. It has been used as recently as 1969, sometimes in conjunction with the emergency powers granted the President in 1933, to justify executive policy in international trade and commerce [Koenig, p. 47]. In short, the executive not only executes policy on the basis of statutes intended originally by Congress to have perished in the Great Depression, but also looks for justification in a proclamation of national emergency that ended almost two decades ago.

I shall make only one observation here concerning the growth of power of the executive as it related to our engagement in Vietnam. When President Johnson brought the Gulf of Tonkin Resolution before Congress, he, like President Truman, justified the speediest of action on the basis of imminent peril. A considerable amount of reliable information has surfaced subsequently that the imminent danger may well have been exaggerated, if not fabricated, in order to promote swift unquestioning support of what turned out to be a justification for protracted war. The question is raised whether a more thorough examination of the resolution by Congress would have foreclosed our defense options in Vietnam. To the contrary, considerable evidence suggests that a more probing Congress, a little less eager to endorse another executive initiative, might have prevented the resulting debacle.

THE PRESIDENTIAL APOGEE AND FALL: FOREIGN POLICY

It is my contention that the celebration of the presidency, which began in 1932, culminated in the early 1960s with the election of President John F. Kennedy and the first 100 days of the administration of President Lyndon B. Johnson. But largely because of two wholly unpredictable developments, the bubble of presidential apotheosis burst. First, full-scale involvement in Vietnam became a nightmare for millions of Americans, particularly liberal intellectuals — theretofore the biggest presidential boosters. Secondly, the abysmal failure of the Great Society to fulfill the expectations of its architects combined with Vietnam to force even the most committed advocate of increased presidential power to rethink his position.

As an important aside, it should be said that for the purpose of this analysis, it is only coincidental that the president we elected in 1960 was the personal embodiment, perhaps excessively so, of inspirational qualities — youth, grace, charm, and handsomeness.

It may be that these qualities allowed the light of the presidency to burn brightest at this point, but in the trend of this century it is a small matter. Similarly what I perceive to be the ebb of presidential power is not much affected by the negative perception of those qualities so often attributed to Presidents Johnson and Nixon. These factors surely affect voter perceptions, but in the century-wide scheme of presidential leadership, personality is a major factor only to the extent that it affects the participant's view of his office and its function.

What culminated in the early 1960s was the lionization of the institution of the presidency, compared to which individual idolatry of an individual president was secondary and derivative. Consider the conclusions reached by James MacGregor Burns in 1963, in his book, *The Deadlock of Democracy:*

> No political system is neutral — certainly not the congressional and presidential . . . . It is not by chance that liberal and internationalist Presidents in this century have been "strong" Presidents, and that men like Taft and Harding are relegated to the ranks of the weak. The stronger the exertion of presidential power, the more liberal and internationalist it will be because of the make-up and dynamics of the presidential party. The stronger the exertion of congressional power, the more conservative and isolationist will be our national policy because of the structure of the congressional forces [p. 264].*

Though I would surely agree with the premise that the presidential-congressional institutional imperative is anything but neutral, the internal logic of the above thought is baffling. The idea that "the stronger the exertion of presidential power, the more liberal and internationalist it will be," clearly implies a domestic and foreign policy dichotomy. It suggests that Presidents Theodore Roosevelt, Nixon, and perhaps Wilson, considered — at this level of generality — conservative influences in

---

*This and subsequent quotations from *The Deadlock of Democracy* by James MacGregor Burns, © 1963 by James MacGregor Burns and published by Prentice-Hall, Inc., Englewood Cliffs, New Jersey, reprinted with the permission of the author and publisher.

domestic policy but internationalist by any standard, are aberrations. Also it is a difficult prescription to apply to President Johnson whose foreign policy in Vietnam, it has been effectively argued, foreclosed opportunities for détente. It was isolationism, even if unwitting. Thus, if you consider Presidents Theodore Roosevelt, Wilson, Franklin Roosevelt, Truman, Kennedy, Johnson, and Nixon as the strong presidents of the twentieth century, there is reasonable doubt about whether four of the seven fit the Burns mold for strong presidents.

Furthermore, with regard to Congress, is it not possible that contrary to what Burns implies, a conservative influence — insofar as it represents restraint — might have been helpful in both Korea and Vietnam? To my mind at least it is possible, as I implied earlier, that in each case an observant Congress might have had a healthy restraining influence that might have averted or shortened two wars. I doubt that the pejorative term of isolationism, used above by Mr. Burns, could be applied to such a case.

Commenting upon still another foreign policy tragedy, Senator Jacob Javits has written:

> The Cuban affair was a prime illustration of the passive congressional role. Although there was substantial opinion in favor of toppling the Castro regime, the President considered the "cover" of the invasion's independent origins to be adequate excuse to go ahead with an armed attack against a neighboring state without congressional authorization. During the missile crisis period, President Kennedy asked Congress to resolve that he already possessed all necessary authority to use "whatever means may be necessary" to prevent Cuba from subverting its neighbors and to prevent the establishment of a Soviet naval base on Cuban soil. When Senator Richard Russell looked at the resolution, he remarked that "I do not believe that the Armed Services Committee is going to make a constitutional assertion that the President of the United States has the right to declare war, and that is what this does." The resolution was redrafted to state that the United States Government, rather than its President, would take the actions suggested by the Kennedy Administration. The difference may have been subtle but it was the first small sign that a reawakening of congressional assertiveness was on the horizon. While the awakening was indefinitely postponed by increasing domestic

turmoil and by the tragedy of John F. Kennedy's stunning and senseless assassination, Lyndon Johnson's Presidency brought it to full flower [1973, p. 257].*

Whether my objections to the Burn's thesis would pan out as important contradictions is less important really than the overwhelming impression he leaves that a strong president is preferable to a weak president and that a strong presidency is preferable to a strong Congress.

In his final chapter, "Strategy for Americans," Professor Burns recommends, in effect, the structural takeover of the federal government by a president capable of achieving what he called the "acme of leadership."

> The presidential leader must, in short, be more than a skillful manipulator or brilliant interpreter. He must be a constructive innovator, who can re-shape to some degree the constellation of political forces in which he operates. To reach the acme of leadership he must achieve a creative union of intellectual comprehension, strategic planning, and tactical skill, to a degree perhaps not paralleled since Jefferson [p. 338].

It was a theme echoed in many ways by politicians and intellectuals and historians. One who was all three, but who shall be nameless temporarily, gave the theme a novel twist. The president, he wrote,

> . . . was fully sensitive — perhaps oversensitive — to the limitations imposed by Congress on the presidential freedom of maneuver. But, though he was aware of the problem within the executive domain, I do not think he had entirely appreciated its magnitude. The textbooks had talked of three coordinate branches of government: the executive, the legislative, the judiciary. But with an activist President it became apparent that there was a fourth branch: the Presidency itself. And in pursuing his purposes, the President was likely to encounter almost as much resistance from the executive branch as from the others . . . .

This problem had assumed its contemporary dimensions after Franklin Roosevelt and the enlargement of government under the

---

*Reprinted from *Who Makes War: The President versus Congress* by Jacob K. Javits with the permission of the publisher, William Morrow and Company, Inc. © 1973.

New Deal. Roosevelt had quickly seen that he could not fight the depression through the Departments of Agriculture, Labor, Commerce and the Treasury (or later, fight the war through State, War and Navy.) He had therefore bypassed the traditional structure, resorting instead to the device of the emergency agency, set up outside the civil service and staffed from top to bottom by men who believed in New Deal policies . . . .

[The President] was determined to restore the personal character of the office and recover presidential control over the sprawling feudalism of government. This became a central theme of his administration and, in some respects, a central frustration. The presidential government, coming to Washington aglow with new ideas and a euphoric sense that it could not go wrong, promptly collided with the feudal barons of the permanent government, entrenched in their domains and fortified by their sense of proprietorship: and the permanent government, confronted by this invasion, began almost to function (with of course, many notable individual exceptions) as a resistance movement. . . .

Is this the work of the architect of President Nixon's super cabinet? Is this the work of those who advocated placing Nixon operatives in each of the agencies in order to ensure that White House policy became federal policy? No, it is not, even though it could even be a draft of the memoirs of Messrs. Haldeman and Ehrlichman. No, this is a passage taken from A Thousand Days [pp. 680-681],* and is the work of Arthur Schlesinger, Jr., whom I doubt would have advocated for President Nixon the same federal takeover he recommended for President Kennedy.

PRESIDENTIAL APOGEE AND FALL: DOMESTIC POLICY

Beyond foreign policy, the celebration of the presidency during the early 1960s was premised in part on the belief that only dynamic leadership from the Oval Office could break the

---

*Reprinted with the permission of the publisher from A Thousand Days by Arthur M. Schlesinger, Jr., published by Houghton Mifflin Company, © 1965.

domestic policy log-jam that gripped that nation after the Eisenhower decade. As the dust settled on the Eighty-ninth Congress, many believed this faith had been fully vindicated.

Under President Johnson's relentless prodding, the long-thwarted liberal domestic agenda had suddenly become the law of the land. In quick succession general aid to education, Medicare, a war on poverty, low-income housing assistance, model cities, an array of manpower-training programs, and a host of other measures designed to ameliorate the conditions of the disadvantaged had been adopted by Congress and implemented all across the nation. While few expected that these problems would be eradicated overnight, the confident belief that extensive government social intervention impelled by a powerful, activist president could transform the social order reigned supreme.

To be sure, it was the shock of a presidential war conducted by stealth and indirection that first punctured the liberal faith in an all-powerful first executive. But I think this rude awakening was compounded by the fact that before many years had elapsed it was apparent that the fruits of domestic presidential activism had soured as well.

- For nearly a decade the Federal government has poured more than $1 billion per year into the compensatory education program, yet we are now confronted with almost overwhelming evidence that these expenditures did next to nothing to close the achievement gap between the poor school children and their more affluent peers.

- The various housing programs launched with so much fanfare during the 1960s as America's belated vindication of the right of every citizen to a decent home have been unceremoniously set aside amidst general recognition of failure.

- Rather than solving the health care problems of the nation, it has been suggested by not a few economists that Medicare and Medicaid may actually have substantially contributed to our current dilemma of skyrocketing hospital costs.

- Finally, even those who conceived and launched the Office of Economic Opportunity's war on poverty have been less than enthusiastic about the results of their progeny.

To social scientists and public policy analysts the dismal failure of the Great Society suggests the limits of governmental social intervention and the intractability and unyielding nature of many of the problems it once so confidently addressed. But for students of the presidency, I think there is an even more important lesson to be drawn: namely, that the uncritical celebration of the Presidency during the early 1960s rested not so much on a principled analysis of the institutional structure of American government and the proper division of powers between the branches, as it did on an expedient judgment that an aggressive liberal Democratic president was the only vehicle by which a particular set of domestic policy ideas and programs could be implemented. When the superficiality and inadequacy of that set of policy prescriptions was revealed by failure in action, the tenuous rationale for a presidentially dominated government came crashing down with it.

CONCLUSIONS

Impact of Watergate

Without the exposure of the Watergate scandals I can imagine myself writing something like the following, "One cannot expect to correct overnight the imbalance between the contemporary executive and the Congress that has developed over the past three decades." In many respects, however, the Watergate scandals have ushered in a period of rapid adjustments. Not since the Civil War has the authority of the executive been so thoroughly scrutinized and its limitations so intensely emphasized. Moreover, individuals holding the highest positions of public office have been reminded harshly through criminal and impeachment proceedings of the legal limitations to their power.

As a result, it seems unlikely that future American presidents will exhibit, as did President Nixon and his aides, an underlying arrogance and insensitivity to the balance of separation of powers. It is also unlikely that Congress, which has begun to demonstrate a willingness to reassert its constitutional prerogatives, will reverse itself in the aftermath of Watergate. The exposure, investigation, and subsequent criminal and impeachment proceedings provided a powerful impetus for striking the balance between the executive and Congress that was intended by the Constitution.

Emergency Powers

Watergate has provided impetus for reforms that before had received little popular attention and support. This applies specifically to the presidential accumulation of emergency powers. The Ninety-third Congress formed a Special Committee on the Termination of National Emergency of the United States Senate. It was created to examine the consequences of terminating the declared states of emergency that now exist and give the president awesome discretionary powers. It has completed cataloguing for the first time the 470 federal provisions that fall into that category. A review of those provisions and legislation to reset the balance between presidential and congressional prerogatives is essential.

In 1973, for example, Congress overrode President Nixon's veto enacting the War Powers Resolution (P.L. 93–148), which asserts the constitutional authority of the legislative branch by establishing certain procedural requirements and checks upon Executive authority to commit U. S. troops to battle. Authority remains in effect (10 U.S.C. 712), however, for the president to detail armed forces to certain nations within the Western Hemisphere during a declared national emergency. This discretion would appear to be in conflict with the spirit of the War Powers law but nonetheless remains in statute. It is this type of provision which the Special Committee to Terminate the National Emergency was created to isolate and analyze. On the basis of the Special Committee's findings, the various standing committees of the Ninety-fourth Congress were scheduled to begin the essential reexamination of which provisions of emergency law should be eliminated, transferred to permanent status, or continued as standby emergency law.

The White House Bureaucracy

As a further example of responsible congressional reform, I cite two provisions I have introduced to the Ninety-third Congress — calling for the Senate confirmation of the Director of the Office of Management and Budget and the Executive Secretary of the National Security Council. As the presidential bureaucracy has grown, and as presidents have moved closer to the Schlesinger ideal quoted earlier, congressional access and input has diminished in proportion. The above reform proposals are ways in which the trend can be reversed, and offer an indication of what kinds of measures should be examined in order to assure the executive will be responsive to legitimate congressional inquiries and demands.

Institutional Shortcomings of Congress

There has been also a general recognition of institutional shortcomings of the Congress and steps have been taken to improve its informational resources and its analytical capabilities. The Legislative Reorganization Act of 1970 expanded the responsibilities of the General Accounting Office and the Congressional Research Service vis-à-vis Congress. The establishment of the Office of Technology Assessment (OTA) ought to improve the capabilities of the Congress to analyze the technical aspects of, for example, military procurement, and thereby directly enhance the ability of Congress to make decisions in the area of national security policy. The OTA also enters into research contracts with private firms, thereby pointing up the possibilities that exist for Congress to make considerably increased use of such private research in fields such as the evaluation of weapons systems, the assessment of the state of technology of alternate energy sources, the analysis of economic conditions as they may affect trade patterns, and so forth. Reform of the budgetary process, already under way, is essential.

Congress should also make use of data-gathering techniques, in particular computerized data, which is applicable in many fields. It is enough to say that congressional capabilities here are all but nonexistent.

Furthermore, it has been suggested that Congress establish a Foreign Policy Research and Analysis Institute of its own patterned after the Rand Corporation. Its staff would include experts from a large number of disciplines. Through such an institute we might well improve considerably our own response to national emergency situations. It is a pattern that executive power expands most, and most uncritically, in national emergencies. A healthy development would be a Congress that responds with complementary speed and efficiency.

Limitations

An implicit danger in this movement toward reform is that we as a Congress and a nation will overreact to the present disillusionment with the executive; that we will, as I said earlier, begin to distrust in the extreme what we earlier embraced in the extreme. We must guard ourselves against reacting like a betrayed lover, tending to reject reflexively what we previously accepted reflexively. It is a worry that I would not have harbored so seriously had it not been for Watergate. The diminution of presidential powers would have progressed at a much more orderly pace without Watergate, but now, I fear Watergate may push us to excess. It is a national imperative that we instead try to strike a balance between the reverential attitudes of the past and the danger now present of executive emasculation.

NOTES

1. For further detail on the executive and war emergency powers see Jacob K. Javits, *Who Makes War: The President versus Congress* (New York: William Morrow & Company, 1973), p. 300.

2. Price was a special assistant to the president and a staff member of the Domestic Council. Mr. Stans was then secretary of Commerce.

BIBLIOGRAPHY

Bishop, Joseph Bucklin. *Theodore Roosevelt and His Time*. New York: Charles Scribner's Sons, 1920.

Bonafede, Dom. "Ehrlichman Acts as Policy Broker in Nixon's Formalized Domestic Council." *National Journal* 3 (June 12, 1971):1240.

Burns, James MacGregor. *The Deadlock of Democracy*. Englewood Cliffs, N. J.: Prentice-Hall, 1963.

Hobbs, Edward H. *Behind the President*. Washington, D. C.: Public Affairs Press, 1954.

Javits, Jacob K. *Who Makes War: The President versus Congress*. New York: William Morrow & Company, 1973.

Koenig, Louis W. *The Presidency and the Crisis*. New York: King's Crown Press, 1944.

Leuchtenburg, William E. *Franklin D. Roosevelt and the New Deal*. New York: Harper & Row, 1963.

Locke, John. *Two Treatises of Civil Government*. London: J. M. Dent & Sons, 1924.

Milton, George Fort. *The Use of Presidential Power*. Boston: Little, Brown and Company, 1944.

Neustadt, Richard. *Presidential Power*. New York: John Wiley & Sons, 1960.

The New York Times, 20 March 1972.

President's Committee on Administrative Management. *Report of the Committee*. Washington, D. C.: Government Printing Office, 1937.

Robinson, James A. *Congress and Foreign Policy-Making*. Homewood, Illinois: The Dorsey Press, 1967.

Scharz, Jordan A. *The Interregnum of Despair.* Urbana: University of Illinois Press, 1970.

Schlesinger, Arthur M., Jr. *A Thousand Days.* Boston: Houghton Mifflin Company, 1965.

Sturm, Albert L. "Emergencies and the President." *Journal of Politics* 11 (February 1949):121.

Taft, William Howard. *Our Chief Magistrate and His Powers.* New York: Columbia University Press, 1916.

U. S. Congress, House. *Inaugural Addresses of the Presidents of United States from George Washington 1789 to Lyndon Baines Johnson 1965.* House Document No. 51, 89th Congress, 1st Sess., 1965.

U. S. Congress, House, Committee on Post Office and Civil Service. *A Report on the Growth of the Executive Office of the President.* Committee Print. Washington, D. C.: Government Printing Office, 1972.

Wann, A. J. *The President as Chief Administrator.* Washington, D.C.: Public Affairs Press, 1968.

8

A Democrat Looks at the Presidency

MORRIS K. UDALL
Member of Congress

M Y BASIC MESSAGE IS THAT THE presidency is in serious trouble. This country was built on optimism and faith. Yet, in recent years, many Americans have stopped believing in their government. This is a very dangerous trend.

I'll give you some examples:

I'm a Democrat. But if I were asked what was the single most important term added to the vocabulary by the Johnson administration, I would have to say it was the term "credibility gap." This is simply a polite way of saying that your government is lying to you.

Twice in 1973, the president of the United States went on national television to tell his fellow citizens that he was not involved in either the Watergate break-in or the subsequent cover-up. But the polls show that two-thirds of the public did not believe him.

In 1972, 45 percent of the adult-age American citizens did not vote. Of course, many of them didn't vote because our archaic registration laws shut them out. But a great number of people didn't vote simply because they felt that they didn't matter or they were turned off to government entirely.

Sadly I report, as a member of Congress, that a Gallup Poll a few years ago showed that the public rated public servants (or politicians) nineteenth out of twenty occupations on an index of trust, just above used car salesmen. They did a survey again recently and now we've switched places with the used car salesmen. We all joked about it, but it's serious.

I think it's time to analyze what's gone wrong, where we're going, and what we can do about it. Let's put the situation into focus first if we can.

CONGRESS, THE PRESIDENCY, AND THE FOUNDING FATHERS

Was the presidency always so powerful and dominating and, if not, how did it get that way? Was it congressional decline or a whole series of strong presidents?

To show you how much we've changed, about a hundred years ago Woodrow Wilson, then a scholar at Princeton, wrote a book entitled *Congressional Government*. His theme was that Congress dominated public life. He said the presidency was weak, that our government was run by congressional chairmen, the powerful barons of the House and the Senate.

I suspect that if Woodrow Wilson would come back to earth today as a scholar, he would have to write a book entitled *Presidential Government*. And yet, I believe our Founding Fathers originally intended for neither of these two branches to get the upper hand.

This idea of divided government is a unique contribution of Americans to political science.

If you were to tell the Harvard Business School, "We're going to start a new country on another planet. Devise us a government that's efficient," the last kind of government they would come up with would be one of divided powers. Efficiency demands a strong man in charge, one who can make decisions and have them carried out quickly. Any such design would stress centralized control and management.

But the Founding Fathers chose another model. They had all come from countries where kings and tyrants had started wars at their pleasure, seized property, and given scant attention to liberty. So they deliberately devised a system in which power was fragmented all over the place.

There were three separate branches. And the genius of the idea was that each branch would be able to check the others. Yet, despite this, the system would be efficient. The compensating factor was that it would promote liberty, and for nearly 200 years the idea has worked and worked very well.

The idea wasn't necessarily that we're supposed to have peace among the branches or that there wouldn't be confusion and a struggle for power. Emmett Hughes, author of *Ordeal of Power* [Atheneum, 1963], said recently that the executive, the legislative and the judicial branches of government were given mandates to "fight fairly, to fight openly and to fight forever." And so they have.

It all sounds kind of crazy and illogical, but somehow it works.

The result of this system has been something we tend to forget. We haven't always had dominant presidents.

Had you gone to Washington in the 1920s and asked a local bartender or cab driver — the oracles of wisdom in places like Washington — who were the five most important men in town, he might have gotten to Calvin Coolidge around number three, four, or five. The most important man in town was Nicholas Longworth, the Speaker of the House of Representatives.

And so it was through much of our history that the most powerful men in our government were the men in Congress. But two shattering events that took place back to back caused, or at least set off, the era of dominant presidents.

THE IMPERIAL PRESIDENCY

I remember the Depression dimly. The great free enterprise system, the most productive nation on earth with all its resources, was in ruin. We worry about 6 percent unemployment today, but in 1932 we had 33 percent unemployment. Half the factory capacity was idle and people were saying, "This system has failed." Socialism didn't really look too bad to a lot of Americans then.

So when Franklin Roosevelt came along fighting this terrible breakdown in our economic system, he asked for any power he wanted, and he got it. Political careers were made on the basis of who could rubber stamp Roosevelt's legislation the fastest.

An old colleague of mine who died a few years ago used to tell us how one night someone held up a piece of paper and said, "The President wants this new law on banking. All those in favor say 'aye.' " The bill was passed and sent down to the White House where the details were filled in by Roosevelt's brain trusters. I don't know if the tale is true, but this was certainly the spirit of the times.

Congress was reasserting its powers and beginning to make a comeback in the late 1930s when all of a sudden along came World War II. It was a shattering event. We were threatened by dictators who we thought were going to stamp out liberty all over the world. And so, if the President wanted battleships, or planes, or unlimited negotiating authority, then Congress gave him battleships, planes, and unlimited negotiating authority.

As a result, a whole generation of leaders grew up with the idea that it was unpatriotic to criticize the President on foreign policy. This continued into the cold war when we believed the Russians were the leaders of a worldwide Communist conspiracy that was going to do us in at any moment. For example, the entire foreign policy of John McCormack, a great and good man who served as majority leader and then speaker during the crucial decades of the 1940s, 1950s, and 1960s, was "support the President." He did not deem it his role in Congress to initiate the kind of foreign policy suggestions we are hearing today from leaders in the House and Senate.

It wasn't always like this. Almost 125 years ago during the

Mexican War, a Congressman by the name of Abe Lincoln criticized America's part in that conflict. Throughout our history it was not out of order or unpatriotic for a member of Congress to criticize the foreign policy or war policy of the president.

But World War II changed all that, and I think this hang-up in part led us into the quagmire of Vietnam and made it so difficult for us to get out. Vietnam, to some degree, shot down this attitude that somehow the president always knows best. But in the early days of the war, many Congressmen felt that if we were in Vietnam at the president's order then we were probably there for a good reason, and we had no right to question the decision.

Harold Ickes, the old curmudgeon who was secretary of the interior during the 1930s and 1940s, suggested that maybe we ought to be willing to distrust our presidents to some degree, to recognize that they're human beings. Ickes said the president is "neither an absolute monarch nor a descendant of the sun god."

During the days of Lyndon Johnson, a senator who had served with him made this comment: "It's a strange psychological phenomenon. When the President was in the Senate, nobody thought he was infallible. He was just another Senator. But he moves 16 blocks and you treat him as if he's infallible and has this private pipeline to God."

Of course that's the way it used to be in medieval times. We're not very far from the divine right of kings.

But the Founding Fathers didn't intend to create a position of imperial power. The man who holds the office of the president is simply the temporary first citizen of a republic, a democracy. He's not a monarch.

This reverence for the president's word is part of another current problem: the great growth of the entire White House operation.

I did a study in the heyday of Ehrlichman and Haldeman, and I discovered a strange thing. Every president in modern times came to power saying, "There are too many people in the White House. I'm going to rely on the cabinet departments. I'm going to get the best people and I'm going to have a tight little White House staff."

Yet everyone left the presidency with a much bigger White

House staff than they began with. Richard Nixon broke all records. He made a very good speech on the need for a small White
House staff in 1968, then surpassed all precedents for concentrating power in the White House.

Let me illustrate the size of the White House staff he built:

Before he became secretary of state, Henry Kissinger headed
the National Security Council. This was one little piece of the
White House operation — two or three percent of it — with assistants and special assistants and secretaries and limousines
and consultants and all kinds of task forces.

This small part of the White House operation had more
bodies than Franklin Roosevelt's total White House staff at the
height of World War II, including cooks, bakers, and gardeners.

It is not in the interest of the country to concentrate power in
the White House for several reasons. Yes, a powerful president
may be more efficient. But it's more important to enlist the consent of the governed, to work through the regular structures than
to have tightened power in the immediate White House establishment in the hands of anonymous assistants and special assistants.

I think this, along with the myth of presidential infallibility,
laid the foundation for the troubles we call Watergate.

This exaltation of the presidency leads to a lot of other serious problems as well. If, for example, the president is an all-
powerful, all-wise ruler, then one must further his programs at
all costs. A burglary becomes patriotism, and destroying material evidence in a criminal case is a positive duty. If he's infallible, he should be able to start wars, and those who oppose him
are always wrong somehow, despite the Constitution, which
says the war powers are vested in the Congress.

Another premise of this imperial presidency is that if the
president is a noble, larger than life-size power, then the career
civil service ought to get in line and do what he says it should
do. In Britain and other countries, the career civil service is a
protection against politicians doing things temporarily for some
kind of political advantage, and that's what our civil service
system is meant to be as well. But the idea of the imperial presidency has changed all that.

The Foreign Service, for example, was largely demoralized during the early Nixon years by the Kissinger takeover of powers that were meant to be in the State Department.

For years, the Bureau of Labor Statistics, an important professional economic wing of the government, put out a monthly consumer-price index. It has been so reliable and so professional that millions of dollars are paid out through labor contracts because of adjustments in the consumer-price index. It's been a thorn in the side of every president because the president will tell us optimistically that unemployment is going down and so is inflation and everything is lovely, and then the BLS comes out with its monthly report, and you find that the president has misled you.

Well, the BLS finally did this to Richard Nixon. So Haldeman and Ehrlichman fired some professional, respected veteran economists and, in effect, said to the others, "You've got to get on the team. You aren't giving figures in accordance with our game plan."

This cast a shadow throughout all other kinds of departments that are supposedly professional and nonpolitical.

Destruction of the Cabinet

An offshoot of the imperial presidency is the destruction of the role of the cabinet.

Before and through the Kennedy-Johnson era, cabinet members were men of national prestige and power. They could stand up to the president, and he'd be reluctant to fire them. Three of the eight original Kennedy-Johnson cabinet members were there at the end of the 8 years.

But only 5 years into the Nixon administration there was not a single member of the original cabinet left. One of the reasons, as I'm sure the former Nixon cabinet members will tell you when they write their memoirs, is that they were being ordered around by 28-year-old hotshots from the Haldeman-Ehrlichman shop.

As a matter of fact, I doubt that there are very many people who can remember how many cabinet positions there are, what the names of all the departments are, and who the individuals are who hold each of these cabinet positions. (I flunked this one myself.)

In my judgment, we are going to have to restore the cabinet and give the president some big men with national reputations who can say "no." And above all, the president is going to have to learn to listen to his cabinet members' advice and give it careful consideration, even if he ultimately rejects their proposals.

It was a sad commentary on the cabinet when former Interior Secretary Walter Hickel was sent back to Alaska for daring to suggest changes in presidential policy. And when former Secretary of State William Rogers criticized administration actions, it was viewed as a sure sign of his impending resignation.

Another dramatic example of the downgrading of the cabinet's role in recent years is the politicization of the Justice Department.

The Justice Department decides who will be prosecuted, whether indictments are to be quashed or carried through, whether ITT will be sued for antitrust, and who will be named federal judges. For most of our history this crucial office has been headed by lawyers of national reputation, judges, law school deans, great men who have earned respect in the bar or on the bench. The postmaster general might be a politician, but the attorney general was someone special. And then, starting in the 1950s, we broke that tradition.

Herbert Brownell, attorney general for President Eisenhower, is a good man and a good lawyer. Bobby Kennedy I loved and fought for, and I cried when he died. He worked for equality and made a good record in the cabinet. But neither of these men should have been attorney general. Both got the job because they had been political managers, and because of personal closeness to the president. Who can have confidence in decisions that have to be made on liberty, life, and prosecution when we have presidential political advisers in the attorney-general's office?

John Mitchell brought home to us all the dangers inherent in politicization of the Justice Department. We have seen the former attorney general of the United States indicted on several counts.

It has been alleged and admitted that a burglary was discussed in his office. Imagine, twice in his public chambers, the highest law enforcement officer in the land discussed the details of a proposed burglary of an opposition political party's office!

Now, he may have agreed to the burglary, or he may have said "don't do it and don't bring it up again" as he claims. But in either case, the fact is that these discussions were held.

I think the president has the right to have a friendly man as attorney general, a man who shares his broad philosophy. But the first priority of the Justice Department still must be justice. I don't think the American people have had that kind of confidence in the Justice Department in recent years.

Another problem with the cabinet is its size. Now John Ehrlichman was right on a couple of things — although he was wrong on most — and one thing about which he was right was the need to streamline the cabinet.

We started out with only five or six cabinet offices, and for a very good reason. There is a basic principle in complicated human affairs that no man can supervise closely on a daily basis more than four or five people. That's why the military has G-1 through G-4, and a well-run company has five vice presidents and not twenty-five. If you go beyond five, you start getting super vice presidents who supervise other vice presidents.

We've always had this pressure to increase the size of the cabinet and it's still going on today. There are people who want a separate Department of Health or a separate Department of Education. There's a proposal for a Department of Peace and a Department of Energy. Every year there are more and more proposals.

John Ehrlichman tried to organize the cabinet into a few compact, comprehensive sections, each answerable to one man. It had become obvious to him that the number of cabinet departments had gone past that magic controllable number.

The changing role of the cabinet and the increasing power of the presidency have raised another problem — the question of executive privilege. You can't find executive privilege in the Constitution or the statutes. It's a custom, and it makes sense within the limits of what was really intended.

Each of the three branches of government is entitled to an area of privacy. The president has no right to come to my office and rummage through my files and ask my secretary about that memo discussing why I voted "yes" yesterday instead of "no," or what I'm planning to do about his favorite bill that he sent up last week. And I have no right to go to the White House and demand access to those advisors to the President with whom he's frankly discussed his alternatives.

Neither of us has the right to go to the Supreme Court and cross-examine a justice or his secretary about how the first draft of an opinion differed from the second draft. There's an area of privacy that each branch has with regard to the confidential operations of that branch.

The corollary of that principle, however, is that the men who make policies and carry out policies in the executive branch are supposed to be available to Congress. This is because Congress is the people's representative in the formulation of executive policies, and it must also legislate related policies of its own. And so the men who advise the president and who are supposed to carry out his policies, including those in the cabinet, can never refuse to come to a congressional committee hearing.

But then we had the case of Ehrlichman and Haldeman, and Kissinger, and dozens of other people of whom you've never heard who were actually making and carrying out more policy than cabinet members, and yet these men were drawing the cloak of executive privilege around them. As a result, Congress couldn't do its job under the system of divided powers.

In testimony before Congress, my fellow Arizonan and former Attorney General Dick Kleindienst said "executive privilege" covers the whole executive branch. Taken to its logical conclusion, this would mean that the postmaster of Muleshoe, Texas, on vacation in California and witness to a murder on the beach, could say "executive privilege" and refuse to testify. Kleindienst said that although he didn't think the president would do that kind of thing, still, in theory, there is no limit to executive privilege. I say this is nonsense. The three contending branches are going to have to get together and define the limits of this much-abused tradition, a process only partially begun in the case of the United States v. Nixon (1974) when the

U. S. Supreme Court limited executive privilege to areas unrelated to criminal prosecution.

Irony of Presidential Office-Seekers

Another mistake has been the idea that the president bears an awesome burden. You see the picture of the lonely chief executive in that Oval Office crushed down by burdens. And yet, no one thrust this office on Richard Nixon or tried to push it on George McGovern. In fact, I distinctly remember both of them traveling far and wide across the country for many years trying to get that awesome burden on their backs.

They're human beings, your presidents. Believe me, they're working, sweating politicians who have been graced by office, not the reverse. They are not pressed into service involuntarily. As a matter of fact, they have been known to pursue this awesome burden rather vigorously and hold onto it with a vengeance.

Now I'll grant you that not everyone is going to give a straight answer to the president on uncomfortable subjects. But I feel that in the long run the isolation of the presidency is pretty much controlled by the person in office. And I daresay President Nixon did little to dispute this.

I remember reading the report of a terrified observer who had been at a White House state dinner. He said Nixon didn't come down and mingle with guests as you might in your own home. Instead, here was all the military resplendent in uniforms; at the proper moment the band sounded the martial music and down the stairs in lock-step came the President and Mrs. Nixon, in marching cadence, into the East Room where everyone lined up to greet them.

QUICK FIXES AND REAL SOLUTIONS

I've painted a rather dismal picture of what's wrong. I would like to suggest some solutions, but first, one nonsolution.

Americans like easy solutions. I think we've gotten into trouble with the environment and our energy supplies because we worship technology, and technology can always give you a "quick fix." We are running out of quick fixes in technology and in the environment.

And so, with the presidency in trouble, we see the quick-fix people saying, "The answer is to give us a six-year term. Let a president be elected, put politics behind him, and for six years he can carry out the will of the people and do the unpopular things and do what is right."

I'm surprised that some distinguished men, such as Senators Mike Mansfield (D., Mont.) and George Aiken (R., Vt.) have pushed hard for this idea. In my judgment, it would be a disaster. The idea simply would not work.

I think we should reject the idea that we need a nonpolitical president, or a nonpolitical governor, or a nonpolitical congressman. I think some of the key things Richard Nixon did that history will honor him for were done only because he was facing the 1972 election.

I question whether he would have found a way to end the war in Vietnam or started talking with the Russians and Chinese if he weren't facing an election in 1972. I know he wouldn't have started his economic program in August 1971, if it weren't for the upcoming election. The program violated everything he had ever talked about.

Clark Clifford, top adviser to several Democratic presidents, once said, "A president immunized from political consideration is a president who need not listen to people, respond to majority sentiment or pay attention to the views that may be diverse, intense and perhaps in variance with his own." The idea of a president who is above politics, in my judgment, is hostile to the genius of democracy.

Many American mothers want their sons to grow up to be presidents like Jefferson and Lincoln, but they don't want them to become politicians in the process. Well, Lincoln was a success as a statesman because he was a politician. He went to Gettysburg, not to give a speech that we could all memorize in the fifth grade a hundred years later, but because some governors were going to be there, and he wanted to be able to talk to them in privacy and get some support for his policies.

We put down our politicians in this country, and we make jokes about them. My favorite is the one about a politician who made a speech to a little group in a small town. "Now ladies and gentlemen," he said, "thems my views, and if you don't like 'em, well then I'll change 'em."

And of course everybody laughs, and it is a cynical story. But the job of a politician is to find a majority, to build that majority, and to lead people forward together. And if he has to adapt and change his policies to do it, then, within the limits of his own honesty and integrity, he does this.

I make this point to suggest that you are not going to have a democracy if you think somehow you can put the president or your public officials above politics. That's a nonsolution. Now, here are some things we can do that I favor.

Congress has begun to regain its war powers with enactment of the War Powers Act. It's ironic that we in Congress should have had to enact a law to get back one power that everyone agrees the Constitution gives to us. To examine budgets, the Budget Reform Act of 1974 provides Congress with a mechanism to look at the large range of priorities and counter the president in this regard.

I think we also have got to insist that the president not isolate himself, so he can expose himself to the ideas of some people of political experience.

I remember the story of Sam Rayburn, the long-time Speaker of the House, watching as John Kennedy came to the White House with all of his glitter and glamour. Someone said to Rayburn, "Isn't it impressive? Look at the brilliant men Kennedy has brought to Washington — Schlesinger and Sorenson and McNamara and Galbraith." And Rayburn said, "Yeah, that may be true, but I'd feel a heck of a lot better if a couple of them had ever run for sheriff."

That was the trouble with Haldeman and Ehrlichman too. Neither of them had ever run for sheriff.

We have to restore a measure of humility to the presidency. Someone tells the story of how Thomas Jefferson took the oath of office, went back to his boarding house for dinner, and found the dining room full. So he stood there a while until one boarder finally finished. The new president took his place at the table, ate his dinner, and went to bed. Jefferson was a powerful president, but he knew he was a human being and not a god.

Today, the president of the United States doesn't have to go to a boarding house. He can have anything he wants to eat at any time, and all of those helicopters and jet planes can take him anywhere he wants to eat at any time.

I've also been personally skeptical about loner presidents who have no cronies and close friends and who never go back-packing or mountain-climbing, or play poker or golf, or walk the beach. I think maybe we'd be better off to have presidents who aren't so intense and who don't work 24 hours a day. Anyone who works that hard will lose his perspective.

And I say deliver us from presidents who can't laugh at themselves or their troubles. I remember Franklin Roosevelt used to have great fun telling stories on himself. One of his favorites was the one about the Wall Street tycoon who hated him because he had changed the economic system.

It seems one of these tycoons would get to Wall Street each day, buy a newspaper from a particular boy for five cents, read only the front page, curse, and throw it into the trash can.

After a week, the boy said, "Sir, why do you waste money to buy a paper, read only the front page and then throw it away?"

The tycoon said, "Son, it's not really any of your business but the fact is I'm looking for an obituary."

The boy said, "But sir, the obituaries aren't on the front page. Try the back of the paper."

"Son," he replied, "believe me. The obituary I'm looking for will be on the front page."

Presidents used to go to gridiron shows where they were roasted, where jokes were told, and fun was poked.

But President Nixon refused to attend nearly all the gridiron shows and radio-TV correspondents' dinners, and all of the other traditional things that say, "I'm human and I'm just a temporary president. I'm one of you and I can take a needle now and then."

Along the same line of thought, I believe the presidency must be put back in touch with the people. President Nixon's problems were compounded by his tendency to isolate himself from the press, from other elected office-holders, and from wide-ranging contacts with businessmen, educators, and other groups.

It's pretty heady stuff to have a band play whenever you walk into the room and to have a mansion and its staff at your disposal. But the one thing that doesn't come with the job and yet is desperately needed is what mayors and congressmen and governors get every day — exposure to people who aren't afraid to criticize or offer frank advice.

I realize that presidential safety measures must be far more stringent than they were in the days when Lincoln could ride his horse through Washington or when Teddy Roosevelt could jog in Rock Creek Park. Maybe it's just not feasible for our president, along with the rest of us, to walk the street now and then, to try and catch a cab at rush hour, or to get caught in a holding pattern over Chicago's O'Hare Airport on a stormy day.

But even if that's the case, at least we could urge presidential candidates to promise regular press conferences and open doors for congressional leaders, governors, and lots of ordinary, plain-speaking citizens.

I don't want to suggest by anything I've said here that a strong measure of respect and reverence for our presidents is bad. Indeed, this is one of the unifying factors in our country's history. It's an unusual factor. In most countries, the first impulse of the citizens is to chop up their leaders, cut them down, give them trouble, throw them out. This is a year-round sport in many countries.

I think what we really need is a balance. We need to put an end to the reverential treatment of the president of the United States, this unquestioning acceptance. But we need to reaffirm our respect for the *office* and the unifying factor that it has been.

Those who simply advocate a strong presidency have given up on the idea of three balancing and checking branches of government in the name of efficiency. They would continue the way things have been going in recent years.

What we need is balance — balance for the president and balance for the other two branches.

One way to strengthen that balance would be to make an

adjustment in our procedure for impeachment. Through all of the recent furor, I have been made aware of the need for a refinement in our procedures for dealing with the problems of a crippled presidency. Most of us in Congress are against tinkering with the basics of our system. In fact, there have been only twenty-six amendments to the Constitution to fill in some of the cracks in the law. But I think we need to take a serious look at some intermediate remedy between the extreme, blunt, divisive instrument of impeachment on the one hand and the problem of a crippled, powerless incumbent under a cloud of suspicion on the other.

I have introduced, along with several cosponsors, a bill that borrows an intermediate procedure from the parliamentary system. It says that if two-thirds of the House and Senate at any time vote "no confidence" in the president because of basic violations of the president's duty to faithfully execute the laws, or violations of the rights of citizens, then we would hold a special election within 90 days.

The incumbent president and vice president could run for reelection. The process is not like impeachment, in which a president is convicted, disgraced, and run out of office. Instead, the president is not convicted or affected in any way. He has simply received a vote of no confidence much as occurs in other systems.

I think we could keep the 4-year term and yet have this option that would help us to avoid situations like impeachment.

Voting for impeachment requires substantial evidence and not a question of what my suspicions are about a president. I just don't want to take so harsh an action without evidence. However, in some situations I could vote with no hesitation for a resolution of no confidence and then ask the people to decide what would be best for the nation.

I have talked a lot about laws and constitutions and structural reforms. These things are important, but none of them will really help in the final analysis.

The thing we've got to do in this country is restore the spirit of civility, restraint, and mutual trust, the spirit that distinguishes between a political adversary and a real enemy.

Some of my closest friends are men like Barry Goldwater. He's a member of another political party, and I don't agree with him very often, anymore than I agree with Senator Thurmond. But we're friends, and I have more in common with him than with a businessman who wouldn't touch politics with a 10-foot pole.

Our system works because of this civility and restraint and trust, because you go through the rituals, you congratulate your opponent on election night when he's clobbered you and you'd rather go off in a corner and cry, or consume some stimulating beverages.

We need to rededicate ourselves to the importance and decency of political life. This way we'll strengthen the presidency and bring it back into balance where it ought to be.

A long time ago, Judge Learned Hand, one of my favorite jurists, put it this way:

> I often wonder whether we do not rest our hopes too much upon constitutions, upon laws and upon courts. These are false hopes. Believe me, these are false hopes. Liberty lies in the hearts of men and women. When it dies there, no constitution, no law, no court can save it. No constitution, no law, no court can even do much to help it. While it lies there it needs no constitution, no law, no courts to save it.

V ☆ THE PRESS

An adversary relationship exists between the president and the press because of their differing objectives. For the president, the paramount goal is to *advocate* a particular *goal* to be achieved, while the press has the duty to *report reality* by chronicling events and placing them in perspective. Here, David Broder offers several suggestions to improve presidential-press relationships and to enhance public understanding of the presidency. A novel and easily implemented suggestion of Broder's is that when a candidate announces for the presidency, the press should obtain a promise from the candidate that in exchange for press coverage of the campaign the candidate will meet with the press for at least one-half hour per week.

David Broder, *The Washington Post* columnist and 1973 Pulitzer Prize winner for political commentary, has been a Fellow at the Harvard University Institute of Government. He appears regularly on television network interview programs and has written two books, *The Republican Establishment* and *The Party's Over*.

9

The Presidency and the Press

DAVID S. BRODER
The Washington Post

PRESIDENTS ALWAYS THINK THEY ARE misunderstood. Those of us in the press know we are misunderstood. Beyond that, there is little one can say with certainty about the relationship of the presidency and the press.

In preparing this essay, I became aware of two dangers in this topic. One is the temptation simply to wade into all of the particulars of the disputes occupying us in Washington, many of which pit the president against the press. That turns the focus on the relationship between this press corps and ex-president Nixon.

The other danger is somewhat at the opposite extreme. It is to rely on quotations from others who have written about this topic. A great deal that is sensible has been said about the relationship between the press and the president, and one could do worse than simply to summarize that commentary.

But I want to try to steer a middle course if I can, borrowing some quotations from others and alluding to some of the current controversies, but also trying to look at the subject from a somewhat broader perspective and to frame the observations from my own experience.

ROLE OF PRESIDENT

First, we have to discuss the role of the president. This is a period of revision in the understanding of that great office. The popular and scholarly literature of at least the last 40 years has described the president not only as the chief administrator but as the chief legislator, chief diplomat, chief politician, and chief national symbol. The power of the office has grown, as has our appreciation and understanding of its weight and significance.

But in the last 10 years — with the Vietnam war and Watergate — the focus has shifted to strategies for reducing the power and the significance of the presidential office. A great many voices are saying the presidency needs to be reduced, restricted, or somehow repositioned in a smaller role inside the American government and political system. Others argue that such a reversal of past trends is impractical or undesirable.

The issues in that debate are at the heart of this book. What I would observe as important for this discussion is that wherever else they may differ, the participants in this debate accept, either implicitly or explicitly, that the president will be the communicator in chief of the country.

That is not a new notion. Theodore Roosevelt talked about the presidency as a "bully pulpit," and Walter Lippmann wrote in 1941, in language characteristic of the "great presidency" view, that

> ... in this tremendous time the American people must look to their President for leadership. Only the President, because he is the chief executive is in a position to know all the facts. Only the President and his advisors are in a position to weigh all the facts; therefore, the President alone can lead the country. It is impossible for the

country to lead the President, yet policy of the government must rest on the support of the nation. So the nation must first be informed and always be dealt with squarely.

The President of the United States cannot administer the whole affairs of the nation, and if he attempts to do these things, he will never have the time or the nervous energy or the physical strength to do well the great things a President must do: to anticipate the future, to determine the great issues of policy, to select the right men to execute those policies, and never to cease explaining to the people, directly and publicly, and also privately and continually through their chosen leaders, what the government is doing and why [1963, pp. 267–268].*

If the rhetoric were muted somewhat, Lippmann's view would seem to me to be valid even today. There is no substitute for the president in this critical function of focusing public attention on those parts of the national agenda that the president thinks are most deserving of attention; of defining the choices that we face in policy areas; of outlining the costs and benefits of various strategies; and then of mobilizing public support, as well as governmental energy, for the course of action that recommends itself.

There is a variety of ways in which the president can fulfill his role as communicator in chief, including his activities as a party leader, a legislative leader, and a leader of the administration. But before looking at those presidential roles, we need to say something about the press, noting for now only that in his role as communicator in chief, the president is simultaneously a subject for coverage by the press, a colleague of the press, and a rival of the press.

ROLE OF PRESS

Now, the role of the press in a democracy is obviously "to inform." But that is a cliché. How does the press inform? In times past, I think, aspiring reporters in journalism schools were

---

*Reprinted with the permission of Louis S. Auchincloss for Walter Lippmann from *The Essential Lippmann*, published by Random House, 1963.

told that their job was to "hold up a mirror to reality," to serve as a proxy for the person unable to be present at some event, and to transmit to that person the impressions, the words, and the actions that person would have seen if he had found it convenient to be present himself.

I must say to you in fairly blunt terms that my experience as a journalist leads me to believe that that concept of journalism is really nonsense. The New York Times, the flagship of our business, prints on its front page every morning the wonderful slogan, "All the news that's fit to print." It is a brilliant slogan, and it is also a complete fraud. If honesty in labeling applied to newspapers, the Times would long ago have been forced to remove that slogan from its front page.

The reason it is a fraud is that neither The New York Times nor The Washington Post, nor any other newspaper has space in its news columns on any given day to summarize all of the events that occur, or all the words that are spoken, in the city of Washington that are of significance to some of its readers — let alone the events in all the other capitals around the world where correspondents are at work.

The basic work of every journalist is deciding what to leave out. Whether you are talking about the individual reporter, or the editor of the Times or the Post, or any of the network news shows, the essential struggle for each of them is how to compress those millions of words, those thousands of events that occur daily, into the available limits of space and time.

Selectivity is the essence of modern journalism. We cannot "hold up a mirror to reality" — not because that is an unworthy goal — because there is no mirror large enough to catch the complex reality of today's political world. If selectivity is the essence of modern journalism, then it follows that journalists must apply some set of values and criteria in selecting the portions of reality they observe that they think most significant and relevant for their readers to understand.

Thus, while there can be — and in my view, must be — standards of professional balance, honesty, and fairness used to judge the work of journalists, the much-sought goal of "objective" or "neutral" journalism is impossible of attainment. No two people, surveying a mass of facts, would select the same set of facts from the mass as being most significant, or display them in exactly the same way.

PRESIDENCY AND PRESS IN CONFLICT

If this is true of journalism as a whole, it is also true of the way in which the press relates to a president. When we are talking about the reporters covering the White House, we are not talking about a group of automatons, value-free individuals performing the strictly mechanical function of recording the words and actions of a president who is — and who must be — consciously aware of the values, goals, and strategies that determine his own actions.

The president, as communicator in chief to a vast republic, must present himself and his purposes through (or around) a press corps whose members hold values of their own, which do not necessarily coincide with his.

That there is potentially and actually a conflict of values between president and press is a proposition that few would dispute. Serious debate begins only when you ask, "What is the nature of that clash of values?"

At this point, I think it is useful to quote from Patrick Buchanan, the former editorial writer for the St. Louis Globe-Democrat who joined Mr. Nixon's staff two years before the 1968 presidential campaign and was the Nixon administration's communications strategist. He has had supervisory responsibility for the daily news summary that went to the president, and he was the principal contributor of the ideas and the language of both President Nixon's and Vice President Agnew's critiques of the press.

Buchanan has a very specific view of the value system of the press, which he outlined in a little book called The New Majority. In it, Buchanan asserts that

> ... an incumbent elite with an ideological slant unshared by the nation's majority has acquired absolute control of the most powerful medium of communication known to man. And that elite is

using that medium monopoly to discredit those with whom it disagrees and to advance its own ideological objectives and is defending that monopoly by beating its several critics over the head with a stick of the First Amendment.

Within the media, many will readily concede this bias and retort, "What else is new?" What is new is not the existence of the liberal bias. What is new in the last decade is the wedding of that bias to unprecedented power. Men who are taking an increasingly adversary stance toward the social and political values, mores and traditions of the majority of Americans have also achieved monopoly control of the medium of communication upon which 60 percent of these Americans depend as the primary source of news and information about their government and society. And these men are using that monopoly position to persuade the nation to share their distrust of and hostility toward the elected government [1973, p. 18].

Now, the Buchanan thesis, in my view, is wrong both in specific and general terms, and is historically inaccurate.

Why do I say that? It is worth recalling the dispute that triggered the Administration's denunciation of the press — particularly, the television networks.

The chapter of Buchanan's book from which I have quoted begins with a reference to the television speech Mr. Nixon gave in the fall of 1969, following the Vietnam moratorium demonstration. It was the speech in which he first invoked the power of "the silent majority" on behalf of his Vietnam policies. Buchanan then goes on to quote the speech he wrote for then Vice-President Spiro Agnew, the famous Des Moines speech in which Agnew attacked the "nattering nabobs of negativism." Agnew's complaint — and Buchanan's — was centered on the way the television networks handled the commentary on Mr. Nixon's address, and particularly on their use of former Ambassador W. Averell Harriman, a Democrat, as a commentator on one of the networks.

Buchanan says that "the reaction of Mr. Harriman, like that of the network analysts, to the President's address was doubt, disappointment and disagreement. They did little to disguise their hostility" [p. 21].

Now, I mention that only because the evidence for that charge is worth examining. You can do so rather easily because another of the president's men, James Keogh, who became director of the U. S. Information Agency, has usefully appended to his book, *President Nixon and the Press*, the text of the president's speech, the network commentaries, and the Agnew speeches criticizing the networks.

Let me quote some of Harriman's words from the interview with John Scali (then of ABC and later Mr. Nixon's ambassador to the United Nations) that apparently gave such offense:

Scali: . . . Do you think that the "silent majority" in the United States will rally behind the President as a result of his speech?

Harriman: I don't know if it's a silent majority or not . . . .

Scali: Well, do you think . . .

Harriman: . . . . or if it's a silent minority. I just don't know . . . . I think he's got the full support of the people. He certainly has my support in his hopes — in hoping that he will develop a program for peace. But I think we've gone so far in Vietnam that this has to be discussed. It can't be accepted without a lot more explanation. And it seems to me that the Senate Foreign Relations Committee would be a very fine place for that discussion.

Scali: I gather then, Governor, that you were somewhat disappointed with the President's approach?

Harriman: Well, I wouldn't say that I was disappointed. I was not surprised, because this was about what I thought that he would say from the positions that he'd previously taken. And he's followed the advice of many people who believe this, many people who advised President Johnson. It wasn't successful, and I don't know — I'm not sure that this advice will be successful in the future . . . . There are so many things that we've got to know about this. But I want to end by saying that I wish the President well. I hope that he can lead us to peace. But this is not the whole story that we've heard tonight" [1972, p. 176].*

---

*Reprinted by permission of the American Broadcasting Company (ABC).

Now, that does not strike me as being a particularly vicious, free-swinging, or vigorous attack on the president, but it was on the frail foundation of this particular incident that the whole case of press bias against President Nixon was built.

As the case is weak in its particulars, so it is weak in its general terms. There simply is no reason to believe that the Washington press corps — or a majority of its leading members — was hostile to the objectives enunciated by the Nixon administration. In the area of foreign policy, if one can postulate that the major goals of the Nixon presidency were extraction of the United States from the Indochina fighting without toppling the security of the independent governments of those lands; normalizing relations with Moscow and Peking, and ending the psychology of the cold war; redistributing the burden of international security more equitably among the western nations; and helping secure peace in the Middle East — then I would say they were enthusiastically endorsed by virtually every reporter I know.

On the domestic side, there was, predictably, more disagreement, but I think a substantial majority of the Washington reporters, after their experiences with the bureaucracy, were sympathetic to Mr. Nixon's goals of decentralizing domestic programs, returning power and revenues to state and local governments, and overhauling the operations of the executive branch.

About the main items on his agenda, there was remarkably little conflict. The conflict arose, as it always does, when the press began to measure the inevitable gap between promise and performance, between rhetoric and reality.

And here, again, I want to quote the views of an observer from an earlier period, who more accurately than Buchanan, in my view, defined the recurring conflict between the presidency and the press.

George Reedy, press secretary to Lyndon Johnson, wrote that

> ... a political leader is essentially an advocate, a man who is seeking to shape the world toward the ends he considers worthy. A newspaperman, on the other hand, is one whose job is to

chronicle daily events and to place the facts before the public in some reasonable perspective. Events and facts have a life of their own. They are independent of the dreams and desires of men. On that basis, it is obvious that there must be a divergence of viewpoints between the political leader who assesses public communications in terms of help or hindrance toward a worthy goal, and the newspaperman who assesses public communications in terms of their consonance with what he regards as reality, however harsh. A democratic society is inconceivable without tension and the objective reporting that democracy requires will always produce tension. I might add that I do not think our country has ever been hurt by a skeptical and rambunctious newspaperman [quoted in Reston 1967, pp. 58–59].

From the viewpoint of the White House, the press must always, I suppose, seem "skeptical and rambunctious." That is not because the press is always opposed to the president's purposes; on the contrary, more often than not reporters share in, and reflect, the currents of public opinion that are reflected in "the making of a president." The rambunctiousness of the press stems from its habit of skepticism about anyone's rhetoric — even a president's. When a "law and order" administration like Richard Nixon's was embarrassed by press disclosures of its own lawlessness, it was not because the press was — as Buchanan would have it — out to overthrow this particular president.

The press was behaving no differently than it did when it insisted on looking behind the slogan of Lyndon Johnson's "war on poverty," and asking, much to Johnson's annoyance, how much of the billions was going to the poor and how much to a new bureaucracy; how much of the effort was directed at organizing the poor for their own causes and how much toward entrenching the Democratic city machines.

Even John Kennedy, whose press relations are now looked back on as some sort of golden age of harmony, was not immune from this treatment. In a very tough column, written shortly before Kennedy's death, James Reston of The New York Times said, "He plays touch politics and does not tackle the tough issues."

The point of this recital — which could be extended back to Jefferson's time — is that the complaints of Buchanan, Agnew, and other Nixon administration spokesmen showed a remarkable lack of historical perspective. The relationship of the press to a president is, and necessarily must be, one of tension. Any good politician who is worth his salt will know that he must try to manage the news. An activist president will try to manage the news on the broadest scale of any politician, because his purposes are the largest. The only modern president with genuinely tranquil press relations was Dwight Eisenhower, who was also the least activist president of modern times. The president must try to shape the news, and journalists, covering him, must resist. There is a built-in conflict in this situation.

PRESIDENTIAL ADVANTAGES

What is important to note at this point is that, of all the actors in the political drama, none has greater advantage in the struggle to shape the news and public opinion than the president of the United States. Again, I want to cite, not a contemporary source influenced by the current dispute, but the observations of James Reston in 1967, when a Democratic president of liberal bent was in the White House. Reston said,

> I believe the power of the presidency has been increasing steadily since World War II, particularly since the introduction of nuclear weapons, and that the power of the press and even of Congress to restrain the Chief Executive has declined proportionately during that period. Almost all the scientific and political trends are enhancing the power of the President more than they are increasing the power of the Congress or the press. No sovereign in history ever had such power or responsibility. Modern communications extend the reach and influence of reporters everywhere, but not so much as they expand the power of the President [pp. 45–46].*

That is particularly the case when you think about the prime medium of political communication today, television. Televi-

---

*Reprinted from James Reston's *The Artillery of the Press*, 1967, with the permission of the publisher. Harper & Row.

sion is a personal medium, and no person looms so large on the television screens as the president. No one else can summon the cameras of all the networks simultaneously, in a setting and at a time of his own choosing, to address the massive national audience that the president can command; no one else has so great an ability to keep the cameras turned off or at a distance when he does not want them. Because the president is the communicator in chief, and his full use of the prime medium of communication is in the national interest, few journalists would ever want to deny a president that unlimited access to television.

RECTIFYING THE IMBALANCE

But there is an imbalance in what Newton Minow has called "presidential television" [1973] that is of concern to journalists and others in the political system. Only rarely in our history is there a Watergate situation, in which a president finds his critics, night after night, dominating the television news shows. That simply does not happen very often to a modern president. Normally, opposition and critical views have much more difficulty getting access to television. Personally, I would like very much to see a provision of law that guarantees the opposition — preferably as designated by the leadership of the opposition political party — some guaranteed access to television. That right of access has so far been denied, as a matter of law, by the Federal Communications Commission and the courts.

It would seem to me desirable to seek a better balance in television debate by providing for a three-way mechanism of discussion, instead of the one-way communication channel that now operates for the president. I think this can be done without, in any way, discouraging the use of television by a president.

What I have in mind is an extension of equivalent time to spokesmen for differing views — again, in my view, preferably those designated by the other political party — whenever the president takes over television to present his views on a public issue.

The third leg of the triangle — as valuable as the other

two — is the acceptance by the president and the opposition spokesmen of an obligation to participate in televised press conferences, where both may be questioned on the issue.

Mention of the press conference brings me to the final topic I want to discuss. There are many shortcomings in the modern presidential press conference, ranging from showboating by reporters to disconnected, confusing questioning. But most, if not all, the faults of the press conference can be corrected automatically if the president meets with the press frequently enough.

It is quite true that an able president will always be able to dominate a press conference. But this in itself is quite proper. It is, after all, a communications device, not a way of showing up a president. What is valuable and important about the press conference is that the president is not in total control. He does not set the agenda. The questions asked are those the reporters want answered, not those the president is disposed to answer. It is a way — an important way — of confronting him with problems that may not be on his agenda at that moment, but which perhaps should be.

The press conference is a way of bypassing the president's staff, and opening the White House and the president to non-programmed items. The press conference actually functioned that way in the Eisenhower and Kennedy years. I can recall members of Congress or agency officials calling and saying, "If you have a chance, would you ask the president about such and such." The answers to those questions gave direct policy guidance to those involved in the issue. The regular presidential press conference is a way of making end runs around a staff system that too often isolates and insulates the modern president. And after Watergate, I think we all recognize the value of removing some of that insulation.

The value of restoring the regular presidential press conference seems great enough to me that I would be willing to join in the very thing that Pat Buchanan always talks about — a press conspiracy.

The conspiracy I have in mind would begin when the 1976 presidential campaign starts. It would be hard to organize, because the press does not have a corporate structure; nobody can call a meeting and get "the press" in a room to discuss anything.

But if it were possible, it would seem to me in the public interest for those of us who cover politics to agree to ask this question of every single individual who announces for president in 1976, at his or her first postannouncement press conference: "In return for the coverage that the networks, the wire services, the news magazines, and the major newspapers will give your campaign, are you willing to commit yourself now, and for as long as you are a candidate, to take one-half hour out of your schedule of 168 hours per week for a news conference open to reporters who are covering you?"

I do not think we would have to raise or invoke the threat that if the answer were no, there might be a diminution in the amount of money and manpower our news organizations invest in the coverage of that campaign. I think that if we put that question to the candidates at the time that our leverage is greatest and their power is least, we might have a chance of extracting that kind of agreement from them. And if the habit of the weekly news conference were inculcated during the campaign, it might conceivably even carry over to the time when one of them is behind the fence at the White House, when the press has very little leverage it can apply.

I do not know whether any of these proposals is practical, or, if adopted, would take us very far down the road toward a healthier relationship between the press and the president. But I am certain that the dilemma we face when we consider the president in his role as communicator in chief is exactly the same today as it was a third of a century ago when Lippmann wrote the words I quoted earlier and which I repeat now in conclusion:

> It is impossible for the country to lead the President. Yet the policy of the government must rest on the support of the nation. So the nation must first be informed, and always it must be dealt with squarely.

BIBLIOGRAPHY

Buchanan, Patrick. *The New Majority*. Philadelphia: Girard Bank, 1973.

Keogh, James. *President Nixon and the Press*. New York: Funk and Wagnall Publishing Company, 1972.

Lippmann, Walter. *The Essential Lippmann*. New York: Random House, 1963.

Minow, Newton; Martin, John Bartlow; and Mitchell, Lee. *Presidential Television: A Twentieth-Century Fund Report*. New York: Basic Books, 1973.

Reston, James. *The Artillery of the Press*. New York: Harper & Row, 1967.

VI ☆ POLITICS AND POLITY

How can a president be held accountable in our turbulent society? How can he govern in the midst of social unrest? These are the key questions addressed by Thomas Cronin and Avery Leiserson. Cronin indicates that it is only through the tradition of American politics that a president can be held accountable to the public. "The problem of making presidents accountable and democratic rests in large measure on whether we have the creativity to turn around this country's escape from politics and flight from partisanship." He concludes that we want politicians in the White House because they are more likely to be accountable to the vicissitudes of public opinion as expressed in the democratic process. Avery Leiserson develops a thorough analysis of the organizational and managerial roles of the president in coping with social unrest and provides a perspective on the limitations of the president in handling such unrest.

Thomas E. Cronin, a graduate of Holy Cross and Stanford University, has been a White House Fellow and a faculty member at the University of North Carolina (Chapel Hill). He is presently a Visiting Fellow at the Center for the Study of Democratic Institutions. He has written numerous articles and books on the presidency, including *The Presidential Advisory System* and *The State of the Presidency*.

Avery Leiserson, former president of the American Political Science Association and Vanderbilt University political science professor, has written five books, served as editor of the *Journal of Politics,* and held governmental positions with the U. S. Bureau of the Budget, National Defense Mediation Board, National Labor Relations Board, and the National Recovery Administration.

10

The Presidency and Politics

THOMAS E. CRONIN
Center for the Study of Democratic
Institutions

Democratic POLITICAL LEADERSHIP is and must be something far more than *personalized popular leadership*. The temptation is considerable today to blame the ills of the recent past on an inadequate, outmoded Constitution, on the lack of character in our leading officials, or on an overly politicized White House. I am skeptical of each of the charges, although, to be sure, there is some merit in each of them.

The factors that have occasioned the swelling of the presidency are likely to be with us for the foreseeable future. Most of them are irreversible. The presidency's potential for good or evil now and in the years to come unquestionably must always be a central concern near the top of the national agenda. The Orwellian fears of remoteness, insulation, regalness, and even contempt for the public's right to know — all of these problems are likely to continue. The truth is, nonetheless, that the modern presidency is unaccountable because in certain areas it is too strong and independent of proper checks and balances, and in many areas too weak and dependent. Awesome restraints and constraints often exist where restraints are undesirable, but adequate brakes are not available where they are very much needed.

The problem of making presidents accountable and democratic rests in large measure on whether we have the creativity to turn around this country's escape from politics and flight from partisanship. Unless we can have elections in which we have national and rational debates, unless candidates debate the issues and ally themselves to the programmatic visions of a party that has integrity and a sense of collective purpose, then government by and for the people may perish. Parties and *political* leadership must be revitalized and substituted for personality cults, charismatic leadership, or the iconizing of the presidency. In the past parties have helped to mobilize creative bursts of popular energy. Parties can also serve as a force to curb excessive presidential power. Should our parties be weakened any more than they presently are, we shall surely see more power shifted to technocrats, bureaucrats, and those already advantaged by the special interest and pressure-group state we now have.

Presidents have too often tried to convince us that political decisions are in the hands of dispassionate, bipartisan experts and that the problems experts deal with are unintelligible to laymen. In May 1962 John Kennedy said,

> Most of us are conditioned for many years to have a political viewpoint — Republican or Democratic, liberal, conservative or moderate. The fact of the matter is that most of the problems . . . that we now face, are technical problems, are administrative problems. They are very sophisticated judgments which do not lend themselves to the sort of passionate movements which have stirred this country so often in the past. [They] deal with questions which are now beyond the comprehension of most men . . . .

There is not one syllable in our Constitution that authorizes presidents to defy that greatest obligation in a democracy — the responsibility to explain themselves, to explain their policies, and to facilitate the public's right to know. As Justice Brandeis once said, "sunlight is the best of disinfectants," and so it is that our parties and political opposition must be rebuilt and professionalized in order that convenient secrecy can be toppled in favor of sustained dialogue. A democracy's foreign and military policies are only as good as the open, avid, and partisan debates that produce them. A democracy without honest reports from its leaders is not a democracy at all. A democratic society can be achieved only if presidents and the public alike are prepared to speak candidly to each other and are equally prepared to criticize and correct the errors made against each other. Basic to these needs in contemporary America is a presidency that listens and speaks as something more than a Hollywood-produced, J. Walter Thompson-staffed, public relations agency. Instead of managing the news, the constructively political president would listen to what is said to him and, within reason, encourage everyone, whether a member of the Washington political community or a mere citizen, to say what is on his mind.

It has become fashionable for presidents and other political leaders to boast that they are "above politics!" This is like a bishop saying he is "above religion." The perception of politics as shameful and of partisanship as undignified have had a grievous impact on the exercise of national leadership in America. In their most manifest form these notions prompt a president to say piously that he is above politics and must act solely as president for all the people.

Theodore H. White's book, The Making of the President — 1972 [1973], tries to clarify many of these developments. His is both an excellent recounting by a gifted storyteller, and a depressing account of perhaps the most embarrassing and unfortunate election in our history.

To White's credit, his series of books on the presidential campaigns [1961, 1965, 1969, 1973] are narratives not just about campaigns, but about America, its popular values, and its public moods. His is a large canvas, his eye is on the American voter as much as on the candidates and their support teams. The uniqueness of the White series derives in large measure from his use of national elections as backgrounds against which to offer us compelling, albeit always sympathetic, portraits of national politicians. He describes them in such a way as to permit provocative discussion of changes in the American mood — what is going on, where people are moving, what they think of their government, and what bothers them.

The ironies and paradoxes in White's book reflect America's ambivalence toward politics and the American dream. For example, as a people we all insist that this is a nation of laws and that no one is above them, yet cynicism is widespread throughout the country, and there is the not unsubstantiated belief that politicians and presidents have abused the laws and misused the authority temporarily granted to them. Perhaps the crowning paradox of the 1972 campaign was that the candidate who spoke so insistently, and sometimes even eloquently, about curbing and braking the centralized power in Washington, took for himself and his immediate staff more power than any president in recent times. In his determined pursuit of reelection-with-honor, he apparently permitted the grossest abuses of power; a veritable treachery against the due processes of competitive elections.

Nixon told Theodore White that the mining of Haiphong and the bombing of Hanoi had been the biggest of gambles, yet also the strategic turning point in his successful pursuit of his own reelection. With the successful execution of the bombing, the grand theme and symbolic issue of war and peace was safe. But if Nixon, Kissinger, Laird, et al., could mine Haiphong and undermine the stability of Hanoi, why could his campaign teams not mine the Democratic National Committee and defame and discredit its leading candidates?

NIXON, THE APOSTATE REPUBLICAN

Time and again Nixon placed distance between himself and party leadership responsibilities. Right after the 1970 elections, decisions were made to "get the politics the hell out of the White House and across the street" as one aide put it. But, more important, the decision was to desert the Republican party and go it alone. Nixon's private, secretive, and often clandestine reelection corporation would mastermind his campaign; the Republican party would run an entirely separate campaign of its own.

Nixon wanted to be above partisan issues, above party, and aloof from nearly all the domestic problems of the day. To do so was to privatize his own election strategy. As Nixon told the nation in his first major Watergate address on April 30, 1973, he wanted to concentrate on the "larger duties" of the office of the president, suggesting rather explicitly that these did not include party leadership, partisanship, or domestic political leadership toward building a better, more decent and just America.

His reasoning, apparently, went like this: people do not respond to presidential leadership in domestic affairs unless there is either a major crisis or it touches them directly (as, for example, busing). Domestic policy leaders are inevitably "losers" because they are cast in the role of national dividers rather than national unifiers. Anyway, getting things done at home costs too much money (which was not available), requires strenuous political bargaining with Congress and the bureaucracies, and necessitates persuasive educational campaigns aimed at the press and the public.

As Nixon aide Leonard Garment told White, "In foreign policy you get drama, triumph, resolution — crisis and resolution. So that in foreign policy Nixon can give the sense of leadership. But in domestic policy, there you have to deal with the whole jungle of home problems . . . . " [White 1973, p. 54].*

Accordingly, Nixon's redefinition of presidential leadership — perhaps for self-serving ends, but, in part, also because he was playing to an apparent American mood — was that a president is really there to make those decisions that no one else can make. The presidency, then, was for him preeminently a place for foreign policy statesmanship, peace making, for being Oversecretary for National Security.

Mr. Nixon proposed to deal with Americans "as they are." Franklin Roosevelt and Woodrow Wilson had both been historic

---

*This and subsequent quotations from Theodore White's The Making of the President — 1972 reprinted with the permission of Atheneum Publishers, 1973©.

models for him, but Nixon viewed them not as the party leaders and domestic political maestros that they also were, but rather as statesmen, shapers of a generation of peace, and as heroic men with a clarity of vision in the foreign policy realm. Whenever Nixon gave interviews in 1972, his conversation always drifted back to his preoccupation with foreign affairs and his apparently compulsive quest for outdoing all previous presidents in the area of foreign policy.

A supreme irony of Nixon's refusal to be a Republican in 1972 (having learned harsh lessons in 1970, especially on election eve when Senator Muskie looked far more presidential than he) was that in 1973 and 1974 he would find himself with an even more hostile Congress (several Republican members had lost, and even many of those who won were bitter at Nixon for ignoring them) than in his first term. This was a fact of no small consequence since to govern the nation — as opposed to running for the Nobel Peace Prize — a president must have a working coalition in the Congress. Here again, though, Nixon the private man, Nixon the apostate Republican leader, and Nixon the disinterested domestic politician — his landslide to the contrary notwithstanding — was in fact contributing to his own undoing. Statistically, Nixon's was the loneliest landslide in the annals of American history.

Nixon often spoke as if he really did want to make things run better, to decentralize power to the people, to streamline the machinery of government, and to make things work. But to run and lead the country you also have to be overt, deal candidly with people, and openly consult (rather than insult) members of Congress. Just the opposite is true, of course, in national security matters; secrecy and covert operations are standard operating procedures.

Nixon's first love was travelling around the world, presidential summitry, "presidency-by-travelogue." And, as H. R. Haldeman told White, it was *also* best for his reelection.

> He doesn't have to campaign, . . . he doesn't have to establish his identity. He's been exposed for twenty-five years because of TV and his trip to China and the man on the moon, he's probably the

best-known human being in the history of the world. For him to campaign would be counterproductive, superfluous [p. 238].

Nixon was both reacting to and playing upon widespread public attitudes toward "Political Man" in America. People in this nation were skeptical and cynical about politics, the selling of the president, the presumed graft and corruption at all levels of government. Public opinion surveys in the early 1970s persuasively pointed out a decline in the public's belief that politicians are honest. People were upset when they read that a president was "playing politics" with an issue or was involved in overt partisan behavior. The temptation, then, was (and still is) for presidents to avoid partisan issues, and whenever possible, to take on problems that the public regards as nonpartisan, bipartisan, or benefitting all regions, classes, and interest groups. Hence the Nixon conception of the presidency as one of concentration on international issues had its roots in his perception of the mood of the people.

NIXON RIDING THE TIDES
OF THE AMERICAN MOOD

Time and again Theodore White suggests that had it been possible, Nixon would not have bothered at all with domestic problems. The problems of managing our economy, of governing our cities, of measurably improving the quality of life, justice, and so forth — these were matters Nixon wished to will away, or proclaim as issues whose time had passed, or delegate down to lower levels of government or the private sector. No Great Societies for him! Liberalism had failed, especially the evangelic McGovern variant. White put it this way:

> There could be no doubt that the candidates of 1972 were addressing a country different from that addressed by John F. Kennedy at his inaugural in 1961. "Ask not," John F. Kennedy had said, "what your country can do for you — ask what you can do for your country!" Public spirit and social conscience had run low by 1972 — a war had worn out the spirit, and random experimenta-

tion had worn out conscience. Few, except for the blacks and deprived, asked what the country could do for them, and fewer still asked what they could do for their country. Most, apparently, by mood and numbers, wanted their country to leave them alone — and leave the rest of the world alone, too. They wanted out of Vietnam, out of world affairs, out of the cities . . . [p. 165].

The truth is, however, that a president cannot for very long avoid being openly political. A president in a democracy has to act politically in regard to controversial issues if we are to have any semblance of government by the consent of the governed — that is, he must negotiate and mediate between groups, compromise polar differences, and find acceptable alternatives. A democratic president must be willing to set priorities, put up trial balloons, and use the prestige of the office to lend a voice of conscience on the side of what, though it may not necessarily be popular, is right and needs to be done.

We can no more take the politics out of the presidency than we can take the presidency out of politics. It is a very political office, and political and partisan leadership are as necessary as foreign policy statesmanship and symbolic leadership. It is, of course, a welcome theme to many Americans that statesmanship means not being political, but such interpretations are misleading and wrong. Everything a president does has political consequences, and each explicitly political act done by a president has consequences for the state of the presidency.

When a president strives to be "above politics," what often results is that he and his aides grow dependent on more secretive and covert political operations. This has long been the case but far more capaciously so in the Watergate affair. The convenience of secrecy and the cloak of "national security" justifications are extraordinarily tempting to those who want to avoid appearing political. Secrecy, no matter what the form or rationale, creates distance and remoteness from the normal set of checks and balances on a presidency. And such secrecy and remoteness invariably can conceal mistakes, deviousness, capriciousness and, as we know now, illegalities of vast proportions.

The attempt to divorce the presidency and politics presupposes a political system significantly different from ours, glued together as it is in such large measure by ambiguity, compromise, and the extensive sharing of powers. In light of the requisites of democracy, the presidency must be a highly open as well as a highly political office, and the president must be an expert practitioner of the art of politics. Quite simply, there is no other way for presidents to negotiate favorable coalitions within the country, Congress, and the executive branch, and to gather the authority needed to translate ideas into legislation, and legislation into accomplishments. *A president who remains aloof from politics, campaigns, and partisan alliances, and dismantles and ignores his own party apparatus, does so at the risk of becoming the prisoner of events, special interests, or his own whims.*

This nation has suffered much during this past decade precisely because presidents have scoffed at the notion that they must serve as the effective heads of their political parties. Once elected, a president permits and often encourages the disintegration of his own political party. In each case, the president has viewed his political party and much of its leadership as intruders into the province of a personalized, and increasingly privatized presidency. Political parties could and should be, however, important vehicles for communicating voter preferences to those in public office. The ideas and commitments of national leaders should clearly be disciplined by the general thrust of partisan thinking. A partyless administration is very likely a conservative one. Furthermore, it has the potential for setting up a very arbitrary and reactionary regime — and one that mainly listens to itself. Bipartisanship rarely has served us well. As James MacGregor Burns aptly notes: "Almost as many crimes have been committed in the name of mindless bipartisanship as in the name of mindless patriotism" [1973, p. 15].

If we would ensure that our presidents will not abdicate their responsibilities as politicians, then we as citizens cannot abdicate ours. Those who want a better America will not realize it by sitting around and waiting for it. The best insurance system for responsive and responsible presidential leadership is an alert citizenry demanding accountability, forming political alliances, debating the issues, and demanding the right to know what is going on. They cannot object to what they do not know. As H. L. Mencken said, "Conscience is the inner voice which warns us that someone may be watching."

So it is that a resort to both pressure politics and party politics is imperative. Presidents will act responsibly when people insist on it through their parties or similar movements. Those who become spectators rather than citizen-activists will suffer the fate clearly outlined by Ogden Nash [1938, p. 194].

> Wherever decent intelligent people get together
> They talk about politicians as about bad weather,
> But they are always too decent to go into politics them-
>   selves and too intelligent even to go to the polls,
> So I hope the kind of politicians they get will have
>   no mercy on their pocketbooks or souls.*

Citizens will be moved to appreciate the role of parties and public interest group lobbies only to the extent that they comprehend the weaknesses and fallibility of their elected leaders. Elected leaders are limited by the accommodations they made to get elected, limited again by their desire to be reelected, and limited, perhaps most importantly, by the prevailing biases of those in the private sector who wield disproportionate influence on those holding office. John Gardner states the problem well:

> Clearly we cannot organize our society in such a way that we are dependent on inspired Presidential leadership, because most of the time it won't be there. We must build creative strength in other parts of the system. And in fact that's the kind of system it was intended to be. It was never intended that we should seek a Big Daddy and lean on him. We shall save ourselves — or we won't be saved [1972, p. 84].

President Nixon realized that the paradox of the presidency requires that a president serve as a national unifier all the while knowing that his partisan and domestic leadership responsibilities also can make him a national divider. Nixon clearly chose the unifier role as often as possible. On the domestic front, Nixon's view seemed to be that there were only two types of problems — those that solve themselves or those that could not be solved.

The record of the Nixon administration was one of trying to keep domestic and foreign policy matters separate when, in fact, it is rare that a foreign policy problem does not have important implications for domestic policy. Nixon responded to domestic problems only when the status quo had become dramatically more painful than what would have been brought about by a new policy. Appraisals of domestic problems occurred only when crises such as the energy shortages or inflation became so exacerbated that the president could no longer avoid a response — even if his response was largely a symbolic gesture or the mere appearance of new directions.

Domestically, the Nixon presidency was largely vacuous; issues were joined only when forced upon it, and then only with symbolic messages. Major problems were totally ignored, and any occasional bright idea or proposal was put forward in the most tentative, timid, and unpersuasive manner. President Nixon rarely spent political capital trying to push anything that verged on being innovative, redistributive, or truly reformist. Rather than transform the executive office and the cabinet into a system for learning, evaluation, and education, Nixon's administration nearly always took the reverse path: they slowed things down, dismantled the Great Society, put a damper on bright ideas, and treated idealism with suspicion.

There is no greater misconception than that our foreign policy can be treated as distinct from our accomplishments here at home. What is it worth to have the best of national security policies and the most impenetrable defenses if what this nation stands for in theory is being eroded in practice? The degrading acts against the ideal of competitive elections need no reiteration here. The inability of our national institutions to respond rapidly and intelligently to the socioeconomic deficiencies of the nation also needs no summation.

Failure to practice democracy and to perfect our democratic institutions at home makes our claims to having a government by and for the people hypocritical at best. Inability to engage in serious community-building at home when we parade around the world exhorting, and claiming to teach, nation-building to others is also a notable contradiction. Our role as a leader and mediator among nations is immeasurably tarnished when a nation as wealthy as ours is unable to be a pace-setter in implementing our great goals of decent housing, full employment, racial equality, and due process. Domestic policy leadership, then, is inextricably intertwined with both our nation's security and our capacity to offer reasoned leadership abroad.

PUTTING POLITICS BACK INTO POLITICS

The quest to be a *popular* rather than a *political* president is fraught with side effects we can ill afford. To mirror public orthodoxy and practice benign neglect is not enough. Even as he listens and consults, the president must educate and provide a vision of a better society, a more exalted definition of national purpose. This is not to say that the people do not have noble values; it is rather to say that these are often latent and passive. The imagination of the citizenry can stretch, and people will support fundamental redistributive changes when the proper appeals are made. An important part of leadership involves paying attention to education and encouraging open debates. Surely we have the money, the talent, and even the wisdom to transform this nation into a far more just and decent society.

The easier path, however, is to treat people as they are, and avoid the controversial. President Nixon often displayed traits that showed that he had some of the political ability of a Franklin Roosevelt. Both were masters at the accumulation of power in the presidency. But in marked contrast to Roosevelt, who strove to use the power for social reforms and redistributive ends, Nixon nearly always used his power for the mere accumulation of enhanced powers, apparently elevating his means to ends unto themselves. When Nixon complained that the "larger duties" of office required his energy, the intention was apparently to propel himself above the tawdry concerns of campaigns and politicians, and emerge isolated and pure, as a statesman.

But the escape from politics, partisanship, and serious commitments at home brought about unanticipated consequences that were worse than those for which they were to be substitutes. The notion of a nonpartisan presidency that delegates or ignores all domestic leadership matters is untenable. The notion that intense conflicts over policy choices can be somehow removed from the presidency is undesirable. The political controversies that surround a president and require him to act as a mediator and coalition-builder mirror existing and potential conflicts over values in the society at large. If our presidents were not asked to resolve political conflicts, they would not be fulfilling the responsibilities we rightly associate with democratic leadership. The human heart, or so it seems, ceaselessly reinvents royalty — or at least a presidency without politics. That is, I gather, why the proposed six-year term with reelection forbidden is currently paraded out as a panacea. It reflects the mistaken illusion that the presidency might be better if it were elevated above the political battles of the day.

Under normal circumstances, a president who retreats into the seemingly safer, "more presidential," and intangible precincts of world affairs is unlikely to achieve much in the way of substantive policy innovation either abroad or at home. And a president who relies too much on direct connections with the public via television and neglects the political institutions and processes risks arousing expectations that he cannot fulfill. Television not only evokes the promise of great deeds, it deludes presidents into believing that they are engaged in dialogue when, quite the contrary, they are merely exploiting a vehicle designed for one-way discussions. James MacGregor Burns notes another critical weakness of consensus politics and the nonpolitical presidency:

> The ultimate tragedy of bipartisanship is the erosion of responsibility. Leaders compromise on politics rather than clarifying the alternatives. They claim to represent some fuzzy national interest rather than group interests or party factions. In seeking to represent everyone the government may end up representing none. The opposition unable to find a clear footing in such a system, follows tactics of opportunism and expediency; it does not offer an alternative program that it will support if given power [1973, p. 15].

Most of the men who have been effective presidents have also been highly political — *in an open, rather than covert, sense of that term.* They loved politics, and they understood the multiple purposes for which the powers of the presidency are granted. The best of our presidents have been those who understood the importance of political parties, who listened to the people and did not condescendingly view the American electorate as childlike and thus dependent on an omniscient president. As a nation, we must mature to the recognition that presidents have to be political, and they ought to be vigorous partisan leaders as well. These attributes cannot and must not be contracted out. And if the presidency is recognized as the highly political office it necessarily is, then we have to strive more rigorously to strengthen and professionalize rival and alternative political institutions that can keep it accountable and pose alternative programs.

It is small wonder that men who have seen alliances formed and villages destroyed at their whim will have little patience for congressional committee chairmen or state party chieftains who demand a respectful hearing before they will do an administration a favor.

By turning up our noses at "politics" in the White House and urging the president to get on to his real business of guiding the nation, we set the two important conditions for the secrecy and duplicity with which we have recently become so familiar. First, with all the apparatus for secret statesmanship at hand, it is much easier for a president to ring up "the Plumbers" when something needs fixing than to persuade the public or Congress to accept his point of view. Second, since the president will look "unpresidential" if he participates in normal party politics, his aides must go through grotesque contortions to prove that their boss never thought about anything except being President of All the People.

The tactic of secrecy, so tempting to those who have it within their grasp, insulates the president from the normal checks and balances of the political system. It will take new bait to lure presidents out of this comfortable sanctuary and into the morass of open politics, for now the enticements are small. The way to prevent future abuses, as has often been noted, is to make the White House more open. The way to do that, as has not so often been suggested, is once more to regard our presidents as politicians.

Plato once said: "What is honored in a country will be cultivated there." We need now, both in and out of the White House, a class of politicians who have objectives in view beyond the enlargement of their own careers. We need now much stronger, more responsible national committees. National chairpersons' posts have not been sought by our ablest leaders because these posts have been without authority and honor, *and* because we have allowed presidents and presidential candidates to misuse and abuse them. But this, perhaps now more than ever, is reversible; especially if greater powers over campaign financing, fairness in campaign practices, and allocation of authority over subsidized television time are redirected through national committee structures. Responsibility will be the much-needed medicine for our sickly national committees, and responsible assignments will be the appropriate lure to entice talented professional politicians to work full time for their parties, and through their parties, in service to their nation.

Politics is not only the art of the possible, it is also the art of making the difficult and desirable possible. The essence of democracy is politics, fairly played; and politics without parties and healthy competition between alternative ideas and candidates is not politics at all. We need more politics, not less. And we need to try more partisanship instead of the secrecy and executive privilegeship we have so often and so regretfully been offered. Citizen-politicians are what we need — tens of millions of them — we need parties that will command the allegiance of the young and all the hopeful who dream the dreams and entertain the visions of a better America and a just world. *Today the principle ground of reproach against president and citizen alike should be that he or she is not a politician.*

BIBLIOGRAPHY

Burns, James MacGregor. "Keeping the President in Line." *The New York Times*, 8 April 1973, p. 15.

Gardner, John. *In Common Cause*. New York: W. W. Norton & Company, 1972.

Nash, Ogden. "The Politician." *I'm a Stranger Here Myself*. Boston: Little, Brown and Company, 1938.

White, Theodore. *The Making of the President — 1972*. New York: Atheneum Publishers, 1973.

11

Social Unrest and the Presidency

AVERY LEISERSON
Vanderbilt University

Wᴴᴬᵀ IS THE RELATIONSHIP BETWEEN American public opinion and the qualities and capabilities of political leadership embodied in the great office of president of the United States?

The types and causes of social unrest, important as they are, will not be our main focus of attention. I assume them to be causal, conditioning factors that establish the conditions and limits of, if they do not precisely define, issues for political determination and choice. The justification for this approach is a desire to focus upon the resources and requirements of the presidency for identifying and dealing with societal disharmony, conflict, and dissent. In no way do I intend to de-emphasize or downgrade the importance of personality and social structure, relative to politics. On the contrary, high among qualities of competent political leaders are: **1.** their sensitivity to social, industrial, cultural, and technological trends, **2.** their quick perception of the impact of such trends upon political fortunes and climates of opinion, **3.** how such tendencies influence the possibilities and limitations for political action.

One of the Framers of the Constitution, President James Madison, stated the problem by saying that the causes of social unrest are sown in the nature of man (and society); hence that form of government is preferable that allows people to express their discontents freely, so that their representatives will know better with what they have to deal. Social unrest arises in part from *personal* frustrations, grievances, and deprivations. These in turn are rooted in the differences, inequities, and consciousness of *group experience* — economic, ethnic, religious, sectional, cultural-educational — by which society is divided. Government itself may be a source of hostility and disruption, as in contests over elective and appointive offices, or deep-seated resentments over military, tax, welfare-spending, and price-wage, or other regulatory, policies.

Whatever the cause or causes of dissatisfaction, and it is important to be able to differentiate and judge them as to scope, intensity, and immediacy, *social unrest is a normal feature of situations with which politicians and public officials are required to deal.* Citizens, intellectuals, and social scientists legitimately differ over whether it is good or bad, healthy or sick, for society to be in a constant or oscillating, low-temperature or highly feverish, state of public excitement. They also differ, and it is to some extent a matter of choice, as to whether the various sources of social discontent should be dealt with piecemeal or in a broadly planned manner, or should be postponed and avoided until they burst forth into some major upheaval. From a political standpoint, what happens depends very much on the quality of analysis, ingenuity, and timeliness with which group, party, and governmental leaders are able to devise and coordinate policies, programs, and jobs to drain off the infection of personal alienation and group destructiveness.

The disturbing feature of social unrest to people who want to believe in the ways of democracy is that at times of unrest, public or popular opinion rarely exhibits itself as a clear majority, a near-consensus or unanimous viewpoint, on public policies, goals, and objectives. Instead of being able to assume a majority view, ordinary or extraordinary, the public seems to face the problem of finding itself, of mobilizing, educating, modifying, and applying its sense of the majority judgment, with the specific question, operative conditions, and the time of decision, all either unknown or uncertain variables. Instead of a clear division between majority and minority on a well-defined issue, popular opinion under conditions of deep social unrest appears to be composed of a number of dissenting minorities, varying on different dimensions, each insisting upon its own perception and definition of the issue and situation.

Diversity and division, not consensus or solidarity, underlie and reinforce the mass-psychological dependence, reliance, and yearning for a trusted, respected, and admired figure like the president, to show us the way out of the clamor of conflicting voices, to help us discern the direction of public national interest, and to persuade us to do what the common good requires. The presidency serves the nation as a vital, unifying center; a focal point for rallying the moral strength and confidence of the people when they are disturbed, at a loss for direction among the clash of contending views and interests. An extremely important indicator of the viability, vigor, or weakness of our political system is the degree to which the president is able to marshal approval and support for his person and policies among the conflicting elements of opinion and power in American society.

But this is only the beginning. In America we expect the president not only to remain in the White House symbolizing unity, but to take the lead in initiating change in public policy. In exercising this role of programmatic leadership, chief executives may undermine unity, divide, polarize, and redivide opinion. In 1937 President Franklin Roosevelt, enjoying a 60 percent electoral majority the previous year, confidently sought congressional legislation to authorize him to add six new appointees to the Supreme Court, one for every justice 70 years old or over, up to a maximum of 15. Not only did he not get the legislation; he practically terminated congressional support for his domestic economic reforms, if not for his spending programs. In 1965 President Johnson, fresh from an even greater majority, sent one-half-million men to resist and punish what he defined as Communist aggression in Southeast Asia without a congressional declaration of war. His policy, if it did not polarize American public opinion, seemed to pulverize it; three short years later L.B.J. felt obliged to announce his retirement from public life. A less clear case is that of John Kennedy. With a popular majority over Richard Nixon of less than one percent, he embarked on a vigorous New Frontier program that included civil rights, medical care, urban redevelopment, foreign aid, and aid to education. It was emasculated, if not wholly rejected, by Congress. Similarly, during their terms of office, President Truman, following Korea, and President Nixon, following the Watergate exposures, saw their popularity ratings in the public opinion polls fall below 30 percent. Did that mean that Mr. Truman and Mr. Nixon forfeited their official right to recommend and seek congressional support for their policies, or incurred the threat of impeachment for those acts of political misjudgment that led to their dramatic loss of popular respect and approval? And what is supposed to happen when, low as presidents fall in public favor according to the polls, Congress stands even lower, or no higher?

The problem is more complex; that is, there are factors involved other than the simple arithmetic of whether the president can muster the votes in Congress to pass his legislative proposals, or is supported by 51 or more percent of a national population sample who approve the way he is doing his job. I want to discuss three such factors: 1. *popular* theories of the presidential office,   2. *system* factors supporting the strong presidency,   3.   the president's *managerial* instruments and opportunities.

POPULAR THEORIES OF THE PRESIDENCY

By 'theory' I do not mean names or labels like the "Imperial" presidency, the "Living" presidency, or the "Twilight" presidency — the latter meaning that the job has grown so big that it is impossible for any human being to do it. By theory I mean the belief-image, the doctrinal standard, the perceptual model of the presidential job that an individual citizen-voter can expect a particular occupant to live by, live up to, and account for. Oversimplifying, there are three such conceptions. They are: **1.** the *plebiscitary*, or *elective monarch*, theory, **2.** the *chief magistrate*, or *lawyer's*, theory, **3.** the *political science*, or *textbook*, theory.

The **plebiscitary-elective monarchy theory** is that every 4 years the American people elect a king in fact, if not in name, to govern them. Constitutionally, he is commander in chief of the armed forces; he is the head of all nonlegislative, nonjudicial civilian agencies of the national government; he represents the nation in our dealings with foreign governments and powers; he is the undisputed leader of his political party as long as he is in office; he is the spokesman for the whole people from the time of his inauguration until his successor is chosen and qualified. He rules, if he does not personally run, the executive branch through subordinates who owe their primary loyalty and responsibility to him. Unless he is impeached by the House of Representatives (which has happened only once since 1789) and convicted by the Senate for high crimes and misdemeanors (which has never happened), the president, during his term of office, may claim that he is responsible and accountable only to the whole people, not to any partisan, partial, self-serving minority or majority. His subordinates may be removed, but except by impeachment, he is beyond legal or political sanction or punishment until his term expires.

For almost 200 years the theory of the presidency as an elective monarchy has been steadfastly rejected by most Americans, by most presidents, by most scholars and authorities. Why? Not because it does not have large elements of fact to support it. For one reason, it has been rejected because, accurately or not, in America the idea that the executive is the effective, de facto source of public authority is felt to be incompatible with the idea of free or democratic government. A no less important reason is that with Lord Acton, most Americans distrust the corrupting effects that nonaccountable authority has upon the personalities who assert it. The kingship theory is what we seemed to hear when Mr. Nixon said he was responsible, but not to blame, for the reprehensible acts of his subordinates. What acts? Burglary, wire-tapping, clandestine espionage of both friends and enemies, refusal or failure to expose illegal practices, use of campaign funds not only for payoffs and hush-money, but to apply pressure from the White House and attorney-general's office to compel access and special favors to campaign contributors. All this constituted such a prevalent style and pattern of decision-making that two White House personal assistants openly sneered that the Watergate break-in and cover-up were only a small-time, "third-rate," low-level piece of foolish incompetence. Only a person who, like a king, cannot distinguish between his own responsible and irresponsible executive authority, says that his subordinates, not he, must lose their jobs and take the blame for exercising his authority illegally, or in a manner he subsequently admits to be constitutionally and politically wrong.

The **lawyer's theory** of the presidency is that he is the country's chief magistrate, or law-enforcer, who directs the executive machinery for putting into effect congressional laws and Supreme Court decisions. A "limited powers" theory, it was perhaps best elaborated by former President and Chief Justice William Howard Taft to describe the predominant attitude of the Supreme Court toward the presidency from 1790 to about 1930. It asserts that the presidential office possesses no inherent powers; the president governs only through those titles and duties expressly named in the Constitution, or so clearly implied as to be retrospectively approvable by the Court. As a theory, it is supported by a considerable foundation of judicial history, and it embodies the constitutional tradition of limited government by men under law.

There are three troubles with the lawyer's theory. One is that it reduces the president to the status of a magnified attorney-general. Second, it assumes that legal norms and precepts enunciated by the Supreme Court prospectively control the premises of presidential thinking about policy decisions in particular situations. This assumption is contradicted by acts of admittedly doubtful legality by such presidents as Jefferson, Jackson, Lin-

coln, the two Roosevelts, and Truman, some of which were subsequently labelled unconstitutional, while others received ex
post facto judicial approval. The second defect is that while the
Supreme Court is the ultimate legal authority under the Constitution, it is not, does not claim to be, and, except perhaps for
short periods of time, has never been the highest *political* authority in the American constitutional system. One of our basic
American constitutional beliefs is that neither the president nor
Congress is politically sovereign in this sense either, but that
does not prove nor even imply that the Supreme Court must be
in charge of our political system.

The **political science, or textbook, theory,** might be better
received if it were called the doctrine of responsible presidential
government. Theodore Roosevelt called it the stewardship
theory of the presidency. Woodrow Wilson said that the president is at liberty to be as big a man as he can, or as his capacities
permit, but this puts it in perhaps excessively psychological
terms. In political language, the theory is that the president
legitimately uses his formal powers under the Constitution, his
informal authority as leader of his political party, and his symbolic status as spokesman for the whole nation, to preserve the
Union, to protect and advance national needs and interests, subject to such limitations as the Congress, interest groups, the
press, public opinion, and the courts are able to impose effectively through legislation, administration, or litigation. The
strength of the theory is that it frankly recognizes   **1.** the *political* sources of presidential power,   **2.** the processes through
which executive power is exercised,   **3.** the legitimacy of the
several political oppositions the president must take into account in order to generate the necessary degree of support for his
acts and policies.

The theory has important defects. As a scientific theory, it is
ambiguous with respect to how it is to be tested and verified.
Some authorities take it to mean that presidential behavior may
be analyzed and evaluated on the basis of the president's personal philosophy; others on the basis of the president's basic
personality structure and character; others on a long-run, historical standard of comparison. Still other advocates urge that the

theory requires a more complex, sociopolitical, structural analysis. That is, the presidency must be viewed as a strategic center of political initiative and diplomacy, moving, shaking, forging new alignments out of the shifting configuration of governmental-nongovernmental supports *and* oppositions. He leads and governs by consent, in contradistinction to the military commander whose power is based upon a concept of ability to destroy the enemy forces or will to resist.

Aside from such ambiguities, there are three other objections to the political responsibility theory. One is the very practical difficulty of distinguishing between true national interests and the president's personal goals and strategies. Second, it is difficult, if not impossible, to carry on the political operations of responsible leadership wholly exposed to public view, and many persons resent and reject decisions reached through informal processes of negotiation, calculated moderation, nonviolent coercion, and compromise. Third, the theory is open to the charge, expressly admitted by Franklin Roosevelt, that as the nation's number one voice, the president is obliged to resort to as much of the political technique of persuasion as is necessary to gain his proximate goals. Since the primary test is popular approval in the crucible of struggle for political success and survival, the inference is that whatever method of persuasion is necessary to obtain that approval is justifiable. In short, the very realism of the theory of responsible presidential leadership suffers from the visceral opposition of people who, disliking the morally ambiguous realities of politics, deliberately reject a theory that explains political facts in favor of a moral or legal doctrine in which they prefer to believe.

These three theories of the presidential office may or may not advance our understanding of the relation of public opinion to the presidency in times of social unrest. Probably not, if you assume either that one or another must be valid, or that it is necessary to choose one or another as a matter of absolute conviction. However, if you are able to grasp and apply each theory *as an alternative standard of reference* to the behavior of particular presidents, you should be better able to arrive at a personal judgment as to how an incumbent has lived up to, or failed to perform, his presidential duties and responsibilities.

SYSTEM-FACTORS
AND PRESIDENTIAL
LEADERSHIP

Let us turn briefly to the "system-factors" that affect the leadership position of the president in times of stress and unrest. These involve the operative practices, normative rules, and institutions regulating access and succession to the presidency, particularly those that have grown up around our electoral and party system and the Congress.

Perhaps most basic is the practice in this country of electing representatives for fixed terms of office, in the president's case for 4 years with one renewable term. Some people, particularly those who like parliamentary forms of government, think it would be better if we dismissed and replaced the chief executive whenever he is defeated on a legislative vote against one of his major policies or on any issue he makes a vote of confidence. For better or worse, that parliamentary practice has never been accepted in American politics. Our political chief executives stay in office for their full terms except in the extraordinary cases of death, resignation, congressional impeachment and conviction, or, in those cities and towns with such provisions for city managers, removal by the city council. Popular removal or recall of an elected official by referendum is practically unavailable in most jurisdictions. The result of fixed terms of office, of course, is to make the elected official less accountable for his position on any particular issue, and obliges the electorate to judge him on his whole record in office. Clearly, this is less than satisfactory to those who think democracy would be better off if the political executive went out of executive office every time he lost a major legislative battle, and it certainly tends to make for greater political stability than would a system that required a new and different legislative coalition upon each major policy issue or constellation of interests. It is not nearly so clear, however, that the parliamentary pattern of compulsory executive resignation and new elections automatically or generally produces the most democratic policy result, or necessarily strengthens the people's faith in their own political efforts to influence and control governing officials. Witness, in the twentieth century, the displacement of parliamentary, two-party government by multiparty co-alition government in so many European political systems, and the replacement of alternating or competitive party governments with one-party or no-party military government in so many Communist and modernizing Asian-African regimes.

The second system-factor affecting the president's leader-ship position is that he is chosen by national popular election for the office, the results of which election must be reflected in a majority vote of state electoral votes in the electoral college. He is *not* chosen because he is the leader of the majority party in Congress. Only in the infrequent case (twice since the Twelfth Amendment of 1804) has a popularly-elected president failed to secure a majority vote in the electoral college. (Now, under the Twenty-fifth Amendment, when the presidency or vice presi-dency is declared vacant, Congress participates in the selection of a presidential or vice presidential designate.) Where a vacancy occurs by reason of death, accident, or emergency, presidential succession laws provide for the possible designation of the Speaker of the House or the Senate president, but there are no historical precedents. Legitimate accession to the presidency re-quires winning a national party convention nomination and nationwide election by the whole people, voting by states. This rule could, of course, be changed by constitutional amendment, but as far as I know there has never been any substantial political opinion in this country advocating that the president be nor-mally or regularly chosen by Congress.

Next, presidents are almost never elected on single issues, and neither party nominations nor platforms turn on the party's or candidate's stand on one overriding issue such as campaign spending, court appointments, impounding of funds, urban riots, school busing, the oil shortage, or controlling inflation. Presidential campaign issues, like voter interests and motiva-tions, are conflicting and manifold, and have somehow to be merged in the voter's estimate of the candidate and party's fitness (capacity) to govern for the period of his office. The suc-cessful candidate receives, it is true, a mandate from the people, but this is indefinite rather than specifically compelling with respect to the precise content of policy; it is fully expected and understood that the fate of executive-legislative proposals is contingent upon the uncertainties of congressional, press, and popular reaction. It is sometimes said that a newly elected president has a honeymoon period of perhaps 100 days when Congress is willing to enact substantially the legislation he requests. But whether a president enjoys rapport with Congress for 100 or 1,000 days, he must work with and through Congress for 4 or 8 years if the system is to function in the constitutional sense.

Last comes the problem of how the American system of separated powers and checks and balances works in the event that the president in office loses his popular and legislative support? We pass quickly over the *notorious absence* at the national level in this country of compulsory party discipline in the face of constituency pressure or the congressman's personal convictions. Furthermore, the overall loss of support or credibility by the president, such as occurred in the aftermath of Vietnam or Watergate, is far less usual than is talked about, and the loss of support on particular legislative issues is far more usual than commonly realized. In the normal situation when the president cannot get a legislative majority for something he considers necessary or advisable, or Congress by resolution or legislative rider tells him to do something he believes quite misguided or wrong, resignation is neither a conventional nor a practical remedy. Abdication of office to the vice president, or leader of the other party, has occurred only once under our system. Vice presidents, according to our constitutional tradition, are elected only to that office, and ascend to the presidency only in the extreme case of the president's death or assassination. If it is so serious or difficult for a nationally elected vice president to replace a president except in case of the ultimate catastrophe, it would be infinitely more difficult under our party system to find a political leader from the defeated party to replace the president merely because Congress rejected an appointment, amended or reduced his budget, attached unacceptable provisions to his legislative proposals, or made his job harder by adverse investigations, votes and resolutions. Undermining to his position as such defeats may be, the American president has always preferred to retain office rather than to resign and give power to the leader of the other party. Why?

The reason lies in the failure of our party system to provide a readily available, clearly acceptable substitute. The defeated candidate in a presidential election immediately loses his status both as a party leader and substitute rival for the presidency.

Party leadership of the defeated party in the last presidential election passes to the national committee chairman, whose authority extends only to interim organization affairs until the next convention selects a new ticket, and to the congressional party leaders, whose authority extends only to the management of House and Senate legislative business. Not once in the twentieth century has a national party chairman advanced to the leadership of his party by means of the qualifying test, a presidential convention nomination, let alone the election. Even in the days of Thomas Reed, Joseph Cannon, Tom Platt, or Mark Hanna, a Senate or House party leader was not considered to have qualified for the national party leadership unless he won the convention nomination. An important element in the question of Nixon's impeachment was the absence of a successor who qualified by this test. Thus, if anything, the American party system does not seem to reduce the president's status, but to put the president up too high. It does not produce a recognized replacement below the level of the president in the majority party, and it leaves the leadership of the defeated party divided between Congress and the national chairman — in limbo for the ensuing 4 years.

The system-factors we have talked about thus add up to an overwhelming bias in favor of the strong presidency. Symbolically and structurally, the unity of the office serves to counterbalance the Congress, the party and electoral system, the states, the First Amendment, even the Supreme Court, all of which make a virtue of diversity, confrontation, dissonance, limitations from the standpoint of governing authority. This is not to say that most intellectual and other critics of the presidency favor a strong presidency in principle. At present most critics seem to feel the office has acquired too much power. The point is that there is practically no critical opinion, radical right or left, conservative or liberal, willing to accept the consequences of dividing up, reducing, or crippling executive responsibility, or to deny the conditions that have led to reliance upon presidential initiative, discretion, and authority. This state of critical opinion is a source of both strength and weakness; strength in the negative sense as a continuing force for stability and continuity, weakness in that it makes for excessive rigidity and polarization, triviality, and utopianism, in thinking about reforms in the instruments and powers of the office.

To repeat, the presidency, looked at from the standpoint of American society with its highly differentiated, strongly organized, pluralistic power structure, and the mass-psychological, perceptual needs of its people, reinforced by the electronic media of radio and television, is firmly established as a unifying focus of popular respect and confidence, rising above the federalized electoral party struggle through which those few who achieve the office are recruited. The presidency symbolizes the nation's unity and the people's faith in their own power. However, when we turn to the instrumental, managerial aspects of the president's job, the sheer size, complexity, and immensity of the task of providing policy leadership for all the controversial issues (energy and the environment, incomes and welfare, production and prices, foreign alliances and military obligations) that arouse and reflect social unrest, it is not the unity and power of the office that seems to be the problem so much as how to divide up the job so that it becomes comprehensible and manageable for any one person to handle.

PRESIDENTS' MANAGERIAL INSTRUMENTS

One fashionable nostrum has been to propose what the British do: separate the ceremonial, symbolic duties from the policy and political functions, and divide them between the crown and prime minister. Another possibility is the Russian system of three executives: the chairman of the Presidium of the Soviet Congress, who handles the ceremonial and judicial functions, the chief of government (the chairman of the Council of Government Ministers), and the party chief (General Secretary, Chairman of the Central Committee and its executive, the Politburo). A third idea, most recently associated with President Eisenhower, is for the president to confine himself to foreign affairs and national security, delegating domestic problems to one or more deputy presidents. All such facile ideas founder against the rock of the essential political responsibility of the American executive. This is not to say that the president is sovereign in the classical sense because 200 years of constitutional experience testify to the fact that governmental powers can be shared effectively among the unitary president, the 535-member Congress, and the 9-member Supreme Court.

In *A Model Constitution*, Rexford Tugwell's inventive mind has extended the pluralistic concept of American government from three to six, suggesting that in addition to the executive, legislative, and judicial branches, we need three more: one comprising a national electoral system and personnel, another grouping together the quasi-judicial regulatory agencies and commissions, a third encompassing the functions of economic and fiscal planning. It is easy to criticize the difficulties involved in such multiple coordination, considering the present problems of executive-legislative relations alone. It is particularly difficult to see how the president and Congress could be politically separated from policy responsibilities for monetary, tax, and expenditure planning; but the idea of devolving out from traditional congressional and executive responsibility two autonomous national systems of economic regulation and elections administration deserves more analysis and discussion than it has had. After all, the French have successfully operated two systems of judicial administration since Napoleon's time, both independent of the political responsibilities of parliament, president, or cabinet.

Basic structural alteration of the tripartite separation of powers, whether by increasing it from three to six, or reducing it from three to two or one, raises the fundamental question of lines of political responsibility to the people through the electoral system. Although we have had with us at least since 1900 F. J. Goodnow's theory of separating policy formation from policy execution, no substantial body of theoretical opinion of which I am aware has advocated any workable way of confining either the executive or congress to one or the other; on the contrary, both have successfully asserted and maintained policy jurisdiction and political responsibility to their constituents over both.

To the best of my knowledge, political scientists who have concerned themselves with public policy have not come up with any significant ideas about altering the existing system of joint presidential-Congressional responsibility for policy development. Their participation in political activity has been devoted either to taking sides on the content or substance of policy issues, or to improving the technical instruments and procedures of policy planning. In short, we lack any serious theory for altering the established, evolving system of executive-legislative political responsibility, the Supreme Court being treated as an implicit independent variable, infrequently emerging explicitly into the political process, as in the civil rights and school-busing issues.

Descending to the administrative level, we should take cognizance of the experience since the Budget and Accounting Act of 1921 with the development of the Bureau of the Budget (now the Office of Management and Budget) as the president's administrative arm for fiscal expenditure management. Further, under the Reorganization Act of 1939, the Executive Office of the President was established, providing an institutionalized staff structure for organizational management of the executive branch, and for conducting special functions in times of war or national emergency. The Employment Act of 1946 and National Defense Acts of 1947 and 1958 extended the same principle to the forecasting of national economic trends and coordination of the armed services under the Joint Chiefs of Staff and National Security Council. These developments have contributed mightily to the strengthening of the institutionalized president, not so much in the sense of enhancing his personal power, as in the extent to which they enable him to delegate more effectively his managerial responsibilities over continuing existing programs, so that he can work on policy change and development of new policy perspectives.

What has not come about (notwithstanding the imaginative efforts made by Nixon in foreign affairs, federal grants-in-aid and revenue-sharing, and the negative income tax for the working poor and welfare population) is any satisfactory solution to the organization of the president's personal, White House office staff. Administratively, there are three problems here: **1.** how he controls his time schedule and access of subordinates to him, **2.** some doctrine or theory for assigning responsibility for coordinating presidential goals, means, and follow-through in selected areas of high priority and policy attention, and, **3.** above all, finding persons of sufficient caliber to handle the intricate negotiations of policy development, to conduct the absolutely essential dialogue with congressional committees, departmental and interest-group representatives, and the news media, which is so necessary to developing public support of presidential initiatives against the opposition of vested interests.

You can now see why I have approached the topic of "Social Unrest and the Presidency" in terms of the resources and requirements of presidential leadership, rather than by analyzing the various sources of social unrest or broad social trends making for social change. The latter procedure either leads to specification of particular policies in one or more social, economic, or technical problem-areas, or to the construction of a generalized model of an emerging or desirable social order, which is then urged upon the president and our other political bodies as a recipe for them to bring about as cooks. This is certainly a possible mode of analysis, indeed a necessary mode if one wishes to acquire competence in a given field of policy. I have not attempted to argue, however, that social unrest and public opinion do not control or compel political change; for upon occasion they do, in which case politicians have very little option but to follow the tide.

In most cases, I assume that politics, or political leadership, guides or controls political and social change, at least in the short run, by translating felt needs and complaints into decisions that introduce policy changes in already existing legislative, administrative, and judicial programs. The existing body of public policy and administrative machinery is so extraordinarily large and complex that such general principles as more nationalization, more centralization, more localization, more planning, more initiative and cooperation, more participation, or more confrontation, make little sense; we need some of each, more of one, less of another, depending upon the issue or field of policy one is concerned about. Applied to the president, the assumption that presidential leadership controls social unrest and policy change means not that he can do anything he wants, or must be in a position to control everything, but that the most the president can do is to break new ground in a very few policy areas during his 4 or 8 years in office. He does so insofar as he is able to mobilize massive shifts in public opinion, thereby enabling him to mediate and persuade the several elements in the power structure of the country — banking and commercial, industrial, labor, educational, technical and scientific, congressional and governmental — to support changes in existing programs for dealing with the needs and requirements of the people.

LIMITATIONS ON THE PRESIDENT
IN SOCIAL REORGANIZATION

Neither politics in general, nor a chief executive in conjunction with Congress can transform society at one fell swoop (any student of totalitarian or communist theory and practice can tell us that). Political biographers tell us that most leaders' social-goal values, except in terms of personal security and welfare, are very broadly and vaguely defined. Political scientists have long since discovered and taught that election campaigns rarely provide specific mandates or commitments to legislative programs. The governing, public policy-making process works quite differently from the electoral process, and is only loosely articulated with it. What a president can do, must do, is initiate through appointments; indicate guidelines by selecting priorities among proposals pressed upon his attention; financially help some, and restrict or reduce support to others; exert his influence through public statements or congressional messages for or against one or another group of political entrepreneurs, participants, or decision-makers. He can demand progress reports, set deadlines, and transfer responsibilities. But he can only move in a very few areas at any one time if he is not to spread his own energies too thin and produce confusion in both public and legislative opinion as to what his urgent, proximate policy aims really are.

In the conception of the presidential role in decision making and new policy planning here advanced, the primary issue is not whether the president has too much power, but whether as a person and a politician he can perform the task that our changing economic and social and political systems have combined to locate in his office. We have strengthened the office, but it looks as if the Congress is moving once again to reconstitute its own budgetary procedures and committee structure to deal more effectively with the enhanced institutional facilities of the chief executive. It is not the presidential office, but incumbent presidents, from Franklin Roosevelt through Gerald Ford, who have yet to develop a satisfactory and consistent manner of organizing their time and keeping the White House staff small enough so they can control it while using it effectively for program evaluation and policy development. We would do well to remember that there are no ideal formulas for solving this problem, if indeed it is soluble. Harry Truman, who perhaps of all post-World War II presidents came closest, fell to 23 percent in popular estimation of how well he was doing his job.

In conclusion, as we recall President Nixon's difficulties with his swollen White House staff, seeing to it that they behave properly not only in relation to the Democratic National Committee, but to the rest of the executive branch, to Congress, the news media, and assuring the proper use of political campaign funds, it seems clear to me that more than ever we need to keep in mind the distinction between the presidency and the president. The office is the measure, the standard, for the man; not he for it. What happens to the man may certainly affect the presidency; but what he does or fails to do during his term of office is far more than a matter of salesmanship and image-making, or of identifying his personality and his acts with the welfare of the institution. We may revere the presidency as a matter of faith, but we evaluate the president as a man of politics, struggling to weigh his personal honor and intregrity against what he is required to do in the name of his country, his party, and his people. For all the powers and facilities that have devolved upon the presidency, there has been no perceptible diminution of Congress' powers to appropriate, to investigate and expose, to originate and influence the flow of legislation, to appoint and to judge.

In sharing the responsibility for taking the lead in policy decisions, the president is sometimes the lever, sometimes the fulcrum; but the same is true of Congress. The American people look upon the presidential office as their instrument, jointly with the Congress, for compelling the economic and cultural system to adjust to and survive the perennial challenge of social unrest.

VII☆THE FUTURE

Can presidential behavior be predicted? James David Barber, Duke University political scientist, thinks so. He has developed a formula for predicting presidential behavior based upon an individual's background and several other ingredients. Knowledge of how a prospective president might behave in office, Barber contends, would enable the public to make better presidential selections. He also notes, of course, that there are many problems inherent in predicting presidential behavior.

James David Barber, professor and chairman of the Duke University political science department, has been professor of political science at Yale University, Guest Scholar at the Brookings Institution, and a Fellow at the Center for Advanced Study in the Behavioral Sciences at Stanford. He is the author of The Presidential Character and editor of Choosing the President.

12

Predicting Presidential Character

JAMES DAVID BARBER
Duke University

Predicting presidential character used to be a lot more fun than it is now. We used to have Teddy Roosevelt, Calvin Coolidge, Warren Harding, and Abe Lincoln — all those dramatic characters to deal with. I must say that a lot of joy has gone out of president-watching in the last little while. I would like to deal with each president, comparatively. One of the most trenchant recent comparisons I have seen is that by Sam Levenson, who used to take violin lessons when he was a child. His father always compared him to Heifetz — "Heifetz, you're not."

Well, Franklin Roosevelt, he's not; T. R., he's not; Lincoln, he's not. But there is Richard Nixon and we have to deal with him, so I will be writing about him against a background of what people expect of a president.

There is much public reaction today that makes you think of some of the more somber passages of the scriptures, like "ashes to ashes, dust to dust." We think of the ashes of the assassinated, the ashes of burned cities in Vietnam and in the United States, the ashes of university presidents burned in effigy, the ashes of our trust — so that in many ways now our presidential music sounds like the Olympia Jazz Band on the way back from a New Orleans funeral.

Now, Richard Nixon wanted us to forget a lot of things. His theme was: "Put it behind us. Get on to the important business of the future." Yet, I think that only by memory can we somehow get a handle on the future — in our own lives or in the society we live in. Part of the responsibility of the university is to maintain the integrity of a tradition and to pass that along to succeeding generations. University people are responsible for not forgetting, for trying to make of the past some guide to the future. How can memory — even back beyond 1974 — help us with that?

PROBLEMS IN PRESIDENTIAL BEHAVIOR PREDICTIONS

It is not easy to predict presidents. You remember that when Franklin Roosevelt was running for president he said he was going to balance the budget. There was all sorts of concern when Harry Truman became president that this farm boy from Missouri would never be able to handle the presidency. Lots of confident predictions were made that Eisenhower, who was, after all, a military man, would attempt to run the White House like the Joint Chiefs of Staff — would be yelling orders to everyone, telling them what to do and where to go. That did not happen. Then we come along to John Kennedy. Wasn't he too wet behind the ears? Wouldn't he sell the country out to the pope? Many such fears were aroused at that time. Then we began to descend into greater difficulties with predictions. I am sure all of you remember as far back as the campaign of 1964. In that campaign there was a Hawk candidate and a Dove candidate; the Dove candidate won. That was Lyndon Baines Johnson, who said again and again how devoted to peace he was, how determined he was that American boys would not wind up in Vietnam. It did not turn out that way.

Mr. Nixon also made a series of predictions when he was running for the presidency. He said that he was going to appoint men who would have great stature and give them independent responsibilities throughout the government. They would be able to speak in their own right, and they would not be subservient to the White House. He said that his was going to be an open administration in which reporters could get the facts they needed — not only from him, but from other members of his administration. He said that we were going to go into a period of "lowered voices," of calm, of quiet — that we had had enough trouble, after all, by the time he took office, that our country needed a more rational, easygoing approach in the presidency. I am not saying the man was lying. I am saying he was mistaken and that presidents have been mistaken time and time again in trying to predict their own actions as they moved into the whirlwind of the White House.

Even when Mr. Nixon repeated something again and again, he could be wrong. Consider the lesson he learned, the one he asserts most frequently in Six Crises: right after you have taken action in a crisis, you go into a period of "letdown," as he calls it. In the "letdown" period, watch out, he says, because you are likely to let down your guard, you are likely to do something that later you will wish you hadn't done. That lesson is repeated over and over in Six Crises [1962]. That book was published one spring, and in the following fall, he ran for governor against Pat Brown in California, met that crisis head-on, and lost. And on election night he delivered his diatribe against the press, "You won't have Richard Nixon to kick around anymore," a bitter outpouring in the letdown period after a crisis.

IMPROVING PREDICTIONS OF PRESIDENTIAL BEHAVIOR

How could we do better at prediction? I want to try an approach that is related to psychology in several ways. Let me first make perfectly clear that I am not referring to psychoanalysis;

that is to say, not to the understanding of human behavior in its deepest manifestations. There one interprets symbols; for instance, the dreams Lyndon Johnson is said to have had. His father had always told him that the real mark of a man was to be able to turn a stampede. Johnson had an aunt, I believe it was, who was paralyzed and confined to a rocking chair. So he had the dream that he was sitting in a rocking chair out on the prairie and along came the stampede toward him, and he couldn't move and couldn't get up to stop the stampede. Then the scene of the dream would switch to the White House. He would think he was in a room where he could hear his advisors making horrible decisions and he couldn't get up to stop them. He would wake up from these dreams, walk through the White House, find the portrait of Woodrow Wilson and remind himself that he didn't look like Woodrow Wilson. All of that is reported in a book on Lyndon Johnson by Doris Kearns of Harvard. I am not really certain what to make of that sort of thing. In Nixon's case, when he was eleven, he wrote a letter to his mother signed, "Your good dog, Richard." The story is that he and his brothers were out in the woods and he fell into the pond and the bees stung him and the old dog wouldn't help him and he ran out the other side. Now if you start multiplying those images, the psychoanalytic interpreters' ears perk up, and they can really see a lot of things in those ponds and bees and dogs and things. I want to stay away from that, because I think it is too difficult when you cannot interview the person directly to make those kinds of judgments.

INGREDIENTS OF THE PREDICTION FORMULA

In the kinds of predictions I try to make, I work with certain basic elements. One is the power situation — for instance, you have to know just how many votes a president can count on in Congress. What was the margin by which he was elected? What is his support in public opinion? What is his relation to the judicial branch? In short, what sort of power box is he in?

The national climate of expectations — the mood of the

country, so to speak — is something else about which one needs to think.

And then the man — his own character, his style, and his views of the world have to be examined. In all of those respects, there are in my judgment, some storms ahead.

Power

Let's use Richard Nixon as an example. Even as early as March 1973, in trying to look at the power situation, there were certain elements that you could see. For instance, the Twenty-second Amendment to the Constitution meant that for the first time in his life, Mr. Nixon could not run for president again. This situation presented him with the loss of power. He became a "lame duck" president. Congress was, and still is, upset about the presidential invasion of the power of the purse, which has traditionally belonged to Congress. Of all the powers that Congress is jealous of, the power of the purse is the greatest. Despite some twenty-five or so court decisions declaring it illegal, President Nixon continued to impound funds. The press was largely hostile, except for the editorial writers. The reporting press, especially the elite press in New York and Washington, was largely anti-Nixon, partly because of dragnet subpoenas and other attacks on civil liberties. He had alienated a great deal of the bureaucracy that he had inherited from the Democrats by dismantling, or trying to dismantle, the Office of Economic Opportunity and by making rather disdainful remarks about bureaucrats. As for the opposition party, the Democrats, there were already Watergate leakages, so that the opposition began to feel not only that they were against Nixon in terms of policy preferences, but also in terms of the basic rules of the game, by which people are supposed to play fairly. So, President Nixon had a lot of people against him. In his own Republican party, the members found it very difficult to relate to him. His famous isolation was there, and the Republicans felt put aside by the Committee to Re-Elect the President, which ran its own campaign and was of very little help to other Republican candidates.

And last, but not least, the universities and the scientific establishments really did not have much use for Nixon and had not
had for a good while.

The power situation can be analyzed similarly for any president. For example, John Kennedy came into office by a paper-
thin margin of votes. Now, if you understand the power situation, you would not, then, expect him to propose imaginative
legislative programs. After all, he was barely president. Lyndon
Johnson, on the other hand, came in on a tidal wave of votes over
Barry Goldwater. He did get a flood of legislation through the
Congress.

Climate of Expectations

The climate of expectations — the mood of the country — is
terribly important now. It is still not entirely clear what happened in the 1972 election, but the preliminary results seem to
show that it was largely an anti-McGovern vote rather than a
pro-Nixon vote. Nevertheless, it was a whale of a vote, and so,
the president went in with high expectations. The public has
traditionally looked up to the presidency. The president is by far
the best-known person in the country; he shows up on polls of
most-admired; he is the first politician that children know anything about, and they have generally felt that he is a good person,
long before they know the sheriff, or the mayor, or the governor,
or any other official. So you have this tradition, at least in the
history of polling, which goes back into the 1930s, of great respect for the president and for the presidential office. You can
see that very dramatically when you look at the assassination or
death of a president. I imagine all readers remember where they
were when John Kennedy was killed, and how they felt, and
what was going on in their minds. A tremendous wave of emotion spread across the country. Many, many people were physi-
cally ill, and a majority of those polled in the country said they
wept. For whom? For someone they had never met, for a public
official, for a hired hand of the government who was supposed to
see that the laws were faithfully executed. This event led

researchers to look back into the death-in-office of other presidents. They found that exactly the same thing had happened, not only for a young, charismatic figure like John Kennedy, but also for Warren Harding — that zero-point on all ratings of presidential greatness — when he died in office. When they brought his body back from the West Coast, children threw flowers on the tracks, farmers stood with their hats over their hearts in the fields. When the cortège reached Chicago, 300,000 weeping people were in the streets, mourning Warren Harding. The same thing happened with McKinley, Garfield, Lincoln — all the way back you find this same kind of terribly intense reaction when a president dies in office. On the other hand, when an ex-president dies, he elicits no such intense reaction. We all feel the loss, we all are sorry about the death of Eisenhower or Truman or Johnson, but there was not this gripping emotion. Something is going on between a president in office and the public, something very deep, involving a strong sense of respect and hopefulness.

These days, we are in the midst of what I am confident is a temporary, if long, slide downward from that kind of trust. For the first time in the history of polling, most Americans are pessimistic about the future of the country. This decline of trust in government as reflected in the polls started long before Watergate and has continued its downward slope ever since. The long slide in Nixon's popularity, in the answer to the question, "Is the president doing a good job?" took place against the background of a slide in confidence that was already going on. This disillusionment with the political order showed up when Gordon Strachan, one of the Watergate witnesses, was asked by one of the senators, "What would you tell a young person thinking about getting into politics today?" Strachan replied, "Stay out of it. Don't get mixed up with that crew or you'll be sorry."

I think that some of this disillusionment comes about because the American people ask a great deal of their presidents. They ask them first, to help them make sense of the political world. Congress is a very complicated thing. The bureaucracy is even more complicated, with all it's alphabet-soup bureaus, agencies, and the like. But everyone can understand the president — he is one man trying to do a job. We can all identify with that, we can understand that. In our thinking, it helps us make sense of the world. Secondly, I think that the people look to the president for reassurance. They look to him for calmness, a surcease of anxiety, a feeling that things are going to be all right somehow. Then they look to him for a sense of activism. The president ought to be in there slugging it out, fighting, working, trying, striving, moving the country forward again. He should be an engine of progress. For instance, Eisenhower was criticized for not working hard enough as president, and thus Kennedy could come in and say he was going to "move the country." And finally, people expect a sense of legitimacy from the president. The people look to the president as guardian of the Constitutional tradition. When he leaves office, they want the flag flying, the Bill of Rights intact, the intentions of the Founding Fathers still being honored — to be able to say to themselves, all's right with the world.

Consider those needs and how they have or have not been met in recent years. The need for making sense of the political world confronts the shocks and confusions that we have had recently. We have reached the point where if there is not some tremendous crisis, we begin to get sort of bored. The constant shock of change and of reorientation has been severe. I think presidents have contributed to that in recent years. Instead of representing the continuity of events, they have represented fragility and changeableness. Look at what we have been through emotionally with respect to the last three presidents. We had John F. Kennedy with his activism — "let's get the country moving again." Young, vigorous, Knight of Camelot, and then he was chopped down. Suddenly the action stops. Then along comes Lyndon Johnson. Remember back when he was first coming into the presidency as Kennedy's successor? He was "Preacher Lyndon," the national president, the symbol of legitimacy. "I shall continue," he said, and he played a great deal on his legitimacy in the presidential office. He ended up with the credibility gap blowing the ground out from under his feet and our trust falling apart. The national psyche was by now deeply disturbed. And then, after all that disturbance, along comes Mr. Nixon, stressing reassurance at first. You remember the "lowered voices." But the voices were not lowered. We went through crisis after crisis after crisis — Cambodia, Haynesworth and Carswell, Phases I and II and III, unheard of shortages, astronomical prices, and finally the threat of impeachment and the act of resignation. These shocks and confusions came along at a time when, for various reasons, public confidence was on the downslide.

What I think that means for the future is that we may become too vulnerable to emotional appeals on the part of the next elected president. I can see these appeals working in two directions. One might be that in our weariness of chaotic events, we would elect a president who would guarantee that he would not do anything. He would promise to just sit there, sign papers, and not disturb our tranquility. That could happen. Or we might look for a man on horseback, someone who would solve all the problems and soothe our anxieties with a kind of phony stability. We have to be wary of both "solutions."

In any case, anything that the current president does has to be understood against the background of this climate of expectations. That is true for every president. It was true for them in the past; it will be true for them in the future. They are very much affected in what they can do by this climate. For instance, when Franklin Roosevelt came in, the nation had fallen apart. Will Rogers said, "As long as he does something, people will rally to him. If he burns down the Capitol, at least they will say he has done something." People were desperate for action from the central government. Roosevelt could build on that.

Character

Then consider the president himself. A familiar question not too long ago was, "Is there a new Richard Nixon?" Barry Goldwater was asked on television whether Nixon would get out of the Watergate problem and, if so, how? Goldwater replied that he thought Nixon would — if he would only reorient himself, take a new stance in solving the domestic problems of the country, then everything would be all right. Now that must have been the "umpteenth" time that someone said there could be a new Nixon. In Theodore White's book about the election of 1972, he was increasingly enthusiastic about Mr. Nixon. White thought that the man had changed; the man had grown; the man was different. Then, when he had just finished writing the manuscript, along came Watergate. White had to do a great deal of hasty rewriting of enthusiastic paragraphs.

I am skeptical about such changes. A president is unlikely to change his basic character when he goes into the White House. Moving from one office to another office in middle age, he is not likely to revolutionize his character. All of us middle-aged folk would like to believe otherwise — that we can change as easily as young people can, but the odds are not great that someone will become a basically different kind of person at the age that most people have reached when they become president. As a result, I think that the first thing to try to understand about a president is what I call his "character."

I have tried to develop a scheme for classifying character that would enable us to see, before the man takes office, what kind of president he is most likely to be. I will sketch out that scheme here. First, divide the presidents into those who are more active and those who are more passive. That makes sense to me because activity and passivity are basic psychological facts about the way people orient themselves to life. Little babies generally tend to be either more active or more passive. The same is true of presidents. Lyndon Johnson, clearly one of the most active politicians ever, went about his job like a human cyclone. He spent half the day and night calling up people, shaking hands, working very hard at the job. In contrast — undoubtedly the most striking contrast — is Calvin Coolidge. Calvin Coolidge slept about eleven hours a night, and he still needed a nap in the middle of the day. He is really one of my favorites, especially for his various sayings, such as "Can't hang you for what you don't say." He said that if you see ten problems coming down the road toward you, if you just sit there, by the time they get there all but two of them will be gone, and one of those won't be worth fooling with. He was known as "Silent Cal" much of the time, but the most recent book about him is called *The Talkative President* because he had more frequent press conferences than Franklin Roosevelt did. He loved to talk to the press. He let them photograph him in all conceivable outfits. There is a wonderful picture of him presenting a sap bucket to Henry Ford. On social occasions, however, he was very silent. One time he was sitting between two matrons at dinner, and one of them said, "Mr. President, what do you think about agriculture?" He did not say anything. "What do you think about business?" He did not say anything. She went all through the alphabet, all the way down to Vermont, and he would not say a word. It was not that he would nod or anything, he just sat there. Finally she said, "Mr. President, I've got a bet with a friend for fifty dollars that you'll say at least three words to me." Cal looked up and said, "You lose." Some presidents manage to get by pretty passively.

Then divide the presidents into those who are positive and those who are negative in a special sense, and that special sense is: do they enjoy doing what they have to do? Or, do they go through the presidency with an air of suffering and martyrdom and struggling and striving, but not seeming to have very much fun? By enjoyment, I don't mean the attitude "I'm struggling along now, but some day I will be happy." I mean "Today it was fun." Today-it-was-fun was Franklin Roosevelt's attitude. He had fun being president. He liked dealing with people in that way of his. For contrast, take Herbert Hoover or Andrew Johnson, who was known as the "Grim Presence" in the White House, who never cracked a smile. Hoover discouraged the presence of people in the White House. He did not like to see the servants in the hall, so when he walked down the halls, the servants would jump into the closets and close the doors, so you had the waiters and waitresses crowding in there with trays. Hoover exuded a sense of suffering, of having a rough time of it rather than enjoying it. That is what I mean by positive or negative. Positive and negative do not mean "good" guys and "bad" guys any more than active and passive do.

Consider some other presidents. Those who were active and positive include Franklin Roosevelt, Harry Truman, and John Kennedy. Those who were active and negative, Woodrow Wilson, Herbert Hoover, Lyndon Johnson, and Richard Nixon.

Those who were passive and positive, William Howard Taft and Warren G. Harding. Those who were passive and negative, Calvin Coolidge and Dwight D. Eisenhower. What that means (and I shall not go into it in great detail) is that each of the types tend toward certain directions. The passive-negative, for example, tend toward withdrawal. Thus, for both Coolidge and Eisenhower, the temptation of the presidency was to escape from politics; Coolidge in the way I have described, Eisenhower by rising above politics. "I will not get down into the gutter with Joe McCarthy," he said, and "Don't worry me about those monkeys in Congress, they can find their own majority leader." Eisenhower did not like to be bothered, and he was always complaining about being bothered in the White House. He had his first heart attack when he was interrupted on the golf course by repeated calls from the State Department. The fault of the Eisenhower presidency (there were also important virtues) was inaction, drift. What that does, of course, is to leave the country without active leadership from the White House.

The tendency of the passive-positive president is to comply, to be agreeable. Harding and Taft both had a tendency to connect with that part of politics that is full of love. It is a much neglected thing in research, but there is a loving aspect of politics, a cameraderie, a kind of inclusiveness of the community that politics can represent. That is what appeals to such presidents as Harding. His father said it was a good thing he was not a girl or he would have been in trouble all the time. He found it difficult to refuse, and he had another problem. He looked like a president, you see. He looked more like a president than any president since George Washington. In fact, the opera singer, Enrico Caruso, took a picture of Warren Harding and drew a wig on it, and it really looked like George Washington. He was a proud speaker, an actor in politics. He made a speech against the League of Nations in the Senate and thought so well of it that he had a phonograph record made with that speech on one side and "Beautiful Ohio" on the other side. You might say that the passive-positives are love bugs in the presidency. I could tell you about William Howard Taft, but that is a larger story.

The danger of the active-negative presidents is that they will freeze around some policy and pursue it despite its highly destructive consequences. They, I think, are the most dangerous types to have in the White House. Historically, Woodrow Wilson was very flexible in the first part of his regime. He put through a lot of progressive legislation. But then he froze up about the League of Nations treaty — about the *language* of the League of Nations treaty — and insisted on what turned out to be rather trivial verbal matters. Therefore, he lost his battle with the Senate, and the United States did not enter the League of Nations. Instead of establishing this connection with Europe, the United States withdrew into isolation. Along came Hitler, along came Mussolini, Europe fell apart, and we had to suffer for it. Hoover, like Wilson, was a good man, a principled man, a man trying to do the right thing. You are not going to spot the president we do not want by looking for a man who gets up first thing in the morning and says, "Today I am going out and do evil." That's not the way it works. These people mean well, but they get into trouble. Hoover got into trouble because he refused direct relief to American citizens at the time of the Depression. It is a complicated story, but Hoover was willing, eventually, to spend money for the relief of business, and would even provide funds to buy feed for cattle, but not for human beings at a time when many families suddenly found their incomes withdrawn from them through no fault of their own. No wonder Franklin Roosevelt was able to knock him over pretty easily.

Lyndon Johnson — that story is too familiar and painful for recounting. You know what he froze up about. It is said that after these active-negative presidents are through, the nation survives. But there are a lot of people who are not surviving because of Lyndon Johnson. There are a lot of families, over in another country, with dead children and dead fathers and dead mothers, and there are a lot of maimed people and homeless people because of what that president did. That is the kind of result that you get from rigidified presidents.

Active and positive presidents are, I think, the most hopeful ones for the presidency. They find it easier to connect with external reality. Think about yourself. You have a powerful resource if you can find some way to work in life so that you can

work hard and enjoy it at the same time. It is an energizing thing
that the active-positive types have. I think genuine achievement
is more likely to come from those resources, although active-
positives have their troubles, too since they tend to get impatient
with tradition, with the rules. Franklin Roosevelt tried to pack
the Supreme Court, for example; Truman seized the steel
industry — both largely out of impatience. But I think generally
active-positive presidents are the ones who work out better.

Style and Worldview

Two final elements complete the framework: style and
worldview. By style, I mean not something so deep as character,
but simply a man's political habits. To determine style, you want
to ask first, "What are the tasks that a president has to do in the
White House — tasks that he can not avoid?" Every president
has to speak to the nation, so he has to be a rhetorician. Every
president has to negotiate up close with other politicians to some
degree. Every president has to do some homework, some paper
work, some fact-finding. All must do some of each, but the *way*
presidents operate in that framework can be very important.
Hoover, for example, had a terrible time making speeches. In the
case of Mr. Nixon, there was universal comment on his difficulty
with negotiations. That is, he was a rhetorician, spoke to the
nation, did his homework, and a lot of close studying. He had a
good record at the Duke Law School, and he put in a lot of time
thinking about what he was doing, but he had desperate difficulties in just relating to people, in close where he could negotiate
with them. It was very hard for him to make that kind of political
connection as far back as the very first time he ran for office in
1946 against Jerry Voorhis in California. Style, then — the president's political habits — needs looking into. What are the gaps?
What are the strengths?

As for the worldview, people make a lot of mistakes in
equating that with ideology. Again, many thought of Richard
Nixon as a rigid anticommunist before he came into office,
which did not prove to be true. Many thought of him as an

economic conservative in the sense of laissez-faire free enterprise and that did not turn out to be true. In short, ideology is not
a very good guide. But if you look at the attitude the man has
toward causality in history, toward how the world works, and
what people are like, you can make better guesses. You can determine whether he, for instance, concentrates on the hopeful
side of human nature or keeps reminding people that most
people are lazy, most people are weak, most people do not have
much imagination. Preachments of this kind from Richard Nixon
represented, I think, attitudes that shaped his action in important ways. Mr. Nixon said that the only way to attack crime in
America is the way crime attacks our people — without pity.
Now pity is something that has been recommended in other
quarters as a desirable thing. How a president feels about such
lasting moral issues as justice and pity is part of his worldview,
his basis for action.

What does all this add up to in the selection of future presidents? This analysis of types of presidents suggests the extreme
care that must be exercised by the people, the political parties,
the press, and all elements engaged in presidential selection.
The type of character found in the president can have enormous
impact on both domestic and foreign policy, as well as on the
level of public trust in the government.

Epilogue: Apocalypse of the Night Watchman

CHARLES W. DUNN
Clemson University

> ...the overloaded powers in the White House were used to transform the presidency into a total government in itself, organized for political overkill to get and hold more power.... Even with Richard Nixon out of office this larger crisis of the presidency would persist.
>
> — Samuel Lubell, *The Future While It Happened* [1973, p. 9].

ACCORDING TO ISAAC NEWTON'S FIRST law, the law of inertia, an object once in motion will continue in motion unless it is acted upon by outside forces. Newton's law enables us to distinguish between two key elements for analyzing the future of the American presidency.

First, constitutional creation of a presidency with the capacity and flexibility to grow in power set in motion an "object" — namely presidential power — which accelerated in momentum during the twentieth century, especially between 1933 and the present. Second, the presidency of Richard Nixon, which was the inheritor, not the creator, of this growth in presidential power, used the power in a manner that caused outside forces to check his exercise of presidential power.

A number of important questions may be asked about the political and personality situation that caused outside forces to check Nixon's exercise of presidential power.

- Would outside forces have checked the power of a Democratic president who conducted himself in the same manner as President Nixon, especially if the Congress were controlled by the Democratic Party?

- Would a president with a different personality, who was, for example, less abrasive in his actions and attitudes toward the courts, Congress, and the press, have had outside forces check his power?[1]

These questions raise the central issue. Did outside forces, according to Newton's law, act just to check the exercise of power by one president or did these forces act to check presidential power itself without reference to a particular president?

The contention here is that outside forces acted largely to check the exercise of presidential power by one president and that whatever effect these forces may have on subsequent presidents will most likely be minimal. Stated another way, while the conditions that caused outside forces to act against Nixon's exercise of power are peculiar to him and his administration, the conditions that caused the quick crescendo in presidential power, beginning particularly in the 1930s, are still with us.

Outside forces acted to check President Nixon's exercise of presidential power, because he sowed the seeds of his own destruction by

- the type of persons he appointed to office;

- his attitudes and actions toward the Congress, the courts, and the press;

- his obsession with secrecy.

Ironically, each of these attitudes or actions later came back to haunt him. Consider what might have happened if the White House had not referred to the House Judiciary Committee as a "kangaroo court." Consider, too, the attitude of blacks serving in large numbers on the Watergate grand jury in the District of Columbia. Could they be expected to look sympathetically upon participants in the Watergate scandal when their people were adversely affected by Nixon's so-called "southern strategy"? It is worth considering as well how Nixon appointees to the U. S. Supreme Court could be expected to look sympathetically upon his position in the tape subpoena case [*United States* v. *Nixon*, 1974] when Nixon himself had indicated his uncertainty about abiding by the court's forthcoming decision? The examples of the ways in which Nixon sowed the seeds of his own destruction could be multiplied; suffice it to say, "they have sown the wind, and they shall reap the whirlwind" [Hosea 8:7].

From the outset, it must be conceded that Watergate and the impeachment proceedings sensitized Congress, the courts, the press, and the public to the possible abuses of presidential power and that as a result certain reforms have either been proposed or enacted. However, the nature of American society today and the nature of the governmental and political system is likely to limit the reform fallout from Watergate to the short run.

THE NATURE OF SOCIETY

There has been substantial commentary in recent years about the decline of the American civilization. One of the best books articulating this thesis is *The End of the American Era* by Andrew Hacker, who argues that the American people are basically selfish and lack a sense of mission — ingredients he considers necessary for continuation of America as a great nation. According to Hacker,

> Most people estimate their opinions too highly to adhere to any consensus, let alone one involving common goals. Moreover, authority tends to be regarded with suspicion, and all codes are continually questioned. Americans remain restless and self-centered, giving priority to individual pursuits and advancement [1970, p. 146].

Another well-known and highly respected commentator on the fate of Western civilization, Malcolm Muggeridge, an esteemed English intellectual, adds a third reason for this decline. Muggeridge believes Western civilization is in a state of moral and spiritual decay; that largely because of television, people have become morally insensitive and incapable of righteous indignation and moral outrage. In his graphic and vivid analogy, Muggeridge says,

> ... Western Civilization is in an advanced stage of decomposition, and ... another Dark Age will soon be upon us, if, indeed, it has not already begun. With the Media, especially television, governing all our lives, as they indubitably do, it is easily imaginable that this might happen without our noticing. I was reading the other day about a distasteful, but significant, experiment conducted in some laboratory or other. A number of frogs were put into a bowl of water, and the water very gradually raised to boiling point, with the result that they all expired without making any serious effort to jump out of the bowl. *The frogs are us, the water is our habitat, and the Media, by accustoming us to the gradual deterioration of our values and our circumstances, ensure that boiling point comes upon us unawares.* It is my own emphatic opinion that boiling point is upon us now ... ["Living Through An Apocalypse," International Congress on World Evangelization, Lausanne, Switzerland, July 22, 1974].*

The Hacker-Muggeridge analysis suggests there are larger forces governing the future of the American presidency besides such contemporary events as Watergate, impeachment, executive privilege arguments, and the hoped-for rebalancing of powers between the president and Congress. Accordingly, these events, merely symptoms of a deeper societal illness, should be understood in relationship to these larger forces.

Who is to referee and umpire the settlement of disputes caused by the increasing entanglement of private interests, or what Hacker refers to as a nation of "200 Million Egos"? The governmental and political processes are, of course, the principal arbiters, and chief among them is the presidency. It is to the

---

*Reprinted with the permission of the International Congress on World Evangelization.

president that the Congress, the press, and the public most often turn for an articulation of the national agenda and the setting of priorities among conflicts and problems to be resolved. Interest groups have recognized for years that to acquire the president's support on an issue generally results in determining the principal focus of attention and debate on that subject. Not only can the president, through such devices as the State of the Union, economic, and budget messages, set the national agenda, but he can also respond more quickly in crisis situations. Congress, large and unwieldy, lacks the capacity and flexibility to effectively challenge the president in articulating the national agenda and in responding quickly to crisis situations. Moreover, the president as party leader and chief foreign affairs spokesman has these assets that are not possessed by the Congress.

For a moment it would be well to shift our focus from Hacker's view of the American people's lack or loss of mission to a focus on the institutional sense of mission in the executive and legislative branches. Clearly, the mission of the executive branch depends primarily on the goals and objectives of the president while the congressional mission depends upon an interaction of 535 individuals. The president can more easily determine the mission of the executive branch of government than can congressional leaders of the legislative, but he also has substantial resources to influence Congress and the public with that sense of mission. Where a president has had a sense of mission and a determination to achieve that mission, historians frequently refer to that period of history in relationship to the president and the slogan which exemplified his mission as with Franklin Roosevelt and the New Deal, Truman and the Fair Deal, Kennedy and the New Frontier, Johnson and the Great Society. Noticeably absent from this list is President Dwight David Eisenhower, who lacked a sense of mission and determination similar to that possessed by other presidents. Generally, we can conclude from modern American history, that if a president has a sense of mission, and the determination to achieve that mission, he will have greater influence over the Congress and will be accorded a special status in history books. Had it not been for Watergate, perhaps Richard Nixon would also have exemplified what a president can do with a sense of mission and the determination to achieve it.

Now, however, back to Hacker's thesis, we may conclude that even though the president will most likely continue to define in large measure whatever sense of national mission there is, he will also experience increasing difficulty in doing so. The ever more personal pursuits of "200 Million Egos" will, according to Hacker, make the task of defining an American mission more difficult. Accordingly, this analysis suggests that presidents will be increasingly unable to articulate a sense of national mission that grasps the imagination of most Americans and that a president's capacity to govern will, of course, be affected. To be sure, Congress plays a role in determining the national mission, but that role is secondary to the president's role, and it would stretch the imagination too far to speculate that the Congress with its many institutional shortcomings could supplant the president as the articulator of a national sense of mission, even if one allows for the increasing number of obstacles that stand in the way of a presidential definition of the national mission.

Because of his determined sense of mission, Richard Nixon, despite Watergate, maintained substantial influence over the Congress during the greater part of that sordid period of over two years that began June 17, 1972. Subsequent presidents, who do not face similar problems, can certainly be expected, if they have a well-developed sense of mission, to have greater influence over the Congress and history except insofar as they are limited by the American people's individual self-interests, which inhibit presidential definitions of the national mission.

It should be pointed out that the Congress until relatively recently had a keen sense of institutional mission and that the congressional sense of mission tended to decline as the presidential role and sense of mission increased. A standing joke in Washington is that most representatives are now elected with the ambition of becoming senators and that most senators are now elected with the ambition of becoming president. In years past, there were many more representatives and senators with a sense of mission and destiny about their respective branches of the Congress, and often with more concern about maintaining their legislative position than in advancing to a higher one. The Senate, however, is now looked upon as the "incubator" of presidential candidates and presidents, and it should easily be recognized that these individuals may sometimes make their decisions more in reference to presidential aspirations than to institutional commitments to the Congress. It may be that the lack of an institutional sense of mission is one reason why major reform proposals to reduce presidential power may not be seriously considered by the Congress.

Malcolm Muggeridge's assessment of the decline in Western civilization indicates that the public may be becoming insensitive to conditions that in years past might have provoked them to righteous indignation and moral outrage. Certainly, Watergate and impeachment proceedings can be used, at least in part, to justify Muggeridge's view. During the two years of Watergate, from June 17, 1972, to August 1974, public opinion polls — although showing a decline in support for Richard Nixon — revealed that this decline was very gradual, and that majority support for impeachment and conviction did not occur until shortly before Nixon resigned. Congress, of course, was criticized by some critics for responding too slowly to Watergate, but that institution that is supposed to mirror at least in part the views of the American public responded at about the same speed as the public.[2]

Should Muggeridge be correct, then we can expect the public to be conditioned to accepting such incidents as Watergate without any immediate and vocal moral outrage or righteous indignation being expressed, but rather, with a rather resigned view that such behavior is either to be expected or may, indeed, even be justifiable.

The foregoing analysis strongly suggests that Watergate may merely be a symptom of far deeper forces at work in American society and that these deeper forces are really shaping these events and the public reaction to them.

THE NATURE OF THE SYSTEM

Upon passing from the public mind, Watergate — cause of a veritable avalanche of reform proposals designed to rectify the evils unveiled by it — will probably reveal that removal of the catalyst for reform proposals will also stifle the initiative for reform. Favorable action on many of these reforms most likely depends upon how long the public is sensitized by Watergate. The central thesis here is that the American governmental and political system responds more directly to crisis and that when the crisis subsides, clamor for change softens.

This avalanche of Watergate-inspired reform proposals can generally be catalogued in three parts: presidential, congressional, and electoral. The list of proposals summarized is not intended to be exhaustive, but rather indicative of the range of proposals which have been made.

Presidential Reform

The American fascination with the parliamentary system has inspired several proposals, including adoption of the parliamentary system itself, which would make the election of the president a function of the Congress rather than of the American people acting through the electoral college. Consequently, the president would be more subject to legislative influence since his election would directly depend upon the legislative branch and the president's party would customarily be the majority party in Congress. This reform, proposed many times during American history, really cannot be taken too seriously since it would mean a major restructuring of the American Constitution and the powers obtained therefrom by the several branches of government. It, like proposals to create a multiheaded presidency in place of just one president, is unrealistic in view of 200 years of experience with the existing system.

Other facets of the parliamentary system have also been proposed for incorporation with our existing structure. The two best known of these proposals are the vote of no confidence and the requirement that the president and/or his cabinet secretaries and aides be required to appear before Congress to answer questions in debate. The vote of no confidence provision, less harsh than our present impeachment provision, would allow the Congress to remove a president from office by a vote of no confidence and then to declare a national election to choose a president. The incumbent president could be a candidate in that election. Thus, where the impeachment mechanism means removal from office with no right to take one's case to the public, the vote of no confidence would allow the president to present his case to the electorate and, if vindicated by them, to return to office. Adoption of this proposal would create some problems, most especially the problem of determining the ground rules for a vote of no confidence. Under the parliamentary system, the party of the prime minister and the majority party in parliament are usually the same, but in our presidential system, the president may be and often is of a different party than the majority party in Congress. To illustrate the problem, on what grounds could a Democratic congressional majority declare no confidence in a Republican president? Although this proposal has certain appeal, the practical difficulties of implementation weigh heavily against its adoption.

The requirement that the president and/or his aides debate or respond to questions, for example, on the House floor also has an appeal, especially in view of Watergate. President Nixon and his aides would, if this provision had been in effect, have had to answer questions put to them by the Congress. Under our present system, the president is largely immune from answering their questions if he chooses to be.

Other principal proposals to alter the structure of the presidency are the single 6-year presidential term and the requirement that certain White House aides, such as the directors of the Office of Management and Budget and the National Security Council, be confirmed by the Senate.

The purpose of the 6-year term is to allow the president adequate time to develop and implement his program without worrying about a reelection campaign in four years and to insulate the president from political considerations in decision-making. The obvious drawback to the provision is that the president would be making decisions as a 6-year lame duck president and without the consideration of how the public would respond to his decisions at the polls. He would be immune from public approval or rejection at the polls. To illustrate, some opponents of this proposal argue that Richard Nixon removed troops from

Vietnam because of his impending campaign for reelection, which would have been seriously impaired had he not withdrawn troops. Had he been in office for a 6-year term, President Nixon would not have had to face the possibility of public rebuke concerning a failure to remove troops.

During the first term of the Nixon presidency, most observers considered Henry Kissinger, not Secretary of State William Rogers, to be the principal architect of foreign policy. Ironically, Rogers had to be confirmed by the Senate and to appear before committees of the Congress. Kissinger did not. The Congress, therefore, had no way to "get at" the principal architect of foreign policy. Top White House aides with significant policy-making responsibilities, according to this proposal, should require senatorial confirmation to prevent policy from being made by persons who do not have to respond to the queries of the legislative branch.

Among other proposals to rectify the imbalance of power in the hands of the president are the requirement that the president report to Congress on steps he has taken to implement new laws, the appointment of a permanent special prosecutor to serve as a watchdog over the executive branch, and the refinement and retailoring of "executive privilege" to prevent presidential abuses. Paradoxically these proposals, which are all congressionally inspired, illustrate the impotence of Congress when it is up against the executive branch. Through its oversight function, that is, its right to investigate the executive branch, Congress has the power to determine presidential compliance with congressional intent concerning the implementation of all laws and to investigate presidential malfeasance, misfeasance, and nonfeasance in office. In reference to executive privilege, the Congress may cite the president for contempt if he fails to provide requested information or bring suit in federal court seeking a court order to provide the information. Congress already has the power to act in these three areas; the question is whether it has the will.

Another recent proposal is one offered by Milton Eisenhower, advisor to several presidents and brother of President Dwight D. Eisenhower. He recommends that the president have two executive vice presidents, one for domestic affairs and one for foreign affairs, who would be nominated by the president and confirmed by the U. S. Senate. They would not stand in line of succession to the presidency nor would they supplant the already elected vice president. In effect, Eisenhower's proposal would institutionalize Richard Nixon's idea of a super-cabinet by making these officials more important than the cabinet secretaries. They would rank as prime ministers and would, therefore, take some of the burden from the president, for example when protocol presently demands that the president meet with certain dignitaries. Under Eisenhower's proposal, the executive vice presidents could perform such chores [*The Charlotte Observer*, August 22, 1974, p. 10 A].

Perhaps the most recent and unusual proposal was that made by Benjamin V. Cohen, an influential advisor to President Franklin D. Roosevelt, who has advocated an executive council to the president of between five and eight persons who would be individuals with the highest public standing, substantial and varied experience, nominated by the president and confirmed by the Senate. These persons would constitute a super-cabinet that would monitor and coordinate the policies and programs of the various departments and agencies — a job now performed by the White House staff. Prior to making any significant decision or commitment, the president would have to consult with his executive council who would be fully apprised of all the facts. Beyond consultation, however, the president would have full responsibility for making the decision. The executive council would have no right to dictate a decision to the president; he would retain full responsibility for decision-making.

Two problems at least are readily apparent with this innovative idea. Would Congressional leaders ever approve an idea that might tend to remove them from the consultative function which they perform for the president? Would this proposal simply be placing another layer of administration on top of an already bloated bureaucracy? These problems alone are probably sufficient to block adoption of this idea, which has as its laudable objective the idea of creating a peer group for the president who, because of his presently exalted position, does not have peers either within his own branch or the legislative branch of government. The idea is to insure that the president has consultative peer advisors like James F. Byrnes, who before becoming an assistant to President Franklin D. Roosevelt had been a governor of South Carolina, United States senator and U. S. Supreme Court Justice. His background, of course, contrasts markedly with John Erlichman, a zoning attorney from Seattle, Washington, and H. R. Haldeman, an advertising executive. The crucial issue, according to Cohen, is having men around the president with sufficient background and experience to stand up to him [Shannon 1974, p. 33].

Congressional Reform

A number of proposals have been made to strengthen the Congress, and a few have even been implemented. These proposals largely fall into two categories: **1.** returning powers to Congress which had been delegated to the president; and **2.** strengthening the capacity of Congress as an institution and thereby giving the Congress more power in coping with the president.

The principal areas in which Congress has sought to regain traditional powers delegated to the president relate to the congressional prerogative to declare war, which has been weakened by the president's commitment of troops without a declaration of war through his power as commander-in-chief, and the repeal of emergency legislation, which the president has because of congressional grants of emergency powers made primarily during the Great Depression and World War II. The Congress already has passed the War Powers Act to limit the time period during which a president could commit troops without a declaration of war, and the Congress is now preparing legislation to remove many emergency powers granted him. Significantly, it should be noted that the War Powers Act would most likely not have been passed over President Nixon's veto had the president's position not been weakened by Watergate.

To strengthen its own capabilities, the Congress has pro-

vided itself with an Office of Technology Assessment to provide
technological advice and data and is now in the process of reforming the budgetary process so that it will have greater control
over setting budgetary priorities and in responding to presidential budgetary initiatives. These proposals, in part, involve providing Congress with the kind of professional bureaucratic expertise that the president already has in these areas. A problem
inherent in these and similar proposals, for example, creation of
a Foreign Policy Research and Analysis Institute, is that the
Congress will merely be creating a legislative bureaucracy to
fight the executive bureaucracy. The result, according to opponents, will be the further removal of elected decision-makers
from actually making decisions. Instead, the Congress will be in
the position of ratifying decisions made by its own
bureaucracy — a situation that would further weaken the Congress as an institution responsive to the public. As the argument
goes, Congress may then become more responsive to the congressional bureaucracy than to the public.

Other types of congressional reform proposals include having the Speaker of the U. S. House of Representatives deliver an
annual congressional State of the Union Message to rival the
president's State of the Union Message. How the Speaker of the
House could speak on behalf of both houses, which include 535
individuals and the leaders of both parties, with any degree of
confidence that his speech had even substantial, let alone complete, support from all members is difficult to fathom. Getting
both parties and both houses to agree to this proposal is one
problem, but assuming adoption, its effectiveness after implementation might be highly questionable unless there is a return to stronger congressional leadership, such as Speakers
Thomas B. Reed of Maine (fifty-first, fifty-second, fifty-fourth,
and fifty-fifth Congresses), Joseph Cannon of Illinois (fifty-eighth
through sixty-first Congresses), and Sam Rayburn of Texas
(seventy-sixth through seventy-ninth, eighty-first, eighty-
second, and eighty-fourth through eighty-seventh Congresses).

A proposal to lengthen the term of office for members of the
House of Representatives from 2 to 4 years has also been made,

but not seriously considered. The purpose of the proposal is to allow representatives a longer period of time before they have to face reelection campaigns, a problem that distracts them from strictly congressional duties every two years. The principal argument against this proposal rests upon the House of Representatives being more responsive to public opinion than the Senate, an objective that would be less obtainable under a 4-year term.

Finally, a proposal to create a congressional legal counsel's office suffers from some of the same problems as the proposal to have a congressional State of the Union Message delivered by the Speaker of the House. Unless the legal counsel's office were divided between majority and minority staffs to represent the respective parties, it might be subject to substantial political turmoil. Typically, of course, congressional committee staffs have majority and minority members to overcome this very problem.

Electoral Reform

Although a variety of electoral reforms have been proposed with many variations, the three principal areas of reform relate to financial disclosure for public officials, the financing of elections, and a national presidential primary. Precluding the misuse of money is the objective of the first two reforms, while eliminating the evils of the national party conventions and allowing greater public participation in the presidential nomination process is the goal of the third. The diversity and quantity of proposals in these three areas merit a more lengthy treatment than permitted here (see The American Presidency: A Selected Bibliography, pp. 344ff., for appropriate citations of relevant works). All of these proposals were not spawned by Watergate, but their public or legislative approval may well depend upon how long the public is concerned about the implications of Watergate. For example, California's adoption by referendum in 1974 of a stringent ethics proposal for public officials and lobbyists benefited from adverse public reaction to Watergate.

Problems in Achieving Reform

Cure Worse than Disease

Reforms, especially those designed to legislate moral purity, are often guarantees for disaster. During the last century, citizens alarmed by bankrupt states and corrupt legislatures called constitutional conventions to write new constitutions to prevent these evils. The result was that these lengthy and restrictive state constitutions have frequently straight-jacketed state governments in responding to critical problems in the twentieth century because of the extraordinary difficulties in proposing and adopting new constitutions. Another example, of course, is with earlier efforts, notably the Federal Corrupt Practices Act and the Hatch Act, to govern campaign expenditures, which failed miserably because ways were found to circumvent these reform laws. The law can only be as good as the spirit of the people and their willingness to abide by the law.

Crises and Reforms

American history documents the fact that reforms are usually brought about by the existence of a crisis. Eliminate the crisis and you eliminate the momentum for reform. The moral here is that the removal of Watergate and impeachment proceedings elimintes the crisis that had created the momentum for reform. Many of the reform proposals would never have been mentioned or even thought of, let alone been taken seriously, had it not been for Watergate. Watergate and impeachment have been catalysts giving currency to reform.

Incrementalism and Reform

Another history lesson indicates that change in American government and politics generally occurs incrementally or slowly. An obvious reason why many of the reforms mentioned will never be seriously considered is that they are either so new or so drastic that our governmental and political system will not respond favorably to them. To illustrate, the proposal for adoption of the parliamentary system's vote of no confidence would require approval by two-thirds of both houses of Congress and by three-fourths of the state legislatures, assuming utilization of the customary amendment procedure. A long and tortuous road generally precludes the adoption of reforms of this magnitude.

Power and the Sum of Its Parts

Powers already delegated by the Congress to the president are greater than the sum of their parts and, therefore, will make the congressional job of cutting back presidential powers very difficult. For example, a congressman interested in obtaining presidential approval for a nomination to an independent regulatory agency is reluctant to oppose presidential wishes in other areas, such as price-support levels. This suggests that the president will hold the upper hand in reform efforts as well as in other areas where the Congress seeks to restore the balance of powers between the two branches.

Congress and the Continuing Presidential Love Affair

It was only after prolonged public debate and repeated presidential efforts to thwart a full investigation of Watergate that the Congress began to act on impeachment of the president. And even then, many members of Congress pointed out that they did not want to weaken the presidency. For example, South Carolina Representative James Mann, a pivotal leader in impeachment efforts, said: " . . . as we look at how the office of the Presidency has been served by an individual, I share the remarks of George Danielson [D., Cal.] that it is not the Presidency that is in jeopardy from us. *We would strive to strengthen and protect the Presidency*" [Judiciary Committee Proceedings, U. S. House of Representatives, July 29, 1974, emphasis supplied].

Mission

Congress has lost the sense of institutional mission it once possessed, and the executive branch needs only a president with a sense of mission to define its mission. This suggests that there is a great likelihood of the executive branch protecting itself from congressional efforts to retrieve lost powers. Moreover, as already established, the president has many ways to obtain support for his position because the sum of his powers is greater than the parts. That is, through approving a congressman's request in one area, he may preclude that individual's opposition in another.

Two Plus Years of Watergate

"Election reform, the offspring of Watergate, may die aborning because of Watergate and congressional preoccupation with impeachment" [Associated Press, August 3, 1974]. One of the major ironies of Watergate is that the reforms it spawned, it also tended to suffocate. Congressional attention to Watergate and the impeachment proceedings diverted the congressional focus from reform proposals.

THE APOCALYPSE

So long as Congress, the courts, future presidents, and the public remain aware of the evils of Watergate, presidential power will most likely not be used in illegal and unconstitutional ways. Within the confines of this central thesis are four interrelated conclusions pertaining to the presidency and Congress, the principal rivals in efforts to rebalance powers among the three branches of the national government.

First, although Congress may reassert itself to some extent, the structural outline of the presidency and its powers will remain largely the same.

Second, with the demise of the Watergate issue, presidential power could actually increase by virtue of the nature of the problems confronting the United States. Historically, the presidency achieved greater powers during times of crisis, times not unlike those of the present with the acute worldwide inflation and the great interdependence of the world's nations in other areas as well. The complexity of these problems and the seeming need for speed and efficiency in their resolution will most likely preclude substantial congressional input in the decision-making process.

Third, the presidential office, unique in history, will continue to hold a magnetic and powerful attraction for the occupant, seekers of the office, and the public. Moreover, this fascination with the office will tend to generate deference to presidential, as contrasted with congressional, leadership.

Fourth, the principal hopes for alteration and reform of the existing configuration in the structure and powers of the presidency will depend upon the already stated conclusions concerning how long the public, the Congress, the president, and the courts will continue to be alarmed by the implications of Watergate, as well as by the nature and expectations of future presidents. In reference to the latter, the election of a passive president with a less well-defined sense of mission and the control of Congress in the hands of the party opposite the president's would allow the Congress to more easily reassert itself in relationship to the presidency. For example, Congress has generally been a much more forceful and effective institution during the tenure of passive presidents, such as William Howard Taft (1909–1913) and Dwight David Eisenhower (1953–1961). Gerald Ford's 25 years in the House and his seemingly more passive nature might allow Congress such an opportunity.

An Eisenhower Renaissance?

Looking at the presidents in this century reveals that following one or more activist presidents come one or more passive presidents. This phenomena, called the "ebb-and-flow theory," is supported by table 1 which indicates that in this century the longest period for either active or passive presidents was a 20-year period between 1933 and 1953, the activist presidencies of

TABLE 1. **Ebb-and-Flow Theory: Active and Passive Presidents, 1905–1975.**

	1905–09	1909–13	1913–21	1921–33	1933–53	1953–61	1961–74	1974–
Active	Roosevelt		Wilson		Roosevelt Truman		Kennedy Johnson Nixon	
Passive		Taft		Harding Coolidge Hoover		Eisenhower		Ford?

Franklin D. Roosevelt and Harry S Truman. The conclusion of
the Nixon presidency, according to the ebb-and-flow theory, may
end 14-years of activist presidents (1961–74), which have included John F. Kennedy, Lyndon B. Johnson, and Richard M.
Nixon. If the theory holds, Gerald R. Ford is likely to have a
passive style in the White House.

Following World War II, the Great Depression, the Korean
War, and many other crisis events during the turbulent 1930s,
1940s, and early 1950s, the ebb-and-flow theorists would argue
that the American people were ready for more tranquil times and
that the times and the man met in President Dwight D.
Eisenhower. Now, having passed through the civil rights strug-
gles of the 1960s, the Vietnam War period, riots in the streets,
campus turmoil, and the Watergate period, are the American
people ready for another Eisenhower and will Gerald Ford be
that type of president?

There are certain obvious differences that exist between
Eisenhower and Ford, and between the 1950s and 1970s. Where
Eisenhower brought to the White House a relatively nonpartisan
background, Ford brings to the White House a background
steeped in partisan politics. Where Eisenhower was a war hero
in the United States and around the world in an age which re-
vered heroes, Ford lacks the hero status in an age that seems
neither to revere nor to have heroes. Beyond these rather sharp
differences, however, there are some similarities.

Like Eisenhower, Ford does not seem to have the same sense
of drive, determination, and mission possessed by his activist
predecessors. Also, like Eisenhower, Ford has those same qualities of honesty and tolerance, and probably even much better
skills as a listener and communicator. Given the high degree of
distrust found in American society today, these skills and
qualities — integrity, tolerance, listening, and communication — appear to intersect the man with the needs of the times.

A note should also be added about President Ford's partisan
background. As he noted himself, on the eve of becoming president "I've been very fortunate in my lifetime in public office to
have a good many adversaries in the Congress. But I don't think I
have a single enemy in the Congress" [New York Times, August

9, 1974, p. 2]. Partisanship has not marred his character, and as a result he brought to the White House a capacity to communicate honestly and openly with people of widely diverse backgrounds. Indeed, in his first address to a joint session of Congress on August 12, 1974, President Ford said, " . . . my motto towards the Congress is communication, conciliation, compromise, and cooperation" [*New York Times*, August 13, 1974, p. 20].

Should Ford's seemingly more passive nature and his traditional ties and loyalty to the Congress continue as president, he may allow the Congress an opportunity to reassert its power. This type of congressional reassertion of power, however, would most likely be limited to the duration of Ford's presidency just as in the post-Eisenhower period, congressional power was eclipsed by three activist presidents. During the Eisenhower presidency, a passive president faced a Congress controlled by the opposite party for all but 2 of his 8 years in office. Ford, of course, also faces a Congress controlled by the opposite party. Thus, if Congress reasserts itself during the Ford presidency, such reassertion will most likely be short lived.

Whether this is an optimistic or pessimistic view probably depends upon one's attitude towards a strong presidency. For those desiring a stronger president, this is most likely an optimistic view, but for those wanting a weaker president, this is most likely a pessimistic view. Regardless of whether it is optimistic or pessimistic, I have sought to portray a realistic view of the future, given past American experience with crisis and reform situations.

Above all, it should never be forgotten that Watergate first became known because there was a watchman in the night, not because of the vigilance of the Congress, the courts, or the press. Each helped to expose the web of Watergate in their turn, but later! In one of his closing remarks before the House Judiciary Committee, James Mann of South Carolina uttered the grim reminder that ". . . next time there may be no watchman in the night" [Judiciary Committee Proceedings, U. S. House of Representatives, July 29, 1974].

NOTES

---

1. These and similar questions are treated in an interesting book by a constitutional lawyer. See Charles L. Black, Jr., *Impeachment: A Handbook* [New Haven: Yale University Press, 1974].

2. For example, the first polls showing a majority of the public for impeachment were taken in early August 1974 (*The Washington Post*, August 7, 1974), and the Judiciary Committee of the U. S. House of Representatives had voted out Articles of Impeachment on July 30, 1974. Despite the many revelations of Watergate wrongdoing between August 1973 and July 30, 1974, the percentage of Americans who believed Watergate was a "serious matter" remained constant at 48 percent, according to the Gallup Poll. Significantly, the two polls taken at the beginning and the end of that period showed that 46 percent and 43 percent, respectively, felt that Watergate was "just politics" [*Congressional Quarterly*, July 20, 1974, p. 13]. It is also of interest that the percentage of Americans who rated the president's job performance as excellent or good never dropped below 50 percent until almost two years after the June 17, 1972 Watergate break-in [*The Washington Post*, August 1, 1974, p. A 6].

BIBLIOGRAPHY

Black, Jr., Charles L. *Impeachment: A Handbook.* New Haven: Yale University Press, 1974.

The Charlotte Observer, 22 August 1974, p. 10 A.

Congressional Quarterly, 20 July 1974.

Hacker, Andrew. *The End of the American Era.* New York: Atheneum Publishers, 1970.

Lubell, Samuel. *The Future While it Happened.* New York: W. W. Norton & Company, 1973.

Muggeridge, Malcolm. "Living Through An Apocalypse." Address delivered at the International Congress of World Evangelization, Lausanne, Switzerland, 22 July 1974.

The New York Times, 9 August 1974, p. 2; 13 August 1974, p. 20.

Shannon, William V. "Reshaping the American Presidency." *The New York Times,* 30 July 1974, p. 33.

The Washington Post, 1 August 1974; 7 August 1974.

The American Presidency: *A Selected Bibliography*

GOVERNMENT SOURCES

Federal Register. Washington, D.C.: Government Printing Office, 1936–present.

Monthly Catalogue of U.S. Government Publications. Washington, D.C.: Government Printing Office, 1895–present.

Public Papers of the Presidents of the United States. Washington, D.C.: Government Printing Office, 1958–present.

United States Government Organization Manual. Washington, D.C.: Government Printing Office, 1935–present.

Weekly Compilation of Presidential Documents. Washington, D.C.: Government Printing Office, 1965–present.

GENERAL BIBLIOGRAPHIC GUIDANCE

Davidson, Kenneth. "The American Presidency: A Bibliographic Essay." *American Studies* 12 (1973): 28–44.

Heslop, David Alan. *The Presidency and Political Science: A Critique of the Work of Political Scientists in Three Areas of Presidential Politics.* Ann Arbor: University Microfilms, Inc., 1969.

Mugridge, Donald H. *The Presidents of the U.S., 1789–1962: A Selected List of References.* Washington, D.C.: Library of Congress, 1963.

FACTS ABOUT PRESIDENTS

Bremer, Howard, ed. *Presidential Chronology Series.* 32 vols. Dobbs Ferry, N.Y.: Oceana Publications, 1968–72.

Harnsberger, Caroline. *Treasury of Presidential Quotations.* Chicago: Follett Publishing Company, 1964.

Kane, Joseph Nathan. *Facts About the Presidents: A Compilation of Biographical and Historical Data,* 2nd ed. New York: H. W. Wilson, 1968.

Taylor, Tim. *The Book of Presidents.* New York: Arno Press, 1972.

ORGANIZATIONS WITH CONTINUING
PRESIDENTIAL STUDIES

American Enterprise Institute
1150 Seventeenth Street, N.W.
Washington, D.C. 20036

The Brookings Institution
1775 Massachusetts Avenue, N.W.
Washington, D.C. 20036

Center for the Study of the Presidency
926 Fifth Avenue
New York, New York 10021

Congressional Quarterly, Inc.,
1735 K Street, N.W.
Washington, D.C. 20006

National Journal Reports
Government Research Company
1730 Main Street, N.W.
Washington, D.C. 20036

MAGAZINES WITH REGULAR PRESIDENTIAL ANALYSIS

National Review
150 E. 35th Street
New York, New York 10016

The New Republic
1244 19th Street, N.W.
Washington, D.C. 20036

Washington Monthly
1208 Connecticut Avenue, N.W.
Washington, D.C. 20036

PRESIDENTIAL CAMPAIGN AND ELECTION DATA

Congressional Quarterly, *Presidential Candidates from 1788–1964.* Washington, D.C.: Congressional Quarterly, 1964.

Cooke, Donald E. *Atlas of the Presidents.* Maplewood, N.J.: Hammond Incorporated, 1967.

Peterson, Svend. *A Statistical History of the American Presidential Elections.* New York: Frederick Ungar Publishing Company, 1963.

Scammon, Richard M., ed. *America at the Polls: A Handbook of American Presidential Election Statistics, 1920–1964.* Pittsburgh: University of Pittsburgh Press, 1965.

Schlesinger, Arthur M., Jr. *History of American Presidential Elections, 1789–1968.* 4 vols. New York: Chelsea House Publishers, 1970.

PRESIDENTIAL CAMPAIGN POLITICS

Bain, Richard C., and Parris, Judith H. *Convention Decisions and Voting Records*, 2nd ed. Washington, D.C.: The Brookings Institution, 1973.

Barber, James David, ed. *Choosing the President*. Englewood Cliffs, N.J.: Prentice-Hall, 1974.

Burns, James MacGregor. *The Deadlock of Democracy*. Englewood Cliffs, N.J.: Prentice-Hall, 1963.

Chester, Lewis; Hodgson, Godfrey; and Page, Bruce. *An American Melodrama: The Presidential Campaign of 1968*. New York: The Viking Press, 1969.

David, Paul T.; Goldman, Ralph M.; and Bain, Richard C. *The Politics of National Party Conventions*. New York: Random House, Vintage Books, 1964.

Davis, James. *Presidential Primaries: Road to the White House*. New York: Thomas Y. Crowell Company, 1967.

Dunn, Delmer D. *Financing Presidential Campaigns*. Washington, D.C.: The Brookings Institution, 1972.

Larner, Jeremy. *Nobody Knows: Reflections on the McCarthy Campaign of 1968*. New York: The Macmillan Company, 1970.

Lubell, Samuel. *The Future While It Happened*. New York: W. W. Norton & Company, 1973.

McCarthy, Eugene J. *The Year of the People*. New York: Doubleday & Company, 1969.

McGinniss, Joe. *The Selling of the President 1968*. New York: Trident Press, 1969.

Matthews, Donald R., ed. *Perspectives on Presidential Selection*. Washington, D.C.: The Brookings Institution, 1973.

Mazmanian, Daniel A. *Third Parties in Presidential Elections*. Washington, D.C.: The Brookings Institution, 1974.

Parris, Judith H. *The Convention Problem*. Washington, D.C.: The Brookings Institution, 1972.

Polsby, Nelson W., and Wildavsky, Aaron. *Presidential Elections*, rev. ed. New York: Charles Scribner's Sons, 1968.

Pomper, Gerald. *Nominating the President*. New York: W. W. Norton & Company, 1966.

Sayre, Wallace S., and Parris, Judith H. *Voting for President*. Washington, D.C.: The Brookings Institution, 1970.

Stavis, Ben. *We Were the Campaign: New Hampshire to Chicago for McCarthy*. Boston: Beacon Press, 1969.

Weinbaum, Marvin G., and Gold, Louis H. *Presidential Election*. 2nd ed. Hinsdale, Illinois: The Dryden Press, 1974.

White, Theodore H. *The Making of the President, 1960; The Making of the President, 1964; The Making of the President, 1968; The Making of the President, 1972*. New York: Atheneum Publishers, 1961, 1965, 1969, 1973.

Witcover, Jules. *85 Days: The Last Campaign of Robert Kennedy*. New York: G. P. Putnam's Sons, 1969.

Witcover, Jules. *The Resurrection of Richard Nixon*. New York: G. P. Putnam's Sons, 1970.

GENERAL WORKS

Bailey, Thomas A. *Presidential Greatness*. New York: Appleton-Century, 1966.

Barber, James David, ed. *Political Leadership in American Government*. Boston: Little, Brown and Company, 1964.

Barber, James David. *The Presidential Character*. Englewood Cliffs, N.J.: Prentice-Hall, 1972.

Burns, James MacGregor. *Presidential Government: The Crucible of Leadership*. Boston: Houghton Mifflin Company, 1965.

Davis, James W., Jr. *The National Executive Branch*. New York: The Free Press, 1970.

Finer, Herman. *The Presidency: Crisis and Regeneration*. Chicago: University of Chicago Press, 1960.

Hargrove, Erwin C. *Presidential Leadership: Personality and Political Style*. New York: The Macmillan Company, 1966.

Hughes, Emmett John. *The Living Presidency*. New York: Coward, McCann & Geoghegan, 1972.

James, Dorothy Buckton. *The Contemporary Presidency.* New York: Pegasus (Bobbs-Merrill), 1974.

Koenig, Louis W. *The Chief Executive,* rev. ed. New York: Harcourt Brace Jovanovich, 1968.

McConnell, Grant. *The Modern Presidency.* New York: St. Martin's Press, 1967.

Neustadt, Richard E. *Presidential Power: The Politics of Leadership.* New York: John Wiley & Sons, 1960.

Polsby, Nelson W. *The President and Congress.* Englewood Cliffs, N.J.: Prentice-Hall, 1964.

Reedy, George E. *The Twilight of the Presidency.* New York: World Publishing Company, 1970.

Rossiter, Clinton. *The American Presidency.* New York: Harcourt Brace Jovanovich, 1960.

Schlesinger, Arthur, Jr. *The Imperial Presidency.* Boston: Houghton Mifflin Company, 1973.

Tugwell, Rexford G., and Cronin, Thomas E. *The Presidency Reappraised.* New York: Praeger Publishers, 1974.

Wildavsky, Aaron. *The Presidency.* Boston: Little, Brown and Company, 1969.

Wise, Sidney, and Schier, Richard F. *The Presidential Office.* New York: Thomas Y. Crowell Company, 1968.

PRESIDENTS AND ADMINISTRATIONS

Anderson, Patrick. *The Presidents' Men; White House Assistants of Franklin D. Roosevelt, Harry S. Truman, Dwight D. Eisenhower, John F. Kennedy and Lyndon B. Johnson.* New York: Doubleday & Company, 1968.

Christian, George. *The President Steps Down.* New York: The Macmillan Company, 1970.

Evans, Rowland, Jr., and Novak, Robert D. *Lyndon B. Johnson: The Exercise of Power.* New York: The New American Library, 1966.

Evans, Rowland, Jr., and Novak, Robert D. *Nixon in the White House.* New York: Random House, Vintage Books, 1972.

Goldman, Eric F. *The Tragedy of Lyndon Johnson.* New York: Alfred A. Knopf, 1969.

Graff, Henry F. *The Tuesday Cabinet: Deliberation and Decision on Peace and War Under Lyndon B. Johnson.* Englewood Cliffs, N.J.: Prentice-Hall, 1970.

Harris, Richard. *Decision.* New York: E. P. Dutton & Co., 1971.

Heren, Louis. *No Hail, No Farewell.* New York: Harper & Row, Publishers, 1970.

Hoopes, Townsend. *The Limits of Intervention.* New York: David McKay Company, 1969.

Kennedy, Robert F. *Thirteen Days: A Memoir of the Cuban Missile Crisis.* New York: W. W. Norton & Company, 1968.

Latham, Earl. *J. F. Kennedy and Presidential Power.* Lexington, Mass.: D. C. Heath and Company, 1972.

Osborne, John. *The Nixon Watch.* New York: Liveright, 1970.

Schlesinger, Arthur M., Jr. *A Thousand Days: John F. Kennedy in the White House.* Boston: Houghton Mifflin Company, 1965.

Sidey, Hugh. *John F. Kennedy, President.* New York: Atheneum Publishers, Crest Books, 1963.

Sorensen, Theodore C. *Kennedy.* New York: Harper & Row, Publishers, 1965.

Sundquist, James L. *Politics and Policy: The Eisenhower, Kennedy, and Johnson Years.* Washington, D.C.: The Brookings Institution, 1968.

Wicker, Tom. *JFK and LBJ: The Influence of Personality Upon Politics.* New York: William Morrow & Company, 1968.

POLICY MAKING, THE PRESS AND PUBLIC OPINION

Allison, Graham T. *Essence of Decision: Explaining the Cuban Missile Crisis.* Boston: Little, Brown and Company, 1971.

Brown, Stuart Gerry. *The American Presidency: Leadership, Partisanship, and Popularity.* New York: The Macmillan Company, 1966.

Campbell, John Franklin. *The Foreign Affairs Fudge Factory.* New York: Basic Books, 1971.

Cornwall, Elmer E., Jr. *Presidential Leadership of Public Opinion.* Bloomington: Indiana University Press, 1965.

Cronin, Thomas E. and Greenberg, Sanford D., eds. *The Presidential Advisory System.* New York: Harper & Row, Publishers, 1969.

Fenno, Richard F., Jr. *The President's Cabinet.* Cambridge: Harvard University Press, 1959.

Fisher, Louis. *President and Congress: Power and Policy.* New York: The Free Press, 1972.

Frankel, Charles. *High on Foggy Bottom: An Outsider's Inside View of the Government.* New York: Harper & Row, Publishers, 1968.

Freeman, J. Leiper. *The Political Process: Executive Bureau Legislative Committee Relations.* Rev. ed. New York: Random House, 1965.

Fulbright, J. W. *The Pentagon Propaganda Machine.* New York: Liveright, 1970.

Gawthrop, Louis C. *Bureaucratic Behavior in the Executive Branch.* New York: The Free Press, 1969.

Harris, Richard. *Decision.* New York: E. P. Dutton & Company, 1971.

Mendelsohn, Harold, and Crespi, Irving. *Polls, Television, and the New Politics.* Scranton: Chandler Publishing Company, 1970.

Mueller, John E. *War, Presidents and Public Opinion.* New York: John Wiley & Sons, 1973.

Pollard, James E. *The Presidents and the Press.* New York: The Macmillan Company, 1947.

Polsby, Nelson W. *Congress and the Presidency.* Englewood Cliffs, N.J.: Prentice-Hall, 1971.

Proxmire, William. *Report from Wasteland: America's Military-Industrial Complex.* New York: Frederick A. Praeger, 1970.

Reston, James. *The Artillery of the Press.* New York: The Macmillan Company, 1966.

Rourke, Francis E. *Bureaucracy, Politics and Public Policy.* Boston: Little, Brown and Company, 1969.

Rubin, Bernard. *Political Television*. Belmont, Calif.: Wadsworth Publishing Company, 1967.

Schultze, Charles L.; Fried, Edward R.; Rivlin, Alice M.; and Teeters, Nancy H. *Setting National Priorities: The 1971 Budget*. Washington, D.C.: The Brookings Institution, 1970.

Schultze, Charles L.; Fried, Edward R.; Rivlin, Alice M.; and Teeters, Nancy H. *Setting National Priorities: The 1972 Budget*. Washington, D.C.: The Brookings Institution, 1971.

Sheehan, Neil, et al. *The Pentagon Papers*. New York: Bantam Books, 1971.

Sorensen, Theodore C. *Decision-Making in the White House*. New York: Columbia University Press, 1963.

Warren, Sidney. *The President as World Leader*. Philadelphia: J. B. Lippincott Company, 1964.

Yarmolinsky, Adam. *The Military Establishment: Its Impacts on American Society*. New York: Harper & Row Publishers, 1970.

Index